D1422214

AS GOOD AS GOD, AS CLEVER AS THE DEVIL

The Impossible Life of Mary Benson

Rodney Bolt

WINDSOR
PARAGON

First published 2011
by Atlantic Books Ltd
This Large Print edition published 2012
by AudioGO Ltd
by arrangement with
Atlantic Books Ltd

Hardcover   ISBN: 978 1 445 871166 5
Softcover   ISBN: 978 1 445 87117 2

British Library Cataloguing in Publication Data available

Printed and bound in Great Britain by
MPG Books Group Limited

For mothers

Love is God

Mary Benson

Contents

List of Illustrations   xi
The Benson Line   xiv
A Word on the Book   xvi
Prologue   xix

PART I   Minnie   1
PART II   Mrs Benson   51
PART III Ben   243

Acknowledgements   346
Select Bibliography   348

p.11 Edward White Benson (Senior) and Harriet Benson. A. C. Benson, *The Life of Edward White Benson, Sometime Archbishop of Canterbury*, Vol 1, 1899.

p.27 Mrs Mary Sidgwick. A. C. Benson, *The Life of Edward White Benson, Sometime Archbishop of Canterbury*, Vol 1, 1899.

p.48 Mary Benson. E. F. Benson, *Mother*, 1925.

p.49 Charles Darwin, *On the Origin of Species*, 1859.

p.54 Revd E. W. Benson and his wife. Reproduced by permission of the Bodleian Libraries, University of Oxford, MS. Benson adds 19, (#14 & #15).

p.62 Wellington College. A. C. Benson, *The Life of Edward White Benson, Sometime Archbishop of Canterbury*, Vol 1, 1899.

p.65 E. W. Benson. A. C. Benson, *The Life of Edward White Benson, Sometime Archbishop of Canterbury*, Vol 1, 1899.

p.75 'Willie We Have Missed You'. Public Domain.

p.78 *The Doubt: Can These Dry Bones Live?* by Henry Bowler, 1855. The Granger Collection/ Topfoto.

p.86 Elizabeth Cooper with Hugh. A. C. Benson, *Hugh, Memoirs of a Brother*, 1915.

p.95 The Benson family at Wellington College. A. C. Benson, *The Trefoil*, 1923.

pp.114–15 Sketches in letters from Mary Benson to Ellen Hall. Reproduced by permission of the Bodleian Libraries, University of Oxford, MS. Benson 3/40, fols 182, 184.

p.120 Nellie and Maggie. A. C. Benson, *Life and Letters of Maggie Benson*, 1917.

p.149 Maggie with some of her pets. A. C. Benson, *Life and Letters of Maggie Benson*, 1917.

p.153 The Family at Lis Escop. A. C. Benson, *The Trefoil*, 1923.

p.184 Fred Benson. E. F. Benson, *Our Family Affairs 1867–1896*, 1920.

p.186 Ethel Smyth. World History Archive/Topfoto.

p.221 Maggie Benson. A. C. Benson, *Life and Letters of Maggie Benson*, 1917.

p.228 Maggie with Nettie Gourlay. A. C. Benson, *Life and Letters of Maggie Benson*, 1917.

p.247 Sketches from Hugh's Egyptian diary. Reproduced by permission of the Bodleian Libraries, University of Oxford, MS. Benson 1/58, fols 151v, 159v.

p.253 Queen Victoria celebrates her Diamond Jubilee. Topfoto.

p.262 Mary Benson with Maggie. A. C. Benson, *Life and Letters of Maggie Benson*, 1917.

p.267 Motorized delivery wagon. Mary Evans.

pp.269 & 271 Tremans. Reproduced by kind permission of the websmaster at horstedkeynes. com.

p.287 A visit to Tremans. Reproduced by kind permission of the websmaster at horstedkeynes. com.

p.295 The 'Boys' at Tremans. A. C. Benson, *Hugh, Memoirs of a Brother*, 1915.

p.325 Beth. A. C. Benson, *The Trefoil*, 1923.

p.337 Mary Benson. E. F. Benson, *Mother*, 1925.

The Benson Line

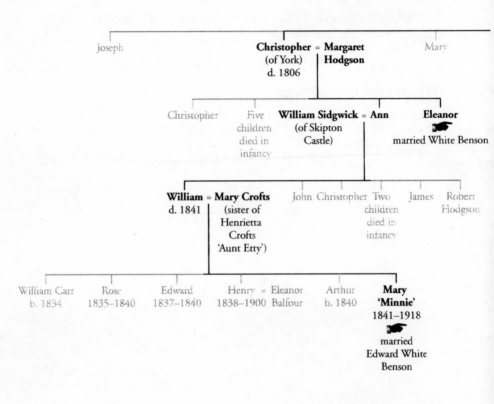

Joseph   **Christopher** = **Margaret**   Mary
(of York)   **Hodgson**
d. 1806

Christopher   Five children died in infancy   **William Sidgwick** = **Ann** (of Skipton Castle)   **Eleanor** married White Benson

William d. 1841 = **Mary Crofts** (sister of Henrietta Crofts 'Aunt Etty')   John Christopher   Two children died in infancy   James   Robert Hodgson

William Carr b. 1834   Rose 1835–1840   Edward 1837–1840   Henry = Eleanor 1838–1900 Balfour   Arthur b. 1840   **Mary 'Minnie'** 1841–1918

married Edward White Benson

m. 1859
Edward White = **Mary 'Minnie'**
Benson   **Sidgwick**
1829–1896   1841–1918

Martin White 1860–1878   Arthur Christopher 1862–1925   Eleanor Mary 'Nellie' 1863–1890

All issue unmarried

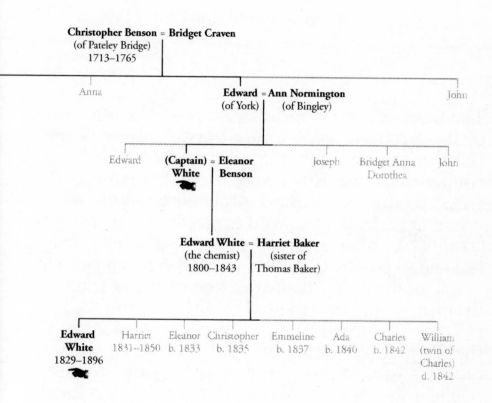

Christopher Benson = **Bridget Craven**
(of Pateley Bridge)
1713–1765

Anna   **Edward** = **Ann Normington**   John
                 (of York)   (of Bingley)

Edward   **(Captain)** = **Eleanor**   Joseph   Bridget Anna   John
        White   **Benson**   Dorothea

Edward White = **Harriet Baker**
(the chemist)   (sister of
1800–1843   Thomas Baker)

Edward   Harriet   Eleanor Christopher   Emmeline   Ada   Charles   William
White   1831–1850 b. 1833   b. 1835   b. 1837   b. 1840 b. 1842 (twin of
1829–1896   Charles)
                                             d. 1842

Margaret   Edward Frederic   Robert Hugh
'Maggie'   'Fred'   'Hugh'
1865–1916   1867–1940   1871–1914

A Word on the Book

The Bensons were hopelessly literate. The offspring of the Archbishop of Canterbury, Edward White Benson, and his wife Mary, formed (said the composer Dame Ethyl Smyth) an 'unpermissibly gifted family'. Mary Benson's children wrote their own magazine, played word games incessantly, kept scrapbooks of stories and poems. As adults, they became so prolific that their sister Maggie remarked: 'Some of the family really must emigrate, or English literature will be flooded.' Maggie produced a philosophical treatise and an archaeological study of the Egyptian Temple of Mut. All three of her brothers wrote novels. A. C. (Arthur) Benson also published poems—most notably the words for 'Land of Hope and Glory'—as well as literary essays, biography and uplifting musings. E. F. (Fred) Benson is today best known for his 'Mapp and Lucia' books, but his vast literary output also included history, biography and writing about sport. None of them ever married. As Maggie once commented: 'The odd burst of books in a non-marrying family is better than marriage.' Mary Benson did not herself join this literary whirligig, but in the novels of her children and in their biographies she frequently flashes by.

In all manner of ways, the Bensons wrote about themselves. Arthur produced biographies of their father the Archbishop, of brother Hugh and of

Maggie. Fred wrote one of their mother (though it is largely about himself); both brothers wrote books on the family as a whole, and Maggie came up with one about their pets. Members of the family appear, thinly disguised if at all, in their fiction. Characters may even bear the names of the author's real siblings. Yet they were a reticent family, locked up and guarded in their relations with others, often not really even in touch with themselves. They fudge issues in their biographies and tell truths in the fiction; sometimes delude themselves in their diaries yet unwittingly reveal themselves in their letters.

When Arthur writes a beautiful account of a childhood walk with his father, something in his tone—and in the eulogizing nature of Victorian biography—creates a niggle of doubt; when, in his novel *Memoirs of Arthur Hamilton*, the boy Arthur writes 'I hate Papa' on a piece of paper and buries it in the garden, the incident has an aura of autobiographical authenticity. The Bensons' writings present an acute version of a well-worn but nonetheless enduring problem, that of the tricky relation between an author's life and work. It is an issue that often leads to tiresome speculation—something I have hoped to avoid. Yet the Bensons, who were at times quite open about the autobiographical nature of their novels, do present something of a special case. When it comes to their own work, one feels, the truth frequently lies somewhere in the interstice between the biography and the fiction.

In grappling with this problem, I became inspired by the idea of a commonplace book—those all-purpose notebooks so beloved of writers, where one page might contain a poem that has caught the eye, another a striking phrase or two, or the opening lines of a novel, and yet another a laundry list. I have also found myself imagining a Benson family scrapbook, full of drawings and word sketches, photographs, memorabilia and stories. These ideas suggested a structure that at the very least would deal with the old problem in a different way.

On the banks of the stream that was Mary Benson's life, I have placed paragraphs of fiction, something to note as you pass by—extracts that may throw a more penetrating light on the flow of the non-fiction. These are an open admission of what has influenced my perception, placed there in the hope that they might contribute a shade or two to the reader's own. As the idea of a commonplace book grew in my mind, I decided, in addition to extracts from Benson novels, to include further Bensonia, fragments compiled from contemporary sources, as well as other images and writings that may briefly divert attention and, without labouring a point, simply say, 'Think on this for a moment'—items that might give a context, provide an illustration, or even a note of contradiction; passages that caught my own eye along the way, and might take the reader on a similar journey. All the while, the main thrust of the narrative tells Mary Benson's story.

There is a sense in which all biography contains an element of fiction, is an *imagined* truth created from the available base of verifiable facts. At one end of the spectrum are those impressive, scholarly studies that record almost all known data and every notable event of a subject's life. This is not such a book. Nor is it a broad cultural history of the subject's times. Its focus is domestic and intimate; its aim to paint a personal portrait of a woman, her marriage, her loves, the trials of her spirit, and of her vivid, difficult, 'unpermissibly gifted' family.

Rodney Bolt *Amsterdam 2011*

Prologue

On Sunday, 11 October 1896, Edward White Benson, Archbishop of Canterbury, insufferable to the end, died on his knees in church saying the Confession, ending a life of relentless success.

At that moment his wife Mary—'Ben' to her intimates—became nobody. Life as consort to the Archbishop had been led in a 'thunderous whirlpool', a 'beating fervent keen pulsating life', of queens and countesses, of discussing politics with prime ministers and dining with poets laureate. William Gladstone had proclaimed her 'the cleverest woman in Europe'; Queen Victoria had on occasion affectionately foregone the royal 'we'. 'All this is over,' Mary wrote in her diary, 'it has fallen to pieces around us.'

Edward White Benson had ruled over his wife, from the moment he wooed the young Minnie Sidgwick (as Mary then was) and throughout their marriage. His death created a vacuum not of intimacy, but of meaning. 'There is nothing within, Good Lord, no power, no love, no desire—no initiative,' she declared. 'He had it all and his life entirely dominated mine. Good Lord, Good Lord— give me a personality.' As Mrs Benson, Mary had held gleaming pearls, 'always on one string, worn, carried about till they seemed as if they had some real coherence. In a moment the string is cut—they roll to all corners of the room—a necklace for glory & beauty no longer, but just scattered beads. Who will string my life together once more?'

When Ben woke up one morning a few days after her husband's death, Lucy Tait, beside her in bed, was already helping her to find an answer. Lucy, the daughter of Edward Benson's predecessor as Archbishop, had long been part of the Benson household. By the time Edward was buried, and Ben and Lucy were seeking respite in Egypt, Ben could assert: *'I have never had time to be responsible for my own life.* In a way I feel more grown up now than I ever have before—strange, when for the first time in my 55 years I am *answerable to nobody* no-one has the right to censure my actions, and I can do what I like. What a tremendous choice!'

PART I

MINNIE

Chapter One

Little Minnie Sidgwick was eleven years old in the spring of 1852. She was a sunny child, plump, high-spirited, nimble of mind, gay and adventurous. 'Minnie is more *volatile* than her brothers,' she overheard her mother remark. Minnie was a little frightened of her mother.

Not too long ago, Minnie had called herself 'Mama's ickle tresor'. She *said* she loved her mother, as a daughter should. Mrs Sidgwick spoke firmly about duty. She was inclined to check the child's natural frivolity. Yet little Minnie was not simply inclined to pleasure; she desired to please. She did not like church, but she said her prayers obediently enough. Her mother wanted her love. Minnie hated disappointing her.

Mrs Sidgwick was practical, matter-of-fact and a formidable trainer of servants. She was fond of moral maxims. 'There's many a poor person would be thankful for that,' was one, or: 'I cannot understand people caring for *luxuries*.' Luxury for Minnie—extreme luxury, to the point even of wicked indulgence—came in the form of the simultaneous enjoyment of a soft chair, a book and an orange. Love, warmth and comfort were to be found in the person of her nurse, Beth, a wiry, twinkle-eyed Yorkshirewoman.

Minnie's father was dead. She did not remember

him at all, as he had gone when she was just a few months old. Her favourite brothers, Henry and Arthur, had but a hazy recollection of him, perhaps conjured for them by portraits and family conversation, but the eldest, William, had known him. Papa had been a headmaster in Yorkshire, near their grandfather's home of Skipton Castle, but Minnie and her family were now planted comfortably in one of the elegant new houses overlooking Durdham Down, on the edge of Bristol, together with her cousins Ada and Eleanor, her maiden aunt Etty, Nurse Beth, Frisk the dog and a canary called Dickey.

Cousin Edward arrived on a visit a short while before Minnie's eleventh birthday. Edward belonged to the mature, mysterious world inhabited by Minnie's mother and aunts, having reached the advanced age of nearly twenty-three. He was Ada and Eleanor's elder brother. Their father and Minnie's father had been cousins, so really that made Edward and Minnie second cousins. He was at Cambridge. He was quite the dandy (his accoutrements for chapel included lilac gloves and a silk necktie decorated with flowers and toucans) and he was strikingly beautiful. He had long, abundant, light golden-brown hair, pale blue eyes under a high forehead, a straight, noble nose and a mouth like an angel's, which curved and dimpled delicately at the corners. His face danced with eager, active looks, and he blushed frequently, through sheer pleasure. Minnie's bachelor uncles in Yorkshire were besotted with him, as was the household at Bristol.

On an earlier visit, when Minnie was only eight, she had impressed Edward by reciting from memory one of Lord Macaulay's *Lays of Ancient Rome*, hundreds of energetically rhythmic lines of poetry peppered with Latin names. This and her knowledge of 'Bible history and English history . . . to say nothing of geography, and writing and drawing' had so delighted Edward that he submitted her to 'a good examination in Latin grammar, to the end of the pronouns'. Minnie had passed.

On this visit, Minnie's 'mighty favourite' was Sir Walter Scott's *The Lord of the Isles*. She loved poetry and relished the romantic and adventurous. Though she was a little dumpy in her ballooning girl's skirt and sausagey ankle-length pantaloons, and a touch plain with her full cheeks and straight, dark hair, Minnie's brightness, bubble and verve transformed her features. As she read *The Lord of the Isles* for Cousin Edward, he was struck by 'the keenness and depth of her thought: how her eye would flash with a fine expression, and the really striking voice and gestures with which she would read through a fine passage'. She also read to him from Tennyson's *The Princess*, and he was much moved by the Prince's declaration that a man who does not love a woman leads a 'drowning life besotted with sweet self . . . Or keeps his wing'd affections clipt with crime'. Love, the inspiring homily continued, encourages men and women to grow together, each absorbing the strengths of the other, a man to 'gain in sweetness and in moral height' (women being morally superior to men in their lack of sordid urges), and a woman (given her naturally weaker mind) to expand in 'mental breadth'—until at last 'she set herself to man / Like perfect music unto noble words'.

One night, as little Minnie half lay on the sofa on which Cousin Edward was sitting, she asked him:

'Edward, how long will it be before I am as tall as if I was standing on that stool?'

'I don't know very well, Minnie, five years perhaps . . .'

'When I am twenty I shall be taller than that?'

'Yes.'

'When I am twenty, how old shall you be?'

'Thirty-two.'

'Thirty-two! Edward, I shan't look so little compared to you, shall I, when I'm twenty and you're thirty-two, as I do now that I'm eleven and you're twenty-three?'

'No, no, you won't, Minnie.'

'This unexpected close [of the conversation] made me blush indeed,' wrote Edward in his diary, 'and the palms of my hands grew very hot.' A few nights later, he spoke to Mrs Sidgwick, saying that 'if Minnie grew up the same sweet and clever girl that she was' he should like to make this 'fine and beautiful bud' his wife.

From the Prologue of Alfred Tennyson's
The Princess

She tapt her tiny silken-sandal'd foot:
'That's your light way; but I would make it death
For any male thing but to peep at us.'

Petulant she spoke, and at herself she laugh'd:
A rosebud set with little wilful thorns,
And sweet as English air could make her, she:
But Walter hail'd a score of names upon her,
And 'petty Ogress', and 'ungrateful Puss',

6

And swore he long'd at college, only long'd,
All else was well, for she-society.

Cousin Edward's visit concluded in a most exciting manner. One Wednesday evening at the end of March, just a few days after Minnie's birthday and the day before Edward's examination results were due to be published, the family sat down to dinner with Edward at the head of the table. He was in the middle of telling a long story when Chacey the butler came in, coughed quietly and said: 'If you please, sir, a gentleman from Cambridge wishes to see you.' An old man called Mr Martin, swathed in coat and shawls and still carrying his hat and carpet-bag, followed, somewhat breathless. Edward fell silent. Mr Martin greeted them all, then said something to Edward that made Minnie's cousin leap about the room and have to hold on to the doorpost to support himself. Frisk the dog, excited by all the rumpus, seized Edward's trouser leg and growled and shook until he had to be pulled off. Mr Martin grasped the young man's hand, stroking, kneading and folding it until it was quite numb. Mr Martin, it transpired, was the Bursar of Trinity College, and Edward's most affectionate protector. His great news was that Edward had won the Senior Medal in the Classical Tripos, the highest of university honours.

A week later, Edward took leave of the family in Bristol and returned to Cambridge.

Chapter Two

Edward White Benson had been fourteen when, in 1843, his father died, leaving a widow and seven children with a very modest income and a patent for the processing of cobalt.

Edward White Senior had studied privately with the chemist and astrologer Dr Sollitt of York back in the 1830s, then experimented in his home laboratory and come up with, amongst other discoveries (and not without the odd window-shattering explosion), a method of making carbonate of soda, and a new process for producing white lead and cobalt for colouring paint. In 1838 he established the British White-Lead Company, with a large factory amidst the flowers and open countryside of Birmingham Heath, but after an initial spurt of success the business ran dry of capital. The company failed in 1842, and Edward White died a few months later, reportedly of an internal canker but quite possibly, given the toxic substances with which he had surrounded himself for much of his adult life, from poisoning. His business partners offered his widow lifetime use of the family home (which was attached to the deserted factory) and a small annuity. Young Edward—or 'White' as he was more often called then—was able, just, to continue as a day boy at King Edward's School in Birmingham, where he

8

had been a scholar since the age of eleven, and where he developed a respect that amounted almost to worship for his headmaster James Prince Lee.

The Curious Case of Dr Sollitt of York
A true tale of the black arts

The great Dr Sollitt of York cast nativities with some success. He was a scholar and magician, and much else besides. Witness what happened in Woodstock some years before Victoria was Queen, at the house of the family of the doctor's acolyte, Edward White Benson, a chemist of Birmingham. Dr Sollitt had long studied the ways of the Evil One, and perusal of his books had led him to believe he could himself summon the Prince of Darkness. In his chambers at Woodstock he drew a circle and went so far in the requisite incantations as to have recited the Lord's Prayer backwards. At this moment he was most violently called in the house, and in dread of detection if any one should come to look for him and find himself either excluded or admitted, the dark doctor rushed instantly out of the room. Scarcely had he reached the lowest stair, when a wonderful crash was heard in the room he had just quitted. The whole household ran thither, and it was found that not a *single* article of furniture, *literally*, was in place. They all lay overturned on the floor. So perturbed by this event was Dr Sollitt that he forswore his art and made a solemn bonfire of his books. And indeed his acolyte Edward White Benson, too, whenever then or later convinced that he had by Astrology acquired such information of future events as he believed improper for a man to attain, he desisted and burned his books also. This tale is true, as told by said Benson to his son, who became Archbishop of Canterbury.

'White' had been a Benson family name for three generations. Young Edward's grandfather, Captain White Benson, was named after Francis White, the unmarried whist partner of his father, one Edward Benson of Ripon. Francis White had bequeathed his entire estate to his card-playing friend, and Edward Benson of Ripon named his son White in gratitude. This young man (later to be Captain White Benson) married his first cousin, Eleanor Sarah Benson. Eleanor was the sister of Ann Sidgwick (née Benson), little Minnie Sidgwick's ancestor at Skipton Castle. The son of White and Eleanor, Edward White, the patent holder of cobalt processing, married Harriet Baker, of a staunch Unitarian family. He had a well-developed sense of humour—he once opened a commonplace book with a Pindaric Ode on a Gooseberry Pie—but he was also the author of a book entitled *Essays on the Works of God* and a fervent Evangelical. Harriet reluctantly joined the Church of England in deference to her new husband.

Young Edward White was their first son—pale and sickly, averse to games, and supremely sensitive. A picture of Bottom wearing an ass's head in a copy of *A Midsummer Night's Dream* struck him dumb with terror and gave him nightmares for weeks; the cry of a wounded hare during a shooting party made him immediately sick, and he swore an oath never to take up a gun in sport. But he was a talkative child, chattering away to strangers and

10

conjuring the most 'monstrous figments'—for which untruths he was frequently beaten. He remained 'White' until a long summer holiday with his Sidgwick cousins in Yorkshire so improved his health and gave him such a tan that the family joked that his name no longer matched his appearance, and that he should be called Edward instead. He was then interchangeably 'White' and 'Edward' until his twenties, when the latter stuck.

In his teens, and particularly after his father died, Edward grew increasingly fervent in his faith, gathering around him like-minded friends for whom discussion of the Council of Trent and the validity of lay baptism was as natural and eager as that of racquets or cricket. With one of them Edward formed a secret, doctrinally conservative Society for Holy Living, 'to bring the kingdom of God to the poor, to promote the spiritual unity of the Church

Silhouettes of Edward White Benson (Senior) and Harriet Benson

and to practise the precepts of the Sermon on the Mount'. His emanations of sanctity once provoked a less pious schoolfellow to ask him, 'And how is the Bensonian Ethereality?' and earn in response a forgiving smile. 'I don't care for the book, nor for the people who write such things,' remarked his mother on finding him engrossed in Tract 90 of John Henry Newman's *Tracts for the Times*, suggesting the possibility of a leaning towards Catholicism that rocked her Unitarian soul, 'but I don't want to stop you reading what you wish: only you ought to think, would your father have approved of it?'

'Yes, mother, I have thought of that and I think he *would* wish me to be acquainted with what is going on in the Church,' was the young man's crushing reply.

Edward had a clear fondness for ceremony and ritual. He converted an office in his father's deserted lead factory into a private oratory, with brass rubbings from nearby churches, a cloth-draped table for an altar, stools to kneel on, and a cross made for him by an old carpenter (who earned rebuke for his pains, as he had rounded off the edges instead of leaving them square). Here he went every day to say the Canonical Hours. Suspecting that while he was at school his sisters were disobeying his injunction on their entering the room, Edward booby-trapped the door, bringing a battering shower of books down on the head of his little sister Emmeline when she peeked in one morning. She did not merit the forgiving smile. It was, after all, *his* oratory.

Though straitened in circumstances Edward Benson was not bereft of achievement. Cambridge beckoned. In 1848 he proceeded from King Edward's School to Trinity College as a subsizar (partially financially supported by the college), then followed a steadily rising path, becoming a full sizar the following year, and finally a scholar (an honour that brought more substantial support). His sister Eleanor wrote to congratulate him: 'What a fine, clever fellow you are, you will soon be Archbishop of Canterbury, and would deserve to be, should you not?', a question Edward surely deemed rhetorical.

Edward lived with ferocious frugality, surviving his first year at university on expenditure of just over £90, less than the earnings of a lowly clerk. (Mr Guppy, in Charles Dickens's *Bleak House*, published in monthly parts from 1852, is comically proud of an annual income of £104, set to rise to £117.) Edward took in pupils to support his finances, one summer acting as tutor to two boys at Abergeldie Castle, on the River Dee near Aberdeen, and catching sight at the Invercauld Highland Games of a young Queen Victoria (the most plainly dressed woman there, he thought) and Prince Albert ('horribly padded and belted'). His mother let go her domestic staff, and did all the cooking, scrubbing, ironing and cleaning herself, with the help of Edward's sisters, but when she wrote to him suggesting that she make use of her late husband's cobalt patent, and set up in business, Edward was horrified. A mother in 'trade' was utterly unacceptable. The rigid strata of society might be beginning to bend, ever so slightly, as all manner of people rubbed shoulders (and made fortunes) in newly industrialized cities and every example of humanity piled into railway trains to speed around the countryside, but the direction of any social mobility should be upwards, not down. A mother who scrubbed her own floors was bad enough, but concealable; one in trade—especially for someone in such an environment as the University of Cambridge, and particularly when it came to career or marriage prospects—was too dreadful to contemplate. Edward would not admit such a stumbling block to his progress. 'I do hope and trust you will keep out of it,' he instructed her. 'It will do me so much harm here, and my sisters so much harm for ever! I trust that the scheme be abandoned once and for all.' Mother complied. She always did.

Instead, Harriet Benson scraped together what she could of her capital and invested it in the railways. The 'roaring and rattling railroad days' had begun, with (as Charles Dickens put it) 'wheezin', creakin', gaspin', puffin', bustin' monsters' shooting around the country at up to 36 miles per hour. ('Not quite so fast next time, Mr Conductor, if you please,' said Prince Albert as he alighted after his first train journey in 1842.) Between December 1844 and January 1849 the network grew from 2,240 to 5,447 miles. In 1849, 60 million journeys were taken by train. Shares in railway companies promised unimaginable riches, and thousands of people joined in a frenzy of speculation that became known as *railway mania*. Harriet Benson can hardly be blamed for secretly becoming one of them. Just months after she did so, the market crashed, with an estimated loss to investors of some £800,000,000. Mrs Benson was ruined.

A few months later, all her offspring in Birmingham fell ill with typhus fever. Not only did Harriet Benson have single-handedly to nurse six children who were tossing and sweating in delirium, but she had to keep the household running without their help. For a while she withheld the seriousness of the situation from Edward, as she did not want to interrupt his work at Cambridge or upset him, but eventually she had anxiously to write for help. 'Do you think,' came the reply, 'it could be managed that instead of my coming down to you, you yourself should come up here for a week and bring one of those who are under ten years old—(that would be half fare by the Railway). This place is so beautiful and fresh now, that I think it would restore the health of the most confirmed invalids.' The house in Birmingham must have been seething with infection. Edward's own health and well-being, all (not least the Good Lord himself) would surely agree, eclipsed that of the rest of the family. In case this part of the letter was too complicated, he trusted his mother would 'not grudge the trouble of reading it over again', and he went on: 'prayers for your restoration in my heart, mingled with prayers that He will not suffer me so to abuse the health and happiness and prosperity that He gives me here (for in all these, my dear Mother, I know that you rejoice) . . .'

Two days later Edward wrote again, wishing he could say something to comfort the invalids, but assuring them that they would comfort each other best—and reminding them that the 'true comfort is of the Comforter'. He was halfway through a third letter when news arrived that his sister, Harriet, had died. She was eighteen. Edward's letter changed course to become a paean to her grace, truthfulness, obedience and saintliness. Finally, he set off for Birmingham.

Mrs Benson herself laid out the wasted body of her eldest daughter and namesake, then retired to

15

bed. At midnight, she got up, lit a lamp and went in for one last look at the body. Back in her own bedroom, exhausted, she lay down with her head on her hand to sleep. She died in the night of heart failure. By the time Edward Benson arrived, he had two funerals to arrange.

Edward's mother's annuity and the right of the family to occupy the house in Birmingham terminated with her death. Her railway shares were worthless. Once expenses had been paid, Edward calculated that the entire family fortune amounted to just over £100. Aunts and uncles rallied round. A Benson half-uncle sent Edward money to meet immediate needs; seventeen-year-old Eleanor and ten-year-old Ada were taken to Bristol to be looked after by Mrs Sidgwick, the widow of their father's cousin, and the rest went—temporarily—to stay with Uncle Thomas Baker, their mother's Unitarian brother.

A rich and generous businessman, Uncle Thomas wrote to Edward offering to take the baby of the family—little Charlie, who was eight—and maybe one of the sisters, and bring them up as his own. He undertook not to 'instil into the child any Unitarian principle', to bring him up according to Edward's religious convictions and to allow Edward 'freely [to] exercise [his] influence by visit or by letter, and hereafter decide on the boy's school'. Edward rejected the offer. He would not permit even the faintest whiff of Unitarianism to taint the air his brother breathed. Better that Charlie live in penury and be poorly educated than imperilled by comforts and ministrations offered by such inappropriate substitute parents as Aunt and Uncle Baker.

16

An Incident in which Edward Benson, Undergraduate of Trinity, Stands by his High Principles
A story told of the African American pastor and abolitionist Alexander Crummel, by the Revd J. Bowman of New Southgate, who was present

On a certain Degree day in 1850 or thereabouts the undergraduate Crummel of Queens' appeared in the Senate House to take his degree. A boisterous individual in the gallery called out: 'Three Groans for the Queens' nigger.' A pale, slim undergraduate in the front of the gallery, very youthful-looking, became scarlet with indignation and shouted in a voice that re-echoed through the building: 'Shame, shame! Three groans for you sir!' And then: 'Three cheers for Mr Crummel!' This hurrah was taken up in all directions, and the original offender had to stoop to hide himself from the storm of groans and hisses that broke out all round him. That pale undergraduate was one Benson, later Archbishop of Canterbury.

Thomas Baker knew how to deal with his objectionable young nephew. He wrote that he had hoped Edward's 'own good sense' would have preserved him from 'such narrow and debasing sentiments'. He withdrew all support, adding: 'I do not see how you can expect from us any sympathy in pursuing an education which has so far taught you not to regard us as friends, but as a class whose influence, beyond a very small range, is to be

17

avoided.' If that was the way Edward felt, he would 'hereafter be bound to provide for [Charlie's] future as he would have been provided for had he been with me'.

Edward flinched a little. His beliefs were, after all, deeply and sincerely held. He noted his uncle's '*uncommon* candour', thanked him for his kindness, and asked his pardon. Then he went on to lecture the older man on Christian doctrine and practice, holding up his own religious principle as 'not a thing of tender feelings, warm comforting notions, unpruned prejudices, and lightly considered opinions' but one that 'consists of full and perfect convictions, absolute belief, rules which regulate my life . . . and tests by which I believe myself bound to try every question, the greatest and the least.' He rounded off his sally with: 'This is a very serious matter; and I hope you will not think bitterly either of the young man's presumption, or the young Churchman's bigotry. Bigot (so-called) thus far, a conscientious Catholic [here meaning orthodox Anglican] must ever be.'

Buffeted between beliefs about which he probably had no inkling, little Charlie Benson was blown on to the cold hard land of brother Edward's 'full and perfect conviction'. This might have spelt disaster for the boy, had it not been for the intervention of the kindly Mr Martin.

Francis Martin, the Bursar of Trinity College, was well into middle age, gruff, grey-haired, solitary, unmarried and rich. He was also a fervent Evangelical. Soon after Edward returned to Cambridge from Birmingham, Mr Martin noticed the beautiful, troubled young man making his desultory way across the Great Court. He knew of the family bereavements, offered his condolences, and invited Edward up to his rooms. The visit marked the beginning of an intense and passionate protectorship.

A fierce figure, with high collars that scraped and rasped at his cheeks, pale grey eyes, parchment-like skin, a rough manner and a resonant voice, Mr Martin commanded Edward's deference, but treated him with a parental tenderness that grew into adoration. The crusty old don softened, and began to make his affection tangible. He offered to pay all Edward's expenses at Cambridge and to continue as long as the money was needed; he furnished Edward's rooms, supplied him with cheques to cover other needs, marked his own birthday by making over £100 as a gift to Charlie and the young ones, rescuing Charlie from the poverty into which his brother's strong conviction would have cast him. Mr Martin even set aside £500 for the Benson girls' dowries.

Edward's sister Eleanor observed that her brother had a disposition to 'make idols', particularly of older men. At school he had formed an 'almost romantic attachment' to his headmaster, James Prince Lee, and at his first sight of the Tutor of Trinity, William Collings Mathison, in chapel, he had been awestruck, thinking he should never be able to approach such a quietly elegant, attractive man, with his 'small intelligent forehead and blue eyes and placid brow'. Yet the intensity of Mr Martin's feeling was confusing. 'I do not worthily return his affection,' Edward wrote. 'I find myself hardly able to understand it.' Nevertheless, he blossomed under the older man's care. The prig who could write such an uncompromising letter to his uncle could also be high-spirited and fancy free; he could be mad with the joy of a summer's morning, and take his mind off on crazy new adventures. Swept along by a fervour for the supernatural that spread countrywide in the 1850s, and echoing his father's and Dr Sollitt's interest in the occult, Edward helped found a Ghost Society, to collect and investigate ghostly tales. He wrote poems, took pleasure tours with Mr Martin and enjoyed silly jokes. In the 1851 long vacation he joined a reading party led by William Collings Mathison in the Lake District and went on long walks, enthusing in his diary that he 'shrieked and shrieked with delight' as he plunged into the Mirror Pool at Rydal Head, climbed up Scardale Fell then scampered down to Windermere, 'jumpy, jerky, wally-shally, boggy-joggy, splashy rushy, thumpy, zany, coky boasty, bathy, warmy, coolly, freshy'.

Lines Written by EWB for his Friend Mr Francis Martin, on Seeing Herons at Grasmere

One floating o'er the gorge, and one
Down dropping o'er the scar,
And one, wide-oaring o'er the wood
The Herons come from far,
From lonely glens where they had plied
All day their feasts and war.

Ah, goodly lords of a goodly land,
How calm they fold the wing:
How lordly beak on bosom couch'd
To their pine-hung eyrie swing,
And stand to see the sun go down
Each like a lonely king.

Mr Martin joined the party at Grasmere. Having twisted an ankle jumping off a coach, Edward sat quietly on a bank beside the lake, watching herons in the sunset and writing a poem about them for his patron and friend. That night he read Mr Martin his poem and received warm praise. The old man read aloud from Terence, Milton and Shakespeare. Edward noted in his diary 'how most pleasant' it was to see Mr Martin, 'with his short cut grizzled hair, and bright face with its constant smile, patting the book and stroking it, and sometimes smiling more and sometimes less, and now and then looking upwards with a scarcely heard Beautiful Beautiful—what *can* be more beautiful . . . leaving off to stroke your hand or lay his hand on your shoulders and play with your hair.'

It was this sentimental, headstrong, self-regarding, absolute, and conscientiously Christian young man for whom Francis Martin had packed his carpet-bag and hastened across the country with news of a first-class degree and the Senior Medal, and whom little Minnie Sidgwick had so aroused with her cleverness and her reading of *The Princess*.

Chapter Three

Mrs Sidgwick was startled by Edward's disclosure, and unsettled by his intentions. Little Minnie was a year below the age of consent and, even so, that was quite young enough. Mrs Sidgwick did not think it proper that a girl should marry before she was twenty-one. She could not entertain the idea of an engagement until, say, eighteen. Seven years away! Who was to say that the boy would not change his mind? Eleanor observed that Edward 'made idols'. Was this not just one? And there were yet so many duties and accomplishments for Minnie to acquire! Besides, there was the child's health to consider. She would soon be passing from girlhood into womanhood, a time that demanded the most anxious maternal supervision if a girl was to emerge unscathed. This was just the moment that any inherent weakness, mental or bodily, might show itself. Minnie was not very strong just now. She was fragile, an unformed child. Certainly, nothing must be said to her for the present. Edward had barely left the house when Mrs Sidgwick picked up her pen to write to him.

Edward was so distracted by events in Bristol that he left his portmanteau behind. Yet he entertained no doubt that he had been correct in speaking to Mrs Sidgwick. Edward explained his conduct to himself quite rationally. It was not surprising that he thought it possible sweet little Minnie should become his wife. They had long been very fond of each other. Besides, there had been tugs at his affections of late that disturbed him, and it would do well to put a stop to such feelings before he had committed any error that would evermore give him cause to repent (he slipped into cipher to record this fear in his diary). Pure little Minnie would help him. Tracing the seamless logic of decisions and circumstances propelled Edward into a sentence of quite extraordinary length:

As I have always been very fond of [Minnie] and she of me with the love of a little sister, and as I have heard of her fondness for me commented on by many persons, and have been told that I was the only person at whose departure she ever cried, as a child, and how diligent she has always been in reading books that I have mentioned to her, and in learning pieces of poetry which I have admired, it is not strange that I, who from the circumstances of my family am not likely to marry for many years to come, and who find in myself a growing distaste for forming friendships (fit to be so called) among new acquaintances and who am fond indeed (if not too fond) of little endearments, and who also know my weakness for falling suddenly in love, in the common sense of the word, and have already gone too far more than once in these things and have therefore reason to fear that I might on some sudden occasion be led [the following in cipher: *into a step I might all my life repent*]—it is not strange that I should have thought first of the possibility that some day dear little Minnie might become my wife.

23

'Dear little Minnie', as she said goodbye to Cousin Edward at Bristol Station on the April morning he headed back to Cambridge, did not cry. When her mother asked her why, Minnie quickly replied: 'I *could* have cried, only I should not think of doing it *on a platform*!' In the days that followed she chattered frequently about Edward. After an outing to 'Gloster' with her mother, she wrote to tell him all about it, ending with: 'All my pets are quite well, With love to you, I remain, Yours *very much*', and including a fluffy yellow feather from her canary for dear old Mr Martin, in a carefully folded piece of paper inscribed: 'A love token from Dicky'. Minnie liked to please people, and for them to feel loved. She was in awe of her big cousin, and very fond of him in her joyous, childish, all-encompassing way. 'I feel quite sure that no one can have put into her head any foolish idea about your notice of her,' wrote Mrs Sidgwick cautiously to Edward, 'and that no such idea has ever entered it, and I think you may quite fearlessly gratify her childish love for several years to come.'

Retrospective Glances from the Adult Diaries of Mrs Mary Benson (née Sidgwick)

I realise that he chose me deliberately, as a child who was very fond of him and whom he might educate—he even wanted to preserve himself from errant fallings-in-love . . . God, thou gavest me a nature which desired to please—and on its natural gaiety and pleasure-lovingness had been planted by my Mother a strong sense of duty.
Desire of pleasing E. because of fear of vexing . . .

Mrs Sidgwick's spinster sister Henrietta, Minnie's Aunt Etty who lived with them in Bristol, sniffed the air and sensed intrigue. Aunt Etty had ink-black hair, a hooked nose, a strong jaw and a voice like a man's. She was fearsome, prone to all-embracing moods that all too often plummeted into a deep enveloping gloom, and she frequently seethed with a consuming jealousy of those about her. Aunt Etty's darker moods could suck the entire household down with her, but when she swooped up again she startled people with her whooping laugh, and a sense of humour the family considered 'incongruous'. One morning after Edward had left, when alone with Mrs Sidgwick, Henrietta, quite unprompted, remarked how fond Minnie and Edward were of each other. She said that she could not help thinking that Minnie might 'some time be his wife'. Mrs Sidgwick did not comment, but side-stepping neatly asked Henrietta whether she would object to such a match. 'Oh, far from it,' boomed the reply. Nevertheless, wrote Mrs Sidgwick to Edward, 'I think it better to say nothing on the subject to anyone at present . . .' Aunt Etty was one more person for Minnie to please.

A prevailing wind of melancholy blew through Mrs Sidgwick's soul. Her grief at her husband's death had been deep and suffocating. It would have smothered her entirely had she not maintained such a strong sense of duty, and been of such sound practical character. She was a dignified and handsome woman, yet there was an air of bewilderment about her and a continued note of mournfulness in her speech. Perhaps this is what led Minnie to want so much to please her mother, and make her happy. Two of her six children lay buried, but she had managed successfully to bring up Minnie and three boys, and to give a roof to Henrietta. When Harriet Benson died, even though the families had not been particularly close, she had willingly taken in Edward's sisters, Eleanor and timid little Ada, who hesitated a full year before calling her 'Aunt Mary', and then only did so in a whisper. She loved Minnie and was fiercely protective of her. Edward's interest in the child caused her deep concern.

Widowhood had fallen upon Mary Sidgwick when she was just into her thirties. Eleven years later, she was still young enough to harbour her own passion for her brilliant, beautiful young relative. She was a handsome woman, with a delicate mouth, a pert, precise nose, large eyes and an abundant head of hair; her late husband had left her in possession of a comfortable fortune. Alone in Bristol one wet Friday evening, having returned from seeing Edward in Cambridge, she wrote 'to repeat how *very, very* much I have enjoyed my visit with you', and then continued, longingly: 'I wish I could just come and take tea with you and stir your fire and stroke your face and have a nice chat with you this windy rainy evening.' And it seems that young Edward's fire was indeed stirred by the woman 'who in all things was more than a mother'. They enjoyed long conversations together, hours after the others had gone to bed, discussing on at least one of Edward's visits whether he would 'ever be a fit companion for one true-hearted woman'. 'I have had a day of you—would that it could have been more in thinking of you only,' he wrote to her from Cambridge. 'How much I thought of you, and how much I wished for you, you may well fancy.'

Duty and pragmatism demanded of Mrs Sidgwick

26

a more motherly role—indeed, that is how Mr Martin encouraged Edward to see her, and Edward had 'affectionately confided' to her all his 'joys and sorrows'. Yet she also had Minnie's health and heart to protect, not to mention her purity. The young man whom she had assured 'that under all circumstances, my affectionate interest in you will *never* cease' had shown an inadmissible regard for her youngest

A Miniature of the Young Mrs Mary Sidgwick

daughter, attention which could 'give rise to thoughts which I hope for some years at least to come will have no existence in her'. Mrs Sidgwick would not permit that. Besides, however sincerely felt, Edward's passion for the child might only be a young man's passing fancy. With heartfelt candour Mrs Sidgwick wrote to him: 'You must allow me to say and from my heart I do say it, that any woman must think herself *most* happy in the possession of your full affections and that I shall think my own dear child singularly blessed to be *the* one when your *maturer* judgement and *older* affection would choose above *every other* and be satisfied with the choice.' These were themes to which, in her letters to Edward, Mrs Sidgwick would frequently return.

Mrs Sidgwick enjoyed a good letter. She would pick up her pen in the morning, again to catch an afternoon post, and sometimes yet again at midnight. Having just dispatched one missive, she began another with: 'I had not intended to write again so soon, but Eleanor's open Envelope lying

27

before me is a temptation I cannot resist', succumbing to the temptation for a full seven pages before running out of paper, having to finish off on a salvaged scrap, and producing a bulletin so heavy it had to be sent under separate cover, after all. Edward became the object of a voluminous correspondence.

Time and again, Mrs Sidgwick implored restraint. Minnie was but a child, and 'I do not wish you to suppose that her love is anything but the childish affection of a little sister'. Nothing should happen that would cause Minnie to 'lose that childlike simplicity which is her great charm'. Minnie was artless, and Edward should not read 'deeper meanings' into her expressions of fondness. If they were there, 'I would feel it necessary for you at once at least to *appear* to lessen your interest in her'. Tactfully, Mrs Sidgwick wrote that Edward was still '*a very young man*' and that her faith was 'not sufficiently strong in the constancy of any man's affection who has not yet attained the age of 23', especially when feelings were as 'warm and earnest' as his were. Edward might well change his mind about Minnie, and would be quite entitled to, but by then the harm would be done. She mentioned the dangers of marriage between cousins (consider the Royal Family!), and pointed out that Minnie was of an age when 'some of the greatest trials of health in childhood and youth are still to come', arguing dramatically that she would not want Edward to have to share her grief if Minnie should die.

Sunny Minnie chirruped along unawares, with bed each night at seven thirty, lessons at home, walks in the garden and games with Nurse Beth, Cousin Ada and her brothers. (Mrs Sidgwick did not approve of outside friends for the children, and the family 'rather gloried in being self-sufficient'.) Minnie always hastened to assure her mother of her love for Edward. 'Mama, I often wish I could be an invisible fairy with wings,' she told her. Then she would fly to Cambridge to see what Edward was doing there. Not that she would upset her awe-inspiring cousin: 'I would fly to Edward's room and hover over him, but I would not disturb him.'

In letter after letter Mrs Sidgwick put up valiant resistance to the untimeliness of Edward's suit, on occasion acknowledging that perhaps she had 'said this all before and may weary you by repetition of it', but continuing nonetheless. She managed to persuade Edward not to say anything to anyone about what they began tangentially to refer to as 'the subject', most of all not to Minnie, who became 'the sweet child', M., or simply __ .

Yet people were beginning to take notice. Edward was talking too much in company about Minnie's 'sayings and doings', even reading her letters aloud. Mrs Sidgwick had specifically to ask Edward to make *his* letters to Minnie suitable to show to others in the family, as people asked to read them and it was difficult to refuse. A friend of his in Cambridge had joked—loudly and while on an omnibus—that Edward treated his little cousin more like a lover than a relation. Edward's sister Eleanor, though concerned that it was 'impertinent in a younger sister' to raise such a topic, had mentioned her misgivings about Edward's behaviour to Mrs Sidgwick.

Mrs Sidgwick was herself concerned that Minnie was now too old for the petting and kissing an adult might lavish on a small child. 'It would seem almost

29

ridiculous to prescribe the degree of interest which it would be safe to show a child of 11 years old,' she wrote, but she hoped that Edward 'would gradually give up such childish fondlings as were only suited to a childish age', or at least 'give them up *for a time*'. But Edward was a most forceful young man, and Mrs Sidgwick's resilience was strongly tested.

Edward demanded regular news of his 'little pet', information he referred to as 'nursery tales'. He pushed to be allowed to speak to her on 'the subject', bombarding Mrs Sidgwick with almost as many letters as she sent to him. Mr Martin, always very much on his protégé's side, joined the cause, pressing with all the authority of an older man and a Cambridge don for Edward to 'speak' (propose) to Minnie. Still Mrs Sidgwick stood her ground. 'I cannot *for a moment* agree with Mr Martin in thinking that any such communication be made to dear Minnie *so early*,' she wrote. 'I really think it would be taking an unfair advantage of a mere child, and not allowing her to be a free agent . . . I have been *wrong* very *wrong* to let your mind dwell so much upon the whole scheme.'

Yet Mrs Sidgwick seemed powerless to resist Edward's fervour. She and Minnie went to Cambridge to visit him, and he came frequently to Bristol. 'There really is no end of him,' proclaimed Aunt Etty, 'one never knows when he is gone.' Always anxious to please, and to assure both Edward and her mother of her love, little Minnie said and did what she perceived would make them happy, even if she had now become a little frightened of her cousin. When Mama wrote Edward a letter, Minnie would ask her to send him her '*very, very, very* best love', and she said how she wished he could come to her room and kiss her goodnight *every* night. After Edward had been dropped at the station at the end of one visit, Minnie sat in his vacated seat in the fly, allowed her eyes to fill with tears and intoned: 'Oh, but for one touch of that vanished hand', on this occasion slightly misquoting her Tennyson. Only once did Mrs Sidgwick find her looking at a portrait of Edward and muttering to herself 'Minnie hates, Minnie hates,' but Minnie assured her mama that she was not in earnest.

Recollections of this Time from Mrs Benson's Retrospective Diary, Written in March 1876

Ed. coming—*fear of him*—love? always a strain—never the love that 'casteth out all fear'.

Mother and Ed. both wanting my love—neither at all satisfied . . . misery. . . utter misery.

I had to satisfy Ed. by expressions of love and after was not true to Mama . . . I was influenced too strongly by him, without really loving.

Go to Beth to comfort me.

On occasions Minnie seemed not to want to visit Edward, or was sulky and uncommunicative once they arrived in Cambridge. That was put down to her 'endeavour to hide the sorrow she felt at parting'. Now she had constantly to be reminded to write to him, and sometimes the simple mention of his name would bring on tears—but again Minnie assured her mother that was because she loved Edward so much and never wanted to do anything to grieve him. When Mrs Sidgwick told her that her drawing needed attention, Minnie promised to improve, because it would gratify her mama, her cousin Eleanor and brother William, 'and she added with tears in her eyes "Edward too—and immediately turned away"'.

Edward persisted in his onslaught. He hinted darkly to Mrs Sidgwick at the temptations that beset him, and at what the consequences might be if he could not express his love for Minnie. The matter-of-fact widow was unmoved. She had been a headmaster's wife and had raised three boys single-handedly. She had, she wrote, an idea, albeit 'undefined', of 'those severe temptations which peculiarly affect boys when they are removed from the sheltering care of home'. She sympathized with the 'anticipation of coming evil' which weighed him down so, and though she advised 'earnest prayer', she knew from experience that there was 'no better antidote than regular and active employment'. As she had with her own boys, Mrs Sidgwick offered Edward a mother's love, the thought of which she hoped would 'present itself in the moment of temptation and sometimes be victorious'.

In his face-to-face encounters with Mrs Sidgwick, Edward did not appear troubled by any misplaced filial respect. He was at various times scathing, hurtful, humiliating her. He had a way of turning on her that devastated her, generally contriving to leave her feeling that she was somehow at fault. Mrs Sidgwick's efforts to protect her child became tempered by an anxiety not to incur Edward's wrath or lose his affection. Her letters grew peppered with apologies, cravings for forgiveness, assurances that he would never lose her love or goodwill. Mrs Sidgwick's resistance was crumbling, and the change in atmosphere was tangible.

A visitor to the house, who had never met Edward, but heard much about him, said: 'I don't know how it is, but if Minnie were a little older, I should be disposed to form quite a *romantic idea* of her and Mr Benson!' Aunt Etty again began to fish for confirmation of her suspicions, saying that when Edward *did* marry, she hoped it would be to a *very* nice woman, adding: 'Well I don't think he will be likely to meet with *anyone* when he comes to see *us*, who will be at all likely to attract him.' When that elicited no response from Mrs Sidgwick, she mentioned the *'peculiar suitableness'* of Minnie's and Edward's characters, and attempted: 'I wouldn't be surprised if in seven or eight years' time they become engaged.' When that still did not loosen Mrs Sidgwick's tongue, Henrietta fired broadside-on with: 'I am sure he thinks of her *as his future wife* and that he has told you so, *has he not*?' Mrs Sidgwick had to acknowledge that yes, he had, and went on to admit to Edward that Henrietta was 'really much pleased with the thought'. There was something magnetic about Edward; something that pulled all around him, particularly women, into his thrall. Edward knew what he wanted, and he always got his way. It had been just a matter of months. After a long conversation alone with him, Mrs Sidgwick relented.

Talk, even in large houses, has a habit of seeping out from the most private tête-à-têtes. Aunt Etty had not been alone in sensing something in the air. 'Mama, it would be curious for me to be engaged

33

now,' said Minnie suddenly one afternoon. 'I should not like it because I would not be able to think properly about it.'

Barely a year after Minnie had read to her cousin from *The Princess*, Edward sat in an armchair in a secluded corner of the Sidgwicks' home and, as he usually did, took the 'little fair girl of twelve with her earnest look' upon his knee. He told her that he wanted to speak to her of something serious, and then 'got quietly to the thing' and asked her if she had ever thought it might come to pass that they should be married.

Minnie was silent. A rush of tears fell down her cheeks.

For just a moment Edward hesitated, then he went on. He told Minnie that she was often in his thoughts, and that he believed he should never love anyone so much as her—provided that she grew up in the manner that it seemed likely she would.

Minnie remained silent.

Edward continued. He said that he thought her too young to make any promise as yet, but that he wished to say this much to her, and if she felt the same she might promise a few years hence.

Still, Minnie said nothing. The tears streamed down her cheeks.

Then, without speaking, she took Edward's handkerchief and—like the heroine of a novel, or a maiden in a poem—she tied a lover's knot in it, and pressed it into his hand.

Edward was 'affected very much'. The gesture was an encouragement. A positive response, indeed.

And thus 'the thing' was settled.

* * *

For the time being, the matter was kept private. Minnie's elder brother William was told, her uncles had been consulted, and of course Mama and Aunt Etty knew, but no official announcement was yet made. Minnie did confide in her comforting nurse, Beth. It was decided that Minnie should sit next to Edward at table, and that he should take a portrait of her to hang on his chimney-piece at Trinity. In the days that followed, Minnie leafed once more through *The Princess*. Edward asked her if the thought of marrying him had ever struck her, when she read to him from the poem. 'Never,' she said. Backward and forward Minnie turned the pages, exclaiming again and again: 'I wonder I never thought of it!' and 'I never understood this passage till today!' Most gratifyingly to her cousin, now fiancé, and no doubt to her mama as well, she recited the line: 'Love, children, happiness', adding: 'Two of those are mine now!'

Chapter Four

Edward had returned to Cambridge, following his First and Senior Medal in Classics, to read German. His rooms in Trinity New Court offered a view over the Backs, with a window so close to the library that he could almost climb across. One morning, towards the end of the academic year and shortly after he had proposed to Minnie, he leaned out. Striding down an avenue of limes by the river was a man he knew by sight as Dr Goulburn, headmaster of Rugby School. Dr Goulburn had succeeded Archibald Tait, who had taken over from the great pedagogue Dr Arnold himself. A moment later there was a knock at Edward's door. The headmaster was standing at the threshold with the surprising announcement that he had come in person to invite Edward to join his staff at Rugby. Edward asked him in. Clearly, someone had been putting in a very good word on his behalf. The terms of Dr Goulburn's offer could hardly have been more favourable.

Edward was to assist the headmaster with the Sixth Form, but would teach for just one hour a day. He would be assigned some boys as private pupils, to supplement his income, but would have the afternoons free to read for a Trinity fellowship. Rugby held an added allure for Edward. As Minnie's brothers were to go to the school, Mrs Sidgwick and Minnie, together with all the company from Bristol, had just moved there, into a suburban villa called the Blue House. Edward himself had persuaded Mrs Sidgwick to disregard her late husband's determination *not* to send his sons to one of the public schools for fear of the poor moral tone that pervaded them (the product of a dissolute aristocracy, in his view). Edward argued that a moral transformation had taken place in public schools since Mr Sidgwick's time. Dr Arnold had led this change at Rugby, imbuing his pupils with a strong work ethic and sound Christian virtues of truthfulness, purity and manliness, combined with healthy exercise—the foundations of what was becoming known as Muscular Christianity. Edward was a firm adherent. He accepted Dr Goulburn's offer.

The Blue House, named for its curiously coloured bricks, was surrounded by a large garden 'agreeably planted with elms'. The household consisted primarily of women—Mama and Minnie, Beth and Aunt Etty, and of course little Ada, nearly Minnie's age and much braver than before, even a touch wilful. Eleanor was now married, brother William was off at Oxford, and Henry and Arthur were at school most of the day. The Blue House swished with silk and tinkled politely with teacups. Piano scales faltered across the morning air, occasionally to be joined by Aunty Etty's booming baritone and whooping laugh, or by the whack of cricket bats if the boys were home. With her slightly bewildered look and melancholy voice, armed with her edifying phrases and belief in 'talking people round', Mrs Sidgwick drifted through the Blue House keeping the entire vessel afloat.

For the twelve-year-old Minnie, life at the Blue

House was lonely. Mrs Sidgwick did not wish her to have friends; in her view, lessons and the family were enough. Minnie walked often in the large garden, and she soon chose a favourite tree. Woods and open fields lay just a few minutes away, and she now had a pony. She also, very soon, had Edward. Shortly after taking up his new position, following a brief stay in lodgings in Rugby, Edward went to live at the Blue House.

Edward went riding with Minnie, and for walks in the garden. She showed him her special tree, and allowed him a kiss under it—something that plagued her conscience, and about which she could not tell Mama. The walks and the rides, and Edward's demands, multiplied. Minnie drew in on herself. Her sulks and tearful silences became more frequent. She was often idle and listless. At times she cried herself to sleep, and she still sought comfort with her nurse, Beth. What was said to Beth, stayed with Beth. She was a fount of warmth and homely maxims; solid, shrewd, and sympathetic. 'Now don't you get to thinking about it,' she might say, 'or you'll not go to sleep.'

Mrs Sidgwick was concerned about Minnie's behaviour. The time for what she might have referred to as Minnie's 'turns' or 'monthlies' was approaching. Doctors warned that this was an age of 'miniature insanity', when even the most well-behaved girls waxed 'snappish, fretful . . . full of deceit and mischief', and that especially the young 'pet of the family' could become inexplicably 'irreligious, selfish, slanderous, false, malicious, devoid of affection . . . self-willed and quarrelsome'. Minnie and her mother had many a long talk, but Minnie had developed 'a fatal want of confidence' in her mother, though she still hated to see her upset. Minnie did not mention difficulties with Edward. She simply hoped that 'complications' would go away.

Misery was most easily banished by not thinking of what Cousin Edward had said, of those dark pools of the past, nor of the turbulent waters of the future, but by splashing happily in the shallows of the present. Minnie's natural cheerfulness was not easily dispelled; the volatility that Mrs Sidgwick had remarked upon proved irrepressible. Minnie clung on to her sunny, spirited, childlike nature as a means of survival. She skated over the surface of difficulties and revelled in the pleasures of the moment, in the butterflies in the garden and the hills growing gold in the autumn. She learned to distil clear nectar from the bleakest situation and to keep her sorrows to herself—and she never forgot how to do this. 'I have long observed in Minnie that she has much difficulty in the expression of her deepest feelings,' noted Mrs Sidgwick, 'remarkably so for a child of her light-heartedness—and yet that she does feel strongly and warmly, I am sure.' A house like the Blue House always has secrets to hold, as those who sit at its tables and slumber in its beds speak, yet say just so much, know and do not know; where so much that really matters remains deep and unsaid.

Swept along by all that was happening to her, Minnie (to her mother and Edward, at least) showed a girlish delight in the secret of her engagement. And she did believe Edward was splendid. For as long as she could remember she had revered her older cousin, adored him—and that was love, was it not?

Jottings from Mrs Benson's Retrospective Diary, *in which she casts a more penetrating adult eye on those childhood sorrows she kept to herself*

. . . that terrible, difficult, amazing, Rugby time . . .

A terrible time. Dreary, helpless . . . He had been allowed to tell me but was not allowed to speak but he *did*—and more—hand-embrace—etc. all weights on my conscience . . . Oh the 1000 difficulties and complications! I lacked courage to bear his dark looks—gloom—but I see now I *did not* love him—Yet he loved me.

Walks. More freedom with Ed.—at last the great complication—Mama wanted me to tell her all that he said, without his knowing of my promise—I made a stand, and, I think, rightly—the 2 walks with Ed to Tree.

I had to strain the truth in order to satisfy Ed. by expressions of love and after was not true to Mama I was influenced too strongly by him, without really loving.

E's disclosure—tears and emotion—why? No real thought about it after. *Really* I think it made me younger. I would not allow any responsibility . . . ride with Edward—*I wasn't true* . . . Here I began to be cowardly—pleasure loving and living in the present.

. . . every interval was to me a kind of holiday in which I drew breath and played, and so it came to pass that I *did not grow up*—not in deep growth, in maturity.

Minnie did fall in love at the Blue House, a few years after moving there, when she was sixteen. Mrs Sidgwick had by then relaxed her strictures on outside friends, and among the visitors Minnie discovered her 'first friendship', a girl who quite captured her heart: 'I fell in love with her and spent a great deal of time with her—and loved her *über alle Massen* [beyond all measure].' Minnie neglected both the others and her duties and this 'vexed Mama', but she kept her feelings to herself. No one else in the Blue House mentions a particular friend. No one, not even Minnie, gives a hint of the girl's name.

Minnie's curious habit of using German to express her innermost feelings was one she picked up from Edward. He had been giving her lessons. Edward's trajectory was effortlessly upward. He had been elected to a fellowship at Trinity during his first term of teaching at Rugby, and was ordained in January 1854, despite being unable to answer a single question put to him by the Bishop of Manchester's chaplain when he arrived for his examination as a candidate for holy orders. The chaplain reprimanded Edward for his ignorance, but when he learned his name (he had missed it at first) realized that he had before him a letter from the Bishop himself, mentioning Edward and including a sealed document which affirmed that Edward had passed 'a most creditable examination'. The young man's influential admirers were once again hard at work. The Bishop was Edward's old headmaster from his schooldays in Birmingham, James Prince Lee.

Edward was clearly destined for high things, and required a fitting consort. In the six years that he lived at Rugby he set about shaping his infant inamorata into a model wife. Not just German, but a range of subjects formed her curriculum. 'Lessons with Edward—so dreaded—architecture and physical geography,' she wrote. There was more: arithmetic, poetic metre, liturgical doctrine. Even in the early days, back in Bristol, Edward and Mrs Sidgwick had embarked on a joint mission to mould and educate little Minnie. Edward made clear when he first spoke to Mrs Sidgwick that he wished to marry Minnie only 'if she grew up as it seemed likely [i.e. in the manner he was expecting]'. Mrs Sidgwick was intent on her ultimately unsuccessful project to temper Minnie's volatility. Edward sent the twelve-year-old girl reading material: books on Pompeii and the Reformation, Ovid's *Epistles*. Minnie complained of too many troublesome words, but Mrs Sidgwick observed that 'a little *hard* reading will do her good'. Edward corrected the style and grammar of the letters Minnie wrote to him (she had a tendency to use the same word more than once). Mrs Sidgwick encouraged his criticism, as what he said 'always makes a deep impression', and for her own part she impressed upon Minnie how good it was of Edward to show such concern, and the necessity that she do her duty.

When, on occasions during the Rugby years, Edward was away from home, he continued Minnie's education by correspondence. On one trip to the Continent with his friends, he dispatched long, crushingly dull letters on the niceties of cathedral architecture, delivered in suffocating prose. Minnie, well-versed in the romantic poems and novels of which her mother rather disapproved, knew what was expected of her and was more flamboyant in reply. How she read and reread his letters, she told him. How she kissed them and devoured them till she knew them half by heart! How she took them up to bed with her and held them to her breast! 'Oh I did indeed put my heart close to yours, and yours echoed back such loving thoughts and beat oh so true—my love, my love, my love!' she wrote. Occasionally, Minnie got into trouble for 'exaggerated affection' in her letters. Mrs Sidgwick read them all.

Not only did the little head require close attention and careful direction, but the little heart, and the little soul, too. Mrs Sidgwick set to work on Minnie's 'characteristic failings' of carelessness and a wandering attention in her lessons, shortcomings that were 'not softened by reproof'. As Minnie grew older, the righteous Edward brought heavier guns to bear:

Believe me though, you will not be *really* nor *permanently* comfortable and happy till you know that you [?deserve] your own respect, and mine, and that of others, by a regular unsparing Crusade against the faults you speak of—like insolence is [sic] conquered and unselfishness is a clear ruling principle . . .

Edward noted that Minnie's 'besetting sin' was thoughtlessness. In his magnanimity, he acknowledged that she was anxious to control herself, 'and grow up a good and useful woman, a *true woman*'—but if she did not attempt to cure

43

herself of this weakness, she would 'go on *always* perpetually giving pain, and perpetually causing trouble to those whom you most love and wish to please'. His masterstroke in provoking a self-regulating sense of guilt was to tell Minnie that if she did not attend to this fault, she would expose her love for others to perpetual suspicion. They would ask: '*could* she do so, if she really and constantly loved me, and thought how she might please me?' Edward exhorted Minnie to read this letter several times.

Minnie had always hated causing others pain, had always wanted 'to make people happy at once'. Now her entire energy, her mirth, charm and vivacity were focused on the desire 'to be worthy of [Edward], to please him, not to disappoint him'— and to please her mother, too, Mama who had ever tried to instil in her a sense of duty. Minnie understood what she should be doing, and set about doing it. She *would* be 'a good and useful woman, a *true woman*'. She would shape herself to Edward. Like the fair love in *The Princess*, she would set herself to him, 'Like perfect music unto noble words'. As Minnie approached womanhood, the foundations for her married life were being firmly laid.

By the time she was sixteen or seventeen, Minnie was already providing emotional support for the man twelve years her senior. Towards the end of his first year at Rugby, Edward had begun to experience periods when he felt bilious and cross, 'with a decidedly low opinion of the world, and a melancholy view of human life'. As time went on, he would sink for days on end into crippling depressions. The doctors diagnosed neuralgia, for which the prescribed cure was a heavy, meat-filled diet, large doses of quinine, and generous quantities of port—which one imagines might not have ensured him much in the way of bright mornings, cheerful clarity of mind or a settled stomach. Edward relied increasingly on Minnie to brighten the mood of her 'affectionate grumbler'.

In Minnie's enclosed world, where Nurse Beth's love and that 'first friendship' with an unnamed girl were solitary beacons of warmth and affection, Edward's volcanic energy, his ardour, beauty and intelligence, drew out a devotion in her. Dry, critical, humourless and didactic he may have been, but he did love her. When, in March 1859, their long-secret engagement was eventually made public, Minnie revelled in the attention this brought her, expressing 'elation' at a 'sense of being interesting'. A few months previously, at the remarkably young age of twenty-nine, Edward had been offered the headmastership of Wellington College, a new public school established by Prince Albert as a memorial to the Duke of Wellington. This gave him the financial stability to summon his ideal wife, and to set a wedding date for 23 June. Minnie was eighteen.

As their wedding day approached, Edward relaxed a little. He wrote a poem on the transformation of his 'Ladylove' to 'Wife'. Some of the stuffiness of his letters to Minnie disappeared. At times they took on a tone reminiscent of the crazy light-heartedness he had recorded many years before, on holiday in the Lake District. 'I find I have no will of my own now, you *witch*!' he wrote to Minnie a month before the wedding, adding with some prescience: 'But I can only console myself by a magnificent threat—"*You won't find it so always*" —There now!' At Minnie's suggestion that they take a long walk together after collecting their banns certificate prior to the wedding, he exclaimed, 'your picture of the walk down the Newbold Road drives me almost wild', warning in a later letter that Minnie had 'better order a strait waistcoat [straitjacket] in case the possession of it [the 'precious certificate'] should involve any extravagances'. He concludes one letter:

Ever with fervent
lover-love and
enduring husband-love
Your own
Edward

In another letter, mentioning the gift of a cameo bracelet to Minnie from Mr Martin, he enthuses in a flurry of underlining: 'you must wear it on the *day*—the 23rd you know—the 23rd the 23rd the 23rd', a few days later surrounding that magical '23rd' with a bursting halo of lines, so that it appears on the page like an explosion, or a holy star.

Edward wrote of his delight at receiving the passport for their wedding journey, as it described him as the Revd E. W. Benson, 'a British Subject travelling on the Continent with his wife'. Just five days before the wedding, he sent Minnie a series of solemn promises, written in German, and 'set to my hand, dear love, that I will do my part faithfully and lovingly in keeping them, and if I ever transgress show me this letter and I will beg your

46

forgiveness on my knees . . .' He asked Minnie to copy out the promises and sign a similar undertaking, adding a cautionary 'I know that I never shall have to show them to you again'.

A Solemn and Personal Contract

1. *Von heute an lebst Du für mich und ich lebe für Dich; und wir wollen nie vor einander das geringste Geheimnis haben, und selbst wenn wir gefehlt haben, es uns einander sogleich offenbaren.*

2. *Wir wollen von unsern häuslichen Sachen Niemandem nichts offenbaren.*

3. *Endlich, wollen wir niemals gegen einander böse werden und nicht einmal zum Scherz mit einander böse thun.*

1. From this day forth you will live for me and I shall live for you; we shall never keep the slightest secret from each other, and even if we do go astray in this, we will confess at once.

2. We shall never reveal anything of our domestic affairs to anyone.

3. Finally, we shall never be angry with each other, and not even act badly towards one another in jest.

The eighteen-year-old Minnie was rather plain, with full cheeks and a snub nose. Her thick hair, parted

Mary Benson,
Aged Nineteen

in the centre, hung in two large loops over her ears, and was gathered at the nape of her neck. Her hands were chubby, her figure dumpy, but there was a mischievous glint in her eyes, and her lips toyed tantalizingly with smiles. She was quite capable of teasing her husband-to-be, telling him she had gone without him to a ball, though had not 'danced with a *single gentleman* except in a Sir Roger de Coverley, and that one was Earnest [sic] Coleridge of the age of 11'.

Edward was sometimes startled at the change in his little Minnie. 'Wherever learned you that sweet charm (so dear to a bridegroom) to be at once so maidenly and so wifely,' he wrote to her after a visit to Rugby from Wellington College, where he had already begun preparations for the opening of the school. 'Wherever learned you to be so maiden-modest yet so wifely-frank, and so womanly-free and so unprudish-pure?' He marvelled at the emergence of the woman he had both moulded and yearned for for seven long years. 'When you loved me with the *child love* you speak of now—oh how sadly sometimes I used to wonder *when* it would ripen, and be *all* like the little flashes of *woman-love* that used to flash out sometimes in the midst.' He looked forward to the night when 'we shall sleep in Paris, married life with all its untried bliss will be a reality and no dream or imagination any more'.

48

ON

THE ORIGIN OF SPECIES

BY MEANS OF NATURAL SELECTION,

OR THE

PRESERVATION OF FAVOURED RACES IN THE STRUGGLE FOR LIFE.

By CHARLES DARWIN, M.A.,

FELLOW OF THE ROYAL, GEOLOGICAL, LINNÆAN, ETC., SOCIETIES;
AUTHOR OF ' JOURNAL OF RESEARCHES DURING H. M. S. BEAGLE'S VOYAGE
ROUND THE WORLD.'

LONDON:
JOHN MURRAY, ALBEMARLE STREET.
1859.

The right of Translation is reserved.

On Bookshelves in the Year of the Bensons' Marriage

Minnie was sent off to sit for a pre-wedding photo-portrait, with an appointment at noon 'because from 12 to 3 is the best time for the sun'. Mrs Sidgwick treated her to a shopping spree in London. Minnie was as excited as a child with her silks and laces, her little light-brown jacket, her wide hat trimmed with white ribbon, her trinkets and fineries. She delighted in the moment. She bathed in the sense of making

Edward so happy, and she 'put away the future'. Edward Benson and Mary Sidgwick were married on 23 June 1859, at St Andrew's Church in Rugby. Dr Frederick Temple, the new headmaster of Rugby School, conducted the ceremony. The couple set off immediately for Folkestone and the Continent.

A Final Backward Glance from Mrs Benson's Retrospective Diary

So childishly, confidently, without stay or guide, though trusting in God . . . only *childish in understanding* I married that June morning . . .

. . . danced and sang into matrimony, with a loving, but exacting, a believing and therefore expecting spirit 12 years older, much stronger, more passionate, and whom I didn't really love—I wonder I didn't go more wrong . . .

PART II

Mrs Benson

Chapter Five

The Revd E. W. Benson, 'travelling on the Continent with his wife', headed first to Paris. Mary bought a diary from the Papeterie Maquet on the Rue de la Paix, most likely at Edward's instigation, as it is Edward's voice that echoes from the pages. While Edward had no sympathy at all for music (his rendition of hymns in church produced 'a buzzing noise that bore no relation to any known melody') or for secular painting, he was absolutely indefatigable when it came to ecclesiastical art and churches. Dutifully, Mary records in her diary opinions on architecture, as the couple march through church after church. She mouths phrases as hollow as those of a child repeating what it has overheard its parents say, passing off their wisdom as its own. 'The west front, which we come upon first, is exceedingly various in detail, though not at all over-ornamented,' she intones. 'There is none of that ugly *matching* which is so often seen in Churches of the present day,' she continues, preaching against 'everything weak and modern'.

To the diary, Mary confides not a word on love or marriage. She barely mentions Edward. Only in a much later journal does she recall her feelings of those first few days of married life:

53

Revd E. W. Benson and his Wife

Wedding night—Folkstone [*sic*]—crossing—
oh how my heart sank—I daren't let it
... misery—knowing that I felt nothing of
what I knew people ought to feel—knowing
how disappointing this must be to Ed., how
evidently disappointed he was—trying to be
rapturous—not succeeding, feeling so
inexpressibly lonely and young ...

Edward's passionate nature can hardly have come
as a surprise to Mary, but she had lived for the
moment, had 'put away the future'. It caught up
with her in Paris: 'How I cried at Paris! poor lonely
child, having lived in the present only ... The
nights! I can't think how I lived.' In retrospect she
wondered 'how hard it was for Edward. He
restrained his passionate nature for 7 years, and
then got *me!*'

Duty to her mother had been supplanted by
duty to her husband, and Mary did her best to

fulfil that duty. It did not take Edward long to break the third of the promises he had made her before their wedding—'the first hard word' came as early as Paris, over laundry arrangements. It is hard to imagine that Mary produced Edward's letter in response to his anger, or required him—as he had vowed he would—to apologize on his knees.

Three Victorian Honeymoons

Amelia Sedley, newly Mrs George Osborne,
contemplates her childhood bed

She looked at the little white bed, which had been hers a few days before, and thought she would like to sleep in it that night, and wake, as formerly, with her mother smiling over her in the morning. Then she thought with terror of the great funereal damask pavilion in the vast and dingy state bedroom, which awaited her at the grand hotel in Cavendish Square. Dear little white bed! How many a long night she had wept on its pillow! How she had despaired and hoped to die there ... Kind mother! How patiently and tenderly she had watched round that bed! She went and knelt down by the bedside; and there this wounded and timorous, but gentle and loving soul, sought for consolation, where as yet, it must be owned, our little girl had but seldom looked for it.

From *Vanity Fair* by William Makepeace
Thackeray, 1847–8

Dorothea Casaubon is found sobbing while on her wedding journey in Rome

Dorothea had no distinctly shapen grievance that she could state even to herself; and in the midst of her confused thought and passion, the mental act that was struggling forth into clearness was a self-accusing cry that her feeling of desolation was the fault of her own spiritual poverty. She had married the man of her choice, and with the advantage over most girls that she had contemplated her marriage chiefly as the beginning of new duties ... that new real future which was replacing the imaginary drew its material from the endless minutiae by which her view of Mr Casaubon and her wifely relation, now that she was married to him, was gradually changing with the secret motion of a watch-hand from what it had been in her maiden dream. It was too early yet for her fully to recognize or at least admit the change, still more for her to have readjusted that devotedness which was so necessary a part of her mental life that she was almost sure sooner or later to recover it. Permanent rebellion, the disorder of a life without some loving reverent resolve, was not possible to her; but she was now in an interval when the very force of her nature heightened its confusion.

From *Middlemarch*
by George Eliot, 1871–2

Married off by her guardian to the first man to express an interest in her, young Janey discovers the nature of married life

Janey, being young, and shy, and strange, was a good deal frightened, horrified, and even revolted, by her first discoveries of what it meant to be in love. She had made tremendous discoveries in the course of a week. She had found out that Mr Rosendale, her husband, was in love with her beauty, but as indifferent to herself as any of the persons she had quitted to give herself to him. He did not care at all what she thought, how she felt, what she liked or disliked. He did not care even for her comfort, or that she should be pleased and happy . . . He took it for granted that, being his wife, she would naturally be pleased with what pleased him, and his mind went no further than this. Therefore, as far as Janey liked the things he liked, all went well enough. She had these and no other. Her wishes were not consulted further, nor did he know that he failed in any way towards her . . . he played billiards in the evening in the hotels to which he took her on their wedding journey; or he overwhelmed her with caresses from which she shrank in disgust, almost terror. That was all that being in love meant, she found; and to say that she was disappointed cruelly was to express in the very mildest way the dreadful downfall of all her expectations and hopes . . .

From *A Story of a Wedding Tour* by Margaret Oliphant, written during the 1870s

The Bensons hurtled onwards to Switzerland. Edward travelled at a relentless tempo. 'There are some interesting places in the neighbourhood,' noted Mary, somewhat wistfully, at Rheims, 'which we had not time to go and see.' Phrases such as 'we intended to go' and 'we determined to try and reach it' pepper her narrative as the sights flash by on a marathon twelve-hour journey to Strasbourg. Even there, the Bensons did not stop: 'There we had such a fine bustle! Edward rushed off to get the tickets, while I bolted into the refreshment room, for the train started for Basle almost immediately.'

At Basle, they stopped for a night at the grand Hotel des Trois Rois, where from their bedroom window the young bride could admire 'the mighty Rhine', which 'rolled along as it seemed beneath our very feet, with a murmuring deep music, glittering in the moonlight'. Next day, sitting in the garden of the equally luxurious Hotel Baur au Lac in Zurich, she stared out across the lake, the first (she notes in her travel diary) she had ever seen, until late in the evening, 'watching the red light of the sun . . . fade away into pale moonlight'. Mary Benson had never been abroad before, and she marvelled at what she saw. As she and Edward travelled into the Alps, her diary finally finds her own voice. She inhales pine forests 'fragrant with the rich smell of rain', glories in wild roses and tufts of Alpine gentians; she is transfixed by 'a roaring river . . . rushing down, foaming and turbid from some far-off glacier'. An Alpine horn blows a 'scale of notes, wild and sweet, up and down—and wilder and sweeter and more faint, the mountains give back the notes, multiplied over and over again'. Pretty Swiss girls catch her eye, decked out

58

for festivity in silver chains and trinkets; a 'charming, motherly woman in a blue gown and spectacles', who waits on her at an inn, pleases her immensely; with chambermaids she collapses in giggles at her own clumsy attempts to speak German.

After Edward's stifling lectures on architecture all the way through France, the Alps rekindled Mary's verve and sense of adventure. Off she set along mountain trails, 'armed with a magnificent Alpenstock' (Edward 'scorning such aid'), and earning the 'wondrous compliment' from the guide that she was a veritable *Gamsenjäger* (mountain-goat hunter). She crossed a glacier, admiring the 'glorious blue-green colour of the ice in the crevasses', tried her hand at rowing on Lake Lucerne, took a dip in its 'clear blue waters' (the most enjoyable bathe she had ever had), and, despite the 'fearful prophecies on Edward's part concerning the damage that was likely to accrue', went sledging on a patch of snow. She found chamois delicious to eat, and improvised with a handkerchief when she needed a veil against the sun. On one walk the young couple had to take shelter from a storm in a country cottage, with three 'nice-looking, intelligent lads and a little demure maiden'; on another she persuaded Edward to buy her 'a noble little St Bernard's puppy', which in fact turned out not to be of that breed at all.

Edward and Mary joined two other newly-weds, the Stephens from Reading, for mule rides and Alpine walks; on one such, they left the other couple behind, 'leaping and running down the steep descent' to the edge of a glacier, where they sat among rhododendrons to gaze down on the ice, as they waited for their companions and guide to catch up. Edward's school and college friend Joseph Lightfoot arrived for a while, with a large party. They went on carriage rides with some Americans (a nation Mrs Sidgwick held in intense disdain), and encountered swarms of insects which caused the ladies to point and scream, and the gentlemen to come to their rescue, walloping with maps and guidebooks.

At night they sat around the log fires of inns, talked with other guests, dozed, and danced the occasional polka (something else of which Mrs Sidgwick deeply disapproved). Mary finished and enjoyed Charles Kingsley's rather bloodthirsty *Westward Ho!*, which she had brought with her to read, and acquired a copy of Thackeray's recently published *The Virginians*, which depressed her 'by the dreadful picture of human nature that it gave'.

Towards the end of July, the Reverend and Mrs Benson packed what they needed into a small carpet-bag, sent their heavier luggage on ahead, and began the journey back to England, settled married life, and Wellington College.

Chapter Six

After a brief stay with Mrs Sidgwick in Rugby, Edward and Mary left for Wokingham, in Berkshire. Wellington College was four miles out of town, set in a desolate part of Bagshot Heath. Mary sat in her bonnet and shawl, amidst the undulating sea of her skirts, as their carriage trundled them across scrubland and heather, over a sandy hill covered in Scotch fir and sword-grass. Her new home rose before her, a startling rendition of a French château, gaunt and imposing with its unweathered red brick and pale Bath stone. Flanking towers with leaden tops gave the unpleasant sensation of 'following one everywhere, it seemed, with hollow melancholy eyes'. Beside the school lay a marsh that Edward intended to turn into bathing pools, beyond that the raised plateau of The Ridges. To the east, the chimney of a stoneworks belched black fumes, surrounded by a garden of broken carvings; to the west was a wild forest known as Bearwood. From the school gates sandy paths ran through groves of pine and across untamed heathland, where, in the distance, stood a cluster of brick kilns with smoky tops. Just over a mile away, the Broadmoor Criminal Lunatic Asylum was being built. Sandhurst Military College lay a little farther off. The carriage rode up a recently planted avenue of Wellingtonia trees, into

61

Wellington College

grounds where heather bound in bundles stood
ready for removal, and the rhododendrons Edward
had ordered were just beginning to flourish.

The Prince Consort, Prince Albert, had
enthusiastically appropriated the plan by the Duke
of Wellington Memorial Fund to establish a new
public school as an enduring monument to the
Iron Duke, who had died in 1852. Prince Albert
wanted to found a school to rival Eton and
Marlborough, based on the classical curriculum
and functioning along sound German educational
lines. Preference for admission would be given to
the sons of deceased army officers, who would be
offered a first-rate education at affordable fees. By
1858, the school building was already well under

way but Albert had rejected all the candidates from a list of over thirty men submitted to him for the post of headmaster. Then he received a letter from Dr Frederick Temple, headmaster of Rugby School, wholeheartedly recommending one of his young masters as 'intellectually a very superior man, a first-rate scholar' and 'one of the best teachers I have ever met with'. Edward White Benson's name was already on the lips of the important and influential. He had been proposed as chaplain to the Bishop of London, commended as having 'very pleasing manners', being the best of his Cambridge contemporaries, 'a very good scholar and divine' and a 'thoroughly religious man'.

After several interviews, and having requested a long letter outlining Edward's vision of the new school, the Prince offered him the position. The new Council of Wellington College confirmed the appointment (though Edward arrived late to meet them, wandering lost through the corridors of the House of Lords) at the handsome salary of £800 a year. When the meeting was over, Edward wrote immediately to Mary to boast that the governors had accepted all his proposals bar the construction of swimming pools, for which there were insufficient funds, with 'the Prince, like a trump as he is, arguing well for every one of them . . . and, when any discussion arose, desiring the Secretary to read my letter aloud'.

Just before Edward and Mary were married, Prince Albert had sent the young headmaster-to-be on a journey to Prussia and the German states to see how schools should be run. Edward was not impressed. The tour, he wrote to his friend

Lightfoot, 'was dullish work, though not uninteresting when contemplated from a sufficient distance, nor uninstructive from the same standpoint', but he was convinced of the 'vast superiority' of English over German schools, and thought 'our run of scholars vastly superior, in sense, feeling and *extent* of reading to theirs'. Edward had his own ideas about education. He was inspired by the methods of Dr Arnold and of his old headmaster James Prince Lee, and he was not going to countenance rule by committee.

Some Victorian Views on the Germans

The land of our Saxon and Teutonic forefathers ... [was] the birthplace of the most moral races of men that the world has yet seen—of the soundest laws—the least violent passions, and the fairest domestic and civil virtues ... the regenerating element in modern Europe ...

Dr Thomas Arnold, on arriving at Cologne in 1828, appearing to disagree with his disciple

The great evil of Oxford is the narrowness and isolation of one study from another, of one part of a study from the other. We are so far below the level of the German Ocean that I fear one day we shall be utterly deluged.

Benjamin Jowett, later Master of Balliol, in a letter to Roundell Palmer MP, 1847

The Germans have taken the lead in historical enquiries, and they laugh at results which are got by groping about in woods with a pocket-

E. W. Benson, Master of Wellington College in 1867

compass while they have made good roads.
Will Ladislaw criticizes Mr Casaubon's
outmoded methods, in George Eliot's
Middlemarch, 1871–2

The headmaster and Mrs Benson settled into the
Master's Lodge, beside the Great Gate. Comely

and kind, Mary soon became known among the boys as 'Mother Benjy', even though, at eighteen, she was barely older than the Sixth-Formers. The boys adored Mother Benjy. They hated and feared their headmaster, and had good cause to. Edward's reputation for violence and for ferocious beatings preceded him from Rugby. Headmaster Benson dominated his realm. As he walked the grounds, porters clipped to attention, boys saluted, gossip ceased. His masters were 'dragooned as diligently as his pupils'. The headmaster fervently held that education was not merely a matter of honing the intellect, but of moral perfection—and he had 'a microscopic eye for the smallest particulars', as well as an unrestrained temper. He instituted Dr Arnold's system of prefects, giving them wide disciplinary powers. Every morning he invited two senior boys to breakfast, to report to him any misdemeanours that might have escaped his attention. He expected them to prowl and to monitor. Any evasion of *their* duty exacted the severest penalties.

Drawn firmly into Edward's orbit, Mary set about married life, feeling 'still no *real* love, but influence', and displaying for her mother (who came on frequent visits), to her husband and the world, her characteristic sunniness. 'I would have died rather than anyone should have thought for a moment I wasn't happy,' she confessed. Before they were married, Edward had written to her from the school, where he had held back on any decoration for the Master's Lodge, saying that if there was one thing he had set his heart on, it was 'that you should *settle* in *your own* house all for *yourself* and according to *your own* ideas, I want no-one to interfere with you.' But straightforward generosity of spirit was not Edward's style, and he went on more characteristically, 'if you love me you will manage it so'.

In his *Manual of Domestic Economy*, published three years before the Bensons moved into the Lodge, J. H. Walsh suggested that a well-to-do family, with two servants, furnishing a three-bedroom house would need a sum of £585. Taste and decoration were not personal concerns, but defined according to status and position. The more prosperous a couple, the greater the percentage of their income would go on the writing desks and sewing tables, the sofas, ottomans and armchairs, the antimacassars, tablecloths and napkins required to make up a respectable home of appropriate appearance. A family with £100 a year might expect to spend £83 on furnishings, while 88 per cent of a £250 income would be swallowed up, and 117 per cent of £500. Edward's handsome £800 salary put him near the top of J. H. Walsh's scale—£1,000 a year, which required £1,391 to establish a home. It was important that the Lodge should be furnished in a manner appropriate to Edward's position. Aristocracy, even royalty, might be received in its drawing room, and correct style amounted almost to a moral duty. Mr Martin would surely have helped out financially, Mrs Sidgwick, too, and surplus from the Blue House eased the situation, but in the early days of their marriage Edward and Mary most likely shared the lot of two other Victorian newly-weds, a young couple named the Berkeleys; their meals (wrote Maud Berkeley, on moving to London with her new husband) 'became meetings of Council, where we debated the virtues of mahogany against teak, planned attacks on furniture warehouses, and worried, worried, worried'. Edward and Mary's first major marital disputes were about money. That, and the way that Mary managed the household.

Mary's chief role was to keep the home neat and clean—society considered this both a virtue and an occupation in itself. She had servants, but she was supposed to advise and instruct them, to check and reprove, to order supplies correctly, to govern what was spent, and to pay bills on time. Mrs Beeton, whose *Book of Household Management* was published the year after Mary moved in to the Lodge, likened the mistress of a house to the commander of an army, asserting: 'A woman must rule her household or be ruled by it.' But Mary's duties as daughter in the Blue House had not prepared her for those as wife in the Master's Lodge. Little more than a girl, she was timid and uncertain. Mrs Sidgwick was rich, and Mary had a taste for good things, was extravagant, and loathed doing the accounts. 'I put them off, let them accumulate, then daren't bring them [to Edward],' she admitted. 'I *knew* it was the one thing he dreaded and disliked—but I disliked the doing them and dreaded the gloom they always brought— and so, cowardly and improvident, I put them off and lived in the present.'

Mary bought a small notebook with a brown marbled cover, and began—in fits and starts—to keep a diary, rather like the travel journal she had so valiantly struggled to keep up on her honeymoon. After her 'usual morning duties' she would sit down to the bills with an 'I wish I could get them finished!', easily to be distracted by a visitor before lunch, a crisis among the servants, or some confusion over what was owing to a tradesman, which would upset her calculations and her temper. On a number of occasions during the first years of her marriage, she secretly borrowed money from her brothers or from Mrs Sidgwick, to cover up a shortfall in the hope that Edward would not notice. At least once, Edward sat her down until way past midnight, forcing her to go through her books until totals balanced, so that tradesmen could be paid in the morning.

Some mornings Mary found it hard to get up, cast down by the dull routine of it all. 'Another blank day. Mist, mist, mist on the world and in my heart and life . . . The evening was a little better than this morning, but it is based on no solid foundation—Oh dear, O dear! My heart feels like a stone.' She tried to stir up her mind to prevent stagnation, reading German with Edward (which made the task easier) and, on her own, tackling Plato, books on mathematics and theology. In a world just beginning to be challenged by Darwin's *On the Origin of Species*, and in which rationalism was leading many people to rethink aspects of the Bible rather than abandon it altogether, Mary occasionally dipped into works which Edward thought heretical, but which for her 'seemed to open my brain . . . and show me a long vista of intellectual delights'.

Once Mary's household duties were seen to, days passed 'as days generally do here. A walk after lunch, and a quiet read in the evening.' The walks were not gentle strolls. Edward would set off at a tremendous pace (with the heavily skirted Mary doing the best she could to keep up) and he continued at a gallop until he had burned off the fret of the morning's work, only then reducing tempo. The marches—through woods, across heathland, up The Ridge and down again, would last at least two hours. Yet days all too easily sank into a round of ordering dinner menus, sponging bonnet ribbons, pointless embroidery—or simple dispirited idleness. 'I think my thinking and reasoning powers are deteriorating with disuse,' Mary complained. As the years crept by, she drew up timetables to impose discipline on her daily routine in the hope of preventing time from draining away unused, but the dullness of everyday tasks seemed to engulf her and produce stasis. 'Ah, my life is wasted,' she noted in her diary as early as 1860, a few weeks after she had turned nineteen. 'I scarcely know whether I can change now or not.' The rest of the page is blank.

Edward was also frequently downcast. His work at Wellington caused him great anxiety. He found these sons of soldiers coarse, unintelligent and difficult to mould. Parents (with some justification) protested at the poor quality of the boys' food. At every turn, Edward clashed with the Board of Governors. He became convinced that they were hostile to him and on the lookout for the first sign of failure. Confiding this to his favourite master, and admitting that he found the Sixth (whom he had to teach himself) heavy and dim, a dead weight he could not budge, Edward burst into tears. 'I wish I were more fit for my work. It is too great a work for me,' he confessed to Mary. 'I feel I am making a sad muddle of everything.' The neuralgia and dark depressions that had afflicted him at Rugby intensified. His moods and furious silences affected all around him, and it fell to Mary to raise him from his low moments.

Diversions did occur. Mary travelled to London—on one occasion to see the great tightrope walker Blondin at the Crystal Palace. Together with Mr Martin, the couple went on holiday in another whirl through France. Mary's travel diary again became an inventory of church architecture. By the time they reached Nantes, she was exhausted. After a 'cursory view' of the cathedral with Edward before breakfast, supplemented by a 'closer survey' immediately afterwards, Mary had had enough: 'I was so tired and knocked up that I could not look at anything, and what I did see I could scarcely remember, so rested all day till nearly evening, when I went to see a new church with Edward (transition between Norman and early French).' Directly afterwards, the party set off for Angers and more churches, cloisters, chapels, hospices and the museum (where the Fine Arts section was closed, so they viewed Natural History instead). Further on, at Ponts-de-Cé, Mary noted, with a touch of relief, that 'there was nothing to see but the bridge'. She records with barely suppressed glee how Edward himself fell asleep sitting on a wall in the middle of sightseeing, with gusto how French fisherwomen dig for eels, and adds a wry note that they listened to a 'long quaint sermon on Patience, which was very appropriate'. But on the whole her journal is a chronicle of how she obliterates her own desires and throws all her energy into pleasing Edward, recording what she ought to be interested in to make herself more worthy, to advance 'the improvement of her life'.

Back at Wellington, Mary watched school football matches, approving that 'all the screaming and shouting that used to be heard has given place to a severe silence, and the immense energy and spirit expressed in the boys faces, if you look at them close, shows that a good deal of the *Rugby* element has been introduced to the game'. Visitors to the Lodge offered Mary further diversion, and often intellectual stimulus. The Wellington schoolmasters came in twos and threes, after Edward's Sunday-morning sermon or in the evenings for dinner. Mary particularly delighted in the company of the aptly named Mr Master, because he 'supplied the very thing in which I have often thought the masters rather lacking—namely *argumentativeness*'. Indeed, Mr Master seemed very fond of it, 'just for the sake of a sport', and that made masters' visits much livelier when he was there. Mary enjoyed a good argument, or rather she enjoyed 'listening to an argument. It seems to stir my thinking powers up.' It would not do for the headmaster's wife to express too strong an opinion.

Other visitors came in their scores—over fifty all told one summer. 'What walks, what talks, what mirth!' exalted Mary. Old friends came from afar, and the better class of neighbour, parents, people on school business, dignitaries and occasionally, before his death in 1861, the Prince Consort himself. Mary found courtiers, 'whose talk consisted chiefly of little polite sentences, and pleasant stories of the Queen, Prince and Royal Family and mixed with a little *mild* politics', rather dull, but was excited by the surprise arrival of Lord Derby, the former Tory Prime Minister, soon after the collapse of his second administration. Derby came with his erstwhile Home Secretary, Spencer Walpole, and his First Lord of the Admiralty, Sir John Pakington, who was considering sending his son to Wellington College. Swept into this grand company for mid-morning tea, Mary was attracted by Lord Derby's 'wonderfully bright blue eyes, that seemed to take in everything almost before it was spoken', by his expansive forehead and a mouth that bespoke sharp wit and 'an enormous amount of energy'. Most of all she was impressed by 'the way he took anyone up if they made a mistake, or came down upon them if they could not understand a thing'. Sir John Pakington was 'not half so sharp at taking things in at once as Lord Derby', but all in all it was a meeting that 'seemed to inspirit one, and make one think'.

Lady Blanche Balfour (mother of a future Prime Minister, and of Mary's brother Henry's wife-to-be) blew in with Lady Salisbury during high winds and torrential rain one February morning, and was 'as hearty and as merry as you would wish to see'. She had read a great deal and thought about what she had read, and could talk of all the news of the day 'in a spirited and interested' way. The stammering, tobacco-addicted, wickedly witty Charles Kingsley, whose *Westward Ho!* Mary had so enjoyed on honeymoon, was rector of Eversley, a brisk walk away. He and his wife Frances, who had black shining eyes and a roguish smile, became particularly close friends. The Bensons and Kingsleys made sure to dine at least once a month together, alone—'on the heights' Mrs Kingsley called it, for all the mirth and good conversation. Soon she was 'Fanny' and Mary was 'Minnie' (Edward and intimate friends often still used her childhood name). At Wellington, Charles and Edward had lively, laughter-filled discussions, pacing energetically outdoors, or tucked away someplace where Kingsley could enjoy his pipe 'without deb-deb-debauching the boys'—a daring occupation, because Edward loathed smoking.

Gradually, the shy Mrs Benson assumed the mantle of local hostess a little more comfortably. On hot summer evenings a table might be laid for dinner guests out on the lawn, the white tablecloth glimmering and dappled under the beech trees, the chink of fork on plate playing lightly over a warm continuo of conversation. On winter's nights, on high occasions, gentlemen shed coats and hats to warm themselves by the hall fire as they arrived, and the ladies, cocooned in plaid and shawls, disappeared into Mary's sitting room, to re-emerge as silk butterflies in pink and green and purple. Then, arm in arm, couples processed into the dining room, with its round-backed mahogany chairs, tapestry curtains, engraving of *The Last Supper* (alongside one of the Prince Consort) and heavy oak sideboard made from two fine sixteenth-century altar panels.

Light from tall, branched candlesticks danced over silver and Spode, glittered off the turbaned Arab, camel and palm tree of a splendid epergne (ornamental centrepiece). Four entrées (two 'brown' of beef, mutton or venison, two 'white' of chicken, brains or rabbit) followed soup and preceded a joint—carved by Mary, rather than Edward, which was thought daring and rather modern. Then came birds, game or duck and heavy puddings, Stilton and lighter desserts, before Mary caught the ladies' eyes, fans snapped shut, and the women rose and like globules of quicksilver came together and flowed out to the drawing room, leaving the men to their male talk and port.

Later, the gentlemen rejoined their wives, and 'there was certain to be a lady present who sang very sweetly, or had a lovely "touch" on the piano . . . [who] was not sure if she had brought her music, but it always turned out that her husband had done so and had left the portfolio with his hat and coat in the hall'. Explaining that she was terribly out of practice, the lady would begin to play or sing, while the audience 'assumed expressions of regretful

'Willie We Have Missed You'

melancholy if the music was sad, or pensive gaiety if it was lively, and fixed their eyes on various points of the ceiling'. Once, feeling the mood rather dull, Mary herself was bold enough to sing 'Willie We Have Missed You', 'Wait for the Wagon' and 'Long Time Ago'. She was not quite certain whether she was wise to do this, but 'I did not vex Edward, and I think that is as good a criterion as I need have'.

Edward's sister Ada came frequently to stay, as did Mrs Sidgwick. Mary's brothers Henry and Arthur visited, too, and one winter's night in 1864, when Edward was away, they held a séance. Mary was fascinated, and thought she might be a medium.

Even before Darwin had published the book that set scholars debating and sent a shudder—of outrage or terror—down many a theologian's spine, among the educated talk had turned to agnosticism. A swell of doubt gathered force throughout the decade. As certainties were borne away, many grasped at spiritualism for rescue. For most, attempts at contact with the afterlife were a palliative to religious insecurity, an assurance of an existence beyond the material world. Others were more sceptical, and, picking up on the language of science, referred to their 'psychical research'.

Henry Sidgwick, who had followed Edward to Cambridge and was now a fellow of Trinity, was a young man of merciless scepticism and rigorous intellect, yet he found that although 'the scientific atmosphere' had paralysed his 'old theological trains of thought and sentiment', he could not discard them completely. A few years earlier, he had abandoned all thought of a clerical career, but felt a deep sense of loss. 'I still hunger and thirst after orthodoxy,' he wrote, 'but I am, I trust, firm not to barter my intellectual birthright for a mess of mystical pottage.' Henry took a deep investigative interest in the occult. He had joined the Ghost Society that Edward had helped to establish as a student, and was in the process of developing it into the respected Society for Psychical Research. Henry felt an intense responsibility for the effect his scepticism might have on others, and he tried to raise such topics with Edward, whom as a boy at Rugby he had revered. Edward was adept at 'avoiding points of fundamental controversy so that one never felt them to be avoided', and that made Henry reluctant to 'degrade the conversation consciously and deliberately into a debate'. Although Henry may also have held back in discussions with his clever and enquiring sister, he was—in the interests of psychical research— prepared to hold an after-dinner séance with her. Edward, when he returned home, was furious.

Despite his student-day dalliance with the Ghost Society, Edward was 'very vexed and spoke very strongly' to Mary, denouncing spiritualism as 'either a sin or a folly'. Later he would dismiss its manifestations as 'phenomena of a class which appears mostly in uncivilised states of society, and . . . in persons of little elevation of intellect', but for the present he forbad Mary further séances, speaking 'harshly' and telling her that if her behaviour were known, it would harm his reputation. 'I *can't* feel it is so wrong,' Mary retaliated, 'when undertaken in a reverent spirit.' She resigned herself to the notion that—for the time being at least—further spiritualist investigations must cease, but she remained this

The Doubt: 'Can These Dry Bones Live?' by Henry Bowler, 1855

argument.' That winter's-night séance at Wellington was by no means the last in which Mary took part.

From time to time, Mary would make a note or unconvinced by Edward's reasoning, in particular by his appeal to his reputation. 'I don't know why it is,' she noted in her diary, 'but I always rebel against two in her diary. Her resolutions to make regular entries in the journal were frequently broken. Her apathy and sense of failure as a wife were persistent themes, as well as her aversion to bills, and a constant determination to do her duty, to please Edward, not to fail or disappoint him—as she pared away at her own personality, effacing herself completely in his favour. 'This ought to be (and to all appearance will be) a time of great trouble and sorrow for me,' she wrote on Ash Wednesday shortly before she turned twenty-three:

I have most woefully neglected my bills, having, in spite of Edward's constant requests and my own most wretched sense of duties undone, gone on from day to day, always deceiving myself and imagining that *this* day had its own peculiar duties, and that tomorrow I would do them. The truth is, I believe, that I dreaded them. It is cowardly I know, and now that I have done them and am going to give them to Edward this afternoon, I find they amount to over £200. What he will say I scarcely dare think, and to crown it all Mamma is here, and it will grieve her terribly. If we were alone, I could bear these hours better, but to have Mamma as witness and make her so unhappy is almost intolerable. I know she takes my part, and that makes it worse still . . . I never again will let my accounts get the least crooked. This I trust is final. And now I am going to keep a regular diary all through Lent, hoping that I may be able to have some true Easter joy and Easter happiness.

Neither resolution—for the diary nor the accounts—held for long. Mary put off the confession for a few days, and with it current entries in the diary end abruptly.

Edward, on his part, had also broken promises. The third pledge of the written vow he had given Mary before they were married—never to be angry with her—had not survived their wedding journey. Now his spells of temper became more frequent, and the second pledge—to keep domestic affairs private—also appeared to be forgotten. Not only was Mrs Sidgwick witness to Edward's displeasure with his wife, but his sister Ada, too, and even a visiting Mr Martin if he happened to be in the room when Edward lashed out. Edward complained of Mary's 'want of tenderness', of her inability to 'pick him up' when he was downhearted, and in particular found fault with her housekeeping. The upsets that Mary called 'jarrings' could seethe on for days, the silent simmering erupting at intervals to the boil.

One morning, as Mary was copying out a letter to Lord Derby (in addition to her domestic tasks, she was Edward's de facto secretary), Edward came storming into the room and 'made some *very strong* remarks on the subject of the Antimacassars'. Mary had to admit to herself that 'they certainly did want changing very much', but the scale of Edward's reaction to something so trivial was derailing. 'It destroys one's whole peace of mind to be spoken to in that way, if one thinks about it, and if one does not I suppose it does one no good.' What made matters worse was that 'Ada was in the room too—I don't think he knows what effect his words produce.'

The ice set in for nearly a week. 'This morning was as bad as the two preceding ones,' Mary wrote two days after the first explosion. When Edward again rebuked her for her carelessness, she and Ada simply, silently, left the room. Later Edward and Mary read German to each other, 'but there was another contretemps before going to bed'. The following morning after breakfast he tackled her on the matter of an overcharged bill. Ada was still in the room.

'It is a *duty* to notice things of that kind even though they give one trouble,' said Edward. 'But some people shrink from things of an unpleasant nature. Especially if they have fat chins.'

Riled, Mary rose from the table. 'I knew you would say something of that kind,' she said, hurt. 'I won't stay.'

'If you leave the room, you will not see me again today,' replied Edward in a perfectly even tone. At this, Ada rose and left. Edward continued, with resolute calm.

'It is a *duty* of the mistress of a household to correct everything going awry in it,' he said. 'One is *bound* to notice mistakes, and to order a household as perfectly as possible. It is a law of God that cleanliness and order lead to godliness.'

Mary listened silently.

'And now,' Edward concluded, 'I think you need not be pettish with me.'

The next day was Sunday. In his sermon in the school chapel, Edward preached that people were divided into three sorts, the followers of Pleasure, of Comfort and of Duty—and it was clear with whom Good lay.

'I *always* feel even when he speaks severely, that he really does it *for my sake*,' Mary wrote miserably in her diary. She blamed herself for 'having behaved badly' and assured herself that she 'went away much happier' for the reprimand. Edward often spoke to her in this manner, saying (she noted in her diary) 'among many other things of the same kind, a paraphrase of:

> *"Oh but she will love him truly*
> *He shall have a cheerful home*
> *She will order all things duly*
> *When beneath his roof they come."'*

Mary still knew her Tennyson. She had most likely also read Coventry Patmore's paean to the perfect woman, *The Angel in the House*, which had been appearing in instalments throughout her engagement and the early years of her marriage, achieving immense popularity as a statement of the Victorian ideals of wives and daughters. Yet Mary had to struggle against her desire to recline on the sofa reading Shelley, rather than doing the accounts or saying her prayers, and against her impulse to answer Edward back. 'A great difficulty is I cannot *obey* as I should,' she noted. 'Please God to help me.' A nugget of rebellion remained.

Ideal Wives

A woman's 'highest duty is so often to suffer and be still'.

Mrs Sarah Stickney Ellis in
The Daughters of England, Their Position in Society, Character and Responsibilities, 1845

How important a work is mine. To be a cheerful, loving wife, and forbearing, fond, wise, thoughtful mother, striving ever against self-indulgence and irritability, which often sorely beset me. As a mistress to be kind, gentle, thoughtful both for the bodies and souls of my servants. As a visitor to the poor to spare myself no trouble so as to relieve wisely and well.

> Marion Jane Bradley, wife of Edward Benson's colleague at Rugby School, George Granville Bradley, in her diary *c.* 1854

The Wife's Tragedy

Man must be pleased; but him to please
Is woman's pleasure; down the gulf
Of his condoled necessities
She casts her best, she flings herself,
How often flings for nought, and yokes
Her heart to an icicle or whim,
Whose each impatient word provokes
Another, not from her, but him;
While she, too gentle even to force
His penitence by kind replies,
Waits by expecting his remorse,
With pardon in her pitying eyes;
And if he once, by shame oppress'd,
A comfortable word confers,
She leans and weeps against his breast,
And seems to think the sin was hers . . .

> From Canto IX of Coventry Patmore's *The Angel in the House,* published in instalments between 1854 and 1863

I married her, thinking her so young and affectionate that I might influence her as I chose, and make of her just such a wife as I wanted. It appeared that *she* married me thinking she could make of me just the sort of *husband* she wanted. I was grieved and disappointed in finding I could not change her, and she was humiliated and irritated at finding she could not change me ... I soon began to observe characteristics which gave me so much grief and anxiety that I wrote to her father saying that there was slight nervous affection of the brain. [The principal cause of which] was her always thinking that I ought to attend *her*, instead of *herself* attending me.

John Ruskin's 'Statement to his Proctor' prepared for the suit brought against him by his wife to annul their marriage, 1854

The voice of a dissenter

Man, on the other hand ... seeks to find in his wife, a sort of upper servant, or female valet, who is to wait upon him, attend to his wants, instinctively anticipate his wishes, and study his comfort, and who is to live for the sole purpose of seeing him well-fed, well-lodged, and well-pleased!

Ann Richelieu in *Can Women Regenerate Society?*, 1844

Chapter Seven

The first child came a little over a year after the Bensons were married, when Mary was still nineteen. Martin was born in August 1860, followed by Arthur in 1862, Nellie in 1863, then Maggie in 1865 and Fred in 1867. After Fred, Mary suffered something of a nervous collapse. In 1871 Hugh was born. After that, Mary broke down completely. Throughout the years at Wellington, as Mary learned to run the household, hide her shyness, and assume the roles of hostess and Edward's secretary; as she struggled with the temptation to put off doing the accounts, repressed any feelings of rebellion and moulded herself to Edward's will, she was almost continuously pregnant or recovering from childbirth.

Mary's old nurse Beth was summoned to Wellington when Martin was born. Elizabeth Cooper was just sixteen in 1834, when she had walked from her village to be interviewed by a young Mrs Sidgwick for the position of nursemaid to her first child. She was forty-two when, having looked after each of the Sidgwick children in turn, she arrived at the Master's Lodge. Once again, Beth remained as the family grew.

Ada visited frequently and offered companionship and support, but much of Mary's listlessness and sapped will in the face of household

Elizabeth Cooper, 'Beth', with one of her Benson Charges

duties was the product of sheer exhaustion. Arthur was a pale, sickly child, and although Beth bore most of the burden of looking after him, worry added to Mary's ill-being. And the Lodge itself played a role: by the time Nellie arrived, thirteen months after Arthur, the family's accommodation had simply become too crowded.

Soon after Maggie's birth, the family moved to a new, more commodious Master's Lodge, built to Edward's design and satisfaction in the workaday Gothic style made fashionable by Ruskin. Commanding gables and tall chimneys signalled a fitting residence for the headmaster. A separate outdoor entrance to Edward's study, main rooms grouped around a large hall with a gallery running round, and a grand drawing room complete with alabaster chimney-piece all added to its authority, but windows clotted by stone mullions meant the interior was dark. Sombre pitch-pine panelling, wallpaper of sullen green or grey, with shadowy vegetation and the odd spray of gold, and a chill lilac distemper (soon dappled with the sticky fingerprints of climbing children) did little to alleviate the gloom. Upstairs, the nursery was brighter and more airy. Fred, its fifth young inhabitant, joined the others a month after little Maggie's second birthday.

Just before Fred's birth, Mary fell in love. This new love was not the timorous, dutiful commitment she felt for Edward. The flood of entirely another force engulfed her, something wilder, more reckless, more akin to her passionate 'first friendship' at the Blue House. Edward was like a god, evoking awe, demanding fealty, creating obligations, requiring abnegation of self. Mary's new love tempted her to shrug off duty and delight in pleasure. The object of her passion was Emily Edwardes, a tall, gentle girl who lived with her widowed mother at Yately Hall, some two miles distant from the school.

Emily was not the first person to awaken Mary's fervour after she married. Five years earlier, just after Arthur was born, George Ridding, the Tutor of Exeter College at Oxford, came down to examine at Wellington. Like Edward, Dr Ridding was an ardent upholder of the Muscular Christian educational ideals of Doctors Arnold and Temple, but he was a mild, tactful man. '*How* I liked him,' Mary wrote, 'was even too excited—head easily upset—Strange to remember the feelings he stirred—it was chaff, I think—on his part, certainly.' But mostly, Mary lost her heart to women. There was a neighbour, Mrs Powell, 'a fascinating little thing . . . I know I shall get very fond of her if I see much of her' (which she did), and a Mrs Price, who came to luncheon one summer's day at the old Lodge. 'I do take to Mrs Price,' Mary noted in her diary, 'there is no denying it. I wonder if I am wrong in thinking that she also takes to me.' She was not. There were others, too often referred to only by their Christian names: 'Annie—she loved me—I led her into some beauty, some good but what might I have done!', and Katie Meyer (the daughter of the Superintendent at Broadmoor) who did not love her so well, but 'Phillie came with her, and did'. Mary experienced the greater intensity of feeling for Annie, 'such love, such delight in each other'. She visited for a month, and they took a trip to Whitby on the North Yorkshire coast. 'Annie and I drew together,' wrote Mary. 'The ways she sat and kissed my hand—our walks—our sittings—and finally the beach—and all the while in an undercurrent I was knowing what love was growing in our hearts for each other . . . and so we spent the month, Annie and I, in most complete fusing.' Mary often fell back on metaphor to express her passion, on images of fusing, of buds, flowing, restlessness and stirrings, of truth in her 'inward parts'. She grew to recognize the first kindling of one of her infatuations, calling these early sensations the 'My God, what a woman!' stage. When Ada was not visiting, Mary wrote to her about her crushes, her *'Schwärmereien'* (enthusiasms), numbering them in succession. Emily Edwardes was number 39.

Innocent Intimacies

Marian Halcombe speaks of her half-sister Laura Fairlie, who, the night before she weds, comes to Marian's bed

I won't live without her and she won't live without me . . . [I] love her better than my own life . . . Poor dear Laura hardly leaves me for a moment, all day; and, last night, when neither of us could sleep, she came and crept into my bed to talk to me there. 'I shall lose you so soon, Marian,' she said; 'I must make the most of you while I can.'

From *The Woman in White*
by Wilkie Collins, 1860

Resting my head in silence on Helen's shoulder, I put my arms around her waist; she drew me to her, and we reposed in silence.

and comforts her as she dies of consumption

'Helen!' I whispered softly; 'are you awake?' [. . .]
'Can it be you, Jane?' she asked, in her own gentle voice [. . .]
I got onto her crib and kissed her . . .
'Jane, your little feet are bare; lie down and cover yourself with my quilt . . . How comfortable I am! That last fit of coughing has tired me a little; I feel as if I could sleep; but don't leave me, Jane; I like to have you near me.'
'I'll stay with you, *dear* Helen: no one shall take me away.'
'Are you warm, darling?'
'Yes.'
'Good-night, Jane.'
'Good-night, Helen.'
She kissed me and I her; and we both soon slumbered.

From *Jane Eyre* by Charlotte Bronte, 1847

Lizzie, who has been pummelled by goblins and covered with the pulp and juice of their fruit, invites her dying sister Laura to partake of the juices in the hope of saving her life . . .

She cried 'Laura,' up the garden,
'Did you miss me?

90

Come and kiss me.
Never mind my bruises,
Hug me, kiss me, suck my juices
Squeezed from goblin fruits for you,
Goblin pulp and goblin dew.
Eat me, drink me, love me;
Laura, make much of me:
For your sake I braved the glen
And had to do with goblin merchant men.'
From 'Goblin Market' by Christina Rossetti,
written in 1859 and published 1862

Old Mrs Edwardes saw ghosts at Yately Hall—
silent, hooded figures, their eyes fixed upon the
ground. (Yately Hall had been built on the site of
a monastery.) Mrs Edwardes was a small,
sprightly woman, whose spiritualist experiences
intrigued and baffled those around her, and who
was eager to use her gifts as a medium. With
Mary present, she had managed to induce a heavy
silver pencil to rise in the air, and to float to the
surface of a vessel filled with water. Despite
Edward's injunction on séances, Mary and Ada
met with Mrs Edwardes and Emily for sessions of
automatic writing and table-turning. The tables
proved remarkably active. First, a velvet-topped
one 'began to creak and start, but went no
further', then the women tried a small candle-
table, 'which tilted and jerked and span around
till we were giddy'. Finally, they lightly placed
their hands on a walnut table with three claws for
feet, not touching each other but with their
thumbs joined; as soon as they did so it ran along
the floor and 'after a try or two' mounted a dais
and attempted to climb on to a seat. 'I dare say if

the door was open it would go out into the passage,' exclaimed Mrs Edwardes. Instantly, the table slid towards a door (the women bustling along beside it, their hands still lying on the walnut surface), rapped it three times, drew back, struck the door with force and immediately became so heavy that none of them could move it. After that they repaired, with no apparent sense of incongruity, to their evening prayers.

Emily had been Ada's friend at first, but Mary—just twenty-six herself—was 'fascinated' by her. 'I tried to make love, but she kept me at arm's length,' she wrote. But as spring moved on into summer, Mary's friendship with Emily 'began to tremble into life'. Soon the pair were 'wild with joy' in each other's company, revelling in 'the hot months. . .' until Fred was born, on 24 July.

Recalled to her duties, strained and exhausted, cast into a melancholy after Fred's birth, Mary grew fractious not only with Edward and Mrs Sidgwick (who had come to Wellington for the confinement) but even with dear Beth. For a while she was seriously ill. The solution was a week's seclusion, then a short holiday in Hastings with Emily, leaving the baby behind. 'O that sweet time with Emily!' declared Mary. Then, with an aside to her Maker: 'How we drew together! Lord it was Thou, teaching me how to love—"friend of my married life"—how I loved her! . . . I remember how thou stirred me to know what Love was.' Mary reluctantly returned to her baby, her toddlers and her husband, with whom she had a long talk about Emily. Edward took his young wife upon his knee, as he had done when she was a child, pronounced a blessing and prayed for her. His usual severity was no doubt tempered by her condition. Pregnancy, after all, was an illness, and the best medical men fully appreciated the connection between a woman's internal organs and all manner of woes, including the low spirits and black moods that followed childbirth, which might develop into 'puerperal insanity'. Edward did not forbid further contact with Emily, but gently urged Mary to resume her neglected duties.

Mary was unmoved: 'My heart shrank within me and became as a stone—for duties stared me in the face—I had gathered no strength to do them— bodily strength of course I hadn't—spiritual strength I hadn't looked for.' Her friendship with Emily 'rose to its height—we met daily, and we lived and loved—walks in woods—talks—she to me, I to her—I wasn't equal to my duties at all— and neglected things terribly.' Mary would walk along a field path through pine woods, up a narrow lane beside a stream, over the wooden bridge that crossed a dark pool edged with meadowsweet and figwort and overhung by alders, on past a timbered mill, mossy and fringed with fern, and up to Yately Hall. She went alone, or with Martin and Arthur as they grew older, sometimes with Edward and the whole family to visit old Mrs Edwardes—then Emily would take the children to pick strawberries or to fish in the pond, while the others sat talking in the shade before tea. Long after the *Schwärmerei* had faded, the family continued to visit, and Mrs Edwardes, Emily and Mary held the occasional séance.

His mother had been married young, and was scarcely more than a girl when he was born; his father was already a man grave beyond his years, full of affairs, and constantly occupied . . . Looking back, it always seemed to be summer in those days . . . The country was very wild all round, with tracts of heath and sand. The melodious buzzing of nightjars in hot mid-summer evenings, as they swept softly along the heather, lived constantly in his memory. In the moorland, half a mile away, stood some brick-kilns, strange plastered cones with blackened tops, from which oozed a pungent smoke; those were too terrible to be visited alone . . . All this life was, in memory . . . a series of vignettes and pictures; the little dramas of the nursery, the fire that glowed in the grate, the savour of fresh-cut bread at meal-times, the games on wet afternoons, with a tent made out of shawls and chairs, or a fort built of bricks . . . The only very real figure was the old nurse, whose rare displeasure he had sorrowed over more than anything else in the world, and whose chance words, uttered to another servant and overheard by the child, that she was thinking of leaving them, had given him a deeper throb of emotion than anything he had before known, or was many years to know.

Wellington College was an exciting place for a child. There were gypsies encamped on the heath and vipers (it was said) in the scrub; there were walks and adventures a-plenty, secret haunts and hiding places, encounters with inmates of Broadmoor out for exercise with their warders, visits to haunted Yately Hall, and to Eversley to see Mr Kingsley, who had now written *The Water-Babies*, had an enthralling collection of stuffed birds, and whose study was a trove of exotic gifts: West Indian nuts, feather ornaments from distant lands. There was Irish Pat who prowled at night with his fierce dog and lantern, an old Roman camp, the belching brick kilns, a Catholic chapel nearby, past which Nurse Beth would hurry with a sense of horror and

The Benson Family at Wellington College
Lizzie Fox Edward Benson
Beth with Maggie Arthur Mary Benson with Nellie Martin Ada Benson

wickedness, resolutely pushing the perambulator and refusing to answer eager questions about what went on inside.

Guests in their scores enlivened the scene: Grandmama Sidgwick in her cap with purple streamers, Aunt Ada, Uncle Henry and Uncle Arthur, and Aunt Etty, regal and startling in swishing silk and with a voice like a man's. Aunt Etty had once almost torn a hymn book in two during a tug-of-war with her lady companion, and then swept from church and hooted with laughter outside. Other visitors were to be observed from behind the railings of the hall gallery, some the object of mirth—schoolboys, for whom the children invented absurd names, embarrassed and shuffling, coming for breakfast; or masters, often just as nervous, it seemed. Some were rather grand, and made even their father appear uncomfortable. Once there was a lady, small but even more dignified than Aunt Etty, with a melodious voice and clothed in black, whom Beth addressed as 'My Majesty'.

Beth, for the Benson children, was the rock—as she had been for their mother. Mary might be ill and away from home, or preoccupied with dinners and guests, but Beth was there always. She never changed; she was totally predictable. Beth never fretted, nor scolded, never inspired fear—though her rare displeasure, or firm 'I don't want your sorrer' at an insincere apology, would cause desolation until beaming forgiveness arrived. She never lost her Yorkshire accent, nor the twinkle in her eye; would gamely join in races, her feet flickering from beneath her skirts in hilariously small steps, until she had to stop with an: 'Eh, dear, I can't run any more: I've got a bone in my leg.' Her stories were few and sorrowful, dwelling deliciously on death, and always exactly the same. She insisted that copper coins would give you 'verdigris' if you put them in your mouth, that the tiniest bit of cork from a ginger-beer bottle, if swallowed, would swell up inside and choke you, and she was wary of the dangers of French beans. Her love could be felt always, instinctively, and solidly. Martin, distressed, asked after her persistently when she left for just a few days when he was two, to visit her sick father. Baby Arthur screamed 'as he has never screamed before' when someone else tried to bathe him. For Arthur, she was the first human being that he was aware loved him; for Fred, she was a 'loved and protecting presence' in almost every childhood memory he had.

From E. F. (Fred) Benson's Novel,
Across the Stream
Archie Morris relates his first memory

. . . it was the face of his nurse Blessington, leaning over his crib. She held a candle in her hand which a little dazzled him, but the sight of her face, tender and anxious, and divinely reassuring, was the point of that memory . . . as by a conjuring-trick, Blessington had appeared with her comforting presence that quite robbed the dark of its terrors. It must still have been early in the night, for she had not yet gone to bed, and had on above her smooth grey hair her cap with its adorable blue ribands in it. At her throat was the brooch made of the same stuff as the shining shillings with which a year or two later she bought the buns and sponge-cakes for tea.

Fred's first word was 'Bef', and as he began to talk a little more, at first only Beth knew what he was saying. His father and mother tried to persuade him to speak more clearly, telling him they could not understand him.

'Bef can,' said Fred.

'Ah,' said Edward, 'but *we* can't, and you are *our* child too, aren't you?'

'Not particler,' retorted Fred.

The children's father was busy, important and fearsome. Martin, the eldest, developed a stammer almost as soon as he could talk, which seemed worse when he spoke to his father. Arthur, next in line, was secretly glad when Papa was late for luncheon—the children chattered freely with their mother, but with Edward about they were almost silent. The threat of his disapproval was ever-present, like thunderclouds on the horizon, and he had a quick eye for the smallest things—an untidy eater; a boy making a rampart of potato to dam up the gravy. He could sniff from afar the phosphorous on the fingers of a son who had picked a match off the floor, and give him a severe lecture on thieving. Yet Martin and Arthur vied for his affection, sending competing quantities of kisses and 'best love' ('ove' in little Arthur's case, as he couldn't say his *l*s) in letters when Edward was away from home. Some of Nellie's earliest words were 'dear Papa', repeated over and over again. The children gathered most mornings, awed, to watch Edward shave (during which he read from the New Testament in Greek, as he abhorred wasting time). He took them on walks, made drawings of castles and cathedrals, and spent hours cutting out pictures with them, to make a beautiful collage that papered the nursery wall (in defiance of the health experts who insisted on whitewash).

From A. C. Benson's Memoirs of Arthur Hamilton, *a Fictional Biography*

He disliked his father, and feared him. The tall, handsome gentleman, accustomed to be obeyed, in reality passionately fond of his children, dismayed him. He once wrote on a piece of paper the words, 'I hate Papa,' and buried it in the garden.

From E. F. Benson's *Across the Stream*

Archie was frightened of his father and always went warily by the door of the room at the dark corner of the hall where this tremendous person lived. There were other dangers about that corner, for on the floor were two tiger-skins which looked as if the animal in question had, with the exception of its head, been squashed out flat ... Archie wished the tigers' heads had been pressed in the same way; as it was, they were disconcertingly solid and life-like, with long teeth and snarling mouths and glaring eyes. He had always made Blessington [his nurse] come right up to his father's door with him when he went to say good-night, so that she should pilot him safely past the tigers on his entry and escort him by them again on his return. But one night his father had come out with him, and, finding Blessington waiting there, had divined, as by some awful black magic, why the nurse should be waiting, and had decreed that Archie

99

should in future make his way across the danger zone unattended. But, next evening, the trembling Archie had fallen down on the glassy sea between the awful Scylla and Charybdis, and, convinced that his last hour had come, when these two cruel heads beheld him prostrate on the floor, had cried himself to sleep from terror of that awful ending. But next day his mother, who understood about things in general better than anybody, had caused the tigers to make friends with him, and in token of their amity they had each of them presented him with a whisker-hair. That assured their friendship, and they wished it to be understood that their snarlings and glarings were directed, not at Archie, but at Archie's enemies. This naturally changed their whole aspect, and Archie, after he had wished his father good-night, kissed the hairy heads that had once been so terrifying, and thanked them for successfully keeping his enemies from molesting him.

Mary was the soft cheek to Edward's bony bristle, the cushioned sofa to Edward's hard leather chairs. Once, when he was still 'the *tiniest* fellow', Martin had stopped as he was leaving a room and said to her: 'Mama, I love you till my heart stands still.' The other children adored her, too. Her laughter bubbled deliciously 'like the sound of cool lemonade being poured out of the bottle'; the worlds she imagined were close to theirs, she was a sparkling fount of different, delightfully dotty ideas. Mama it was who bought a live parrot to entertain Arthur in the crib when he was a baby; who had a looking-glass carried in to calm a tantrum of

Maggie's, by showing her how ugly it made her. She might retire early for the night, claiming sleepiness, and behold, a short while later Fairy Abracadabra would appear in the hall, with golden wings, a hat embowered in flowers and a dress of jewels, blowing a trumpet and distributing gifts from what looked like the nursery clothes basket, but could not, surely, actually have been so.

As the children grew older, it was Mary, rather than a governess or Beth (who could not read or write very well), who gave them lessons. For two or three hours every morning, she made history and geography, especially, come excitingly alive. Little Arthur would concentrate 'till his face came out in large drops', Maggie dissolved easily into tears of frustration over sums and reading, Martin was transported by pride and delight when, aged five, he discovered that he could read a letter written to him by an absent Edward, all on his own. He read it again the moment he saw Beth, giving Mama all the kisses he had been commissioned to do, but saving one for his nurse, 'as he evidently thought she should not be neglected'. It was Mary who read to the children on winter's evenings, from *Ivanhoe* or George MacDonald's fairy romance *Phantastes*, or she told them stories, more vivid than Beth's, tales of an underground hall of giants, or of an enchanted bell that rang every evening in the woods.

In the autumn of 1871, just as the leaves were beginning to turn, the children noticed that a new crib had appeared in the night nursery. It contained 'a small, pink creature called Hugh', who had as yet no conversation.

A short while later, their mother left Wellington for a very long time.

101

Chapter Eight

Charles Dickens's wife Catherine bore ten children in sixteen years, as well as enduring a number of miscarriages. Queen Victoria set a firm example to the nation by producing nine offspring, at a comparable rate. The birth of Hugh brought Mary up to no more than the national average of six, but her youth, the stresses of life with Edward at Wellington College, of giving lessons to her elder children, which often left her 'utterly done up', and her struggles with disabling post-natal melancholy took a severe toll. Recovering from Martin she felt 'wretched'. Arthur was born with 'suffering'; after the third baby, Nellie, she wanted no more, yet was pregnant with Maggie within a year. Her illness after Fred's birth had been serious enough, even though, Mary admitted, there 'was at first a great pleasure in the importance of it', in the attention and pampering. Illness was enticing, it brought interest from others and relief from obligations to duty. A week in Hastings with Emily Edwardes, and without the baby, had helped no end. But Mary's collapse after Hugh was born was of a different order entirely.

Mary began to experience headaches and have difficulty sleeping. She lost her appetite, felt pressure on the top and sides of her head. The ground seemed to rise and fall beneath her feet, and she became uncertain in walking. As time went on, she appeared to lose all sense of the present, and became extremely distressed, feeling 'very depressed and ill and incapable'. Doctors diagnosed nervous prostration, or as it was becoming known in more advanced medical circles, neurasthenia, a label that carried a sense of social acceptability, even a touch of prestige. Neurasthenics, one doctor declared, were generally of a refined and unselfish nature, 'just the kind of women one likes to meet with'. They were 'sensible, not over sensitive or emotional, exhibiting a proper amount of illness' and, what was more, if treated with care showed a 'willingness to perform their share of work quietly and to the best of their ability'.

Clearly, Mary required rest before she could be expected to resume her role at Wellington. She was sent to Scotland to recover, and when that had no real effect, to stay with close friends, the Wordsworths, at Riseholme Hall, a magnificent pile set in fields and forests and fronting a large lake, three miles out of Lincoln. Christopher Wordsworth (a nephew of the poet William) was Bishop of Lincoln and had first met Edward through his son John, who was briefly a master at Wellington. In the summer of 1869, shortly after Christopher had been consecrated, the two families took a momentous holiday together in Whitby.

Edward and Mary were going through a time of 'bickerings and unlovingness', but Whitby with the Wordsworths turned into 'a glorious month'. Edward was already firm friends with the Bishop, but it was the Wordsworth progeny who provided the greater delight. The women adored Edward, and he 'revelled' in the 'love poured out on him'. In

103

particular Elizabeth Wordsworth, an intelligent young woman of Mary's age, was fired by his conversation, drawn by his unusual magnetism, and thought him supremely handsome, with the hands 'of an enthusiast, every finger full of character and vigour'. After the holiday, the two kept up a close and affectionate correspondence. 'I have often wished for you by the half hour together,' he wrote to her, one lonely day at Wellington.

To Miss E. Wordsworth
14 July, 1871

Dearest Elizabeth,
Last Sunday I had a singular and interesting change, I went to Windsor to preach to the Queen and saw something of and *much admired* Mr Gladstone. His eyes alone afford sufficient reason for his being Prime Minister, and we talked of anything and everything (except Cathedrals), as if he had not another thought in his mind except to know all the knowable in literature . . .

Your ever affectionate,
EWBenson

Mary felt the glimmerings of a *Schwärmerei* for Elizabeth, but realized 'oh my vanity! how I fancied attracting her—how I thought she was thinking of and looking at me when far other nobler things occupied her. . .' Elizabeth, for her part, was rather irritated by Mary, thought her 'all over the place arguing with you at every turn and insinuating herself into everything like tooth-powder into the man's dressing-case compartments in *Somebody's*

Luggage'. Instead, it was Elizabeth's younger sister Susan with whom Mary fell in love, drinking ''arf pints' late at night in Susan's bedroom, and writing long, passionate letters to her in the months to come.

At Riseholme, Mary was assured of comfort and close attention, but by June of 1872, some seven months after Hugh had been born, she was still not well. Edward wanted her to return to Wellington for Speech Day on 18 June, to perform her wifely duties at his side. The doctor advised strongly against her travelling, and Elizabeth Wordsworth did everything she could to make Edward change his mind. Susan wrote imploring him to remember that Mary required care, and to be sensitive to her needs, but he was resolute. Mary must return. A few days before Speech Day, she set off, travelling alone. She could not even break her journey in London, as she had hoped to do. By the time she arrived at Wellington she was so weak she had almost to be carried into the Lodge. She found the spirit to write for the Wordsworths a mock-heroic account of her journey entitled 'Adventures of a Timid Englishwoman', complete with sarcastic asides from Edward, but was soon once again seriously ill. Shortly after Speech Day, Mary's brother Arthur intervened and persuaded Edward to allow Mary time to make a complete recovery, staying for a while with Christopher Benson, Edward's youngest brother, at Wiesbaden, in a newly unified Germany.

Mary travelled to Wiesbaden in September, most likely with Arthur, by boat to Ostend and then southwards via Cologne. It could not have been absent from her mind that her neurasthenia might

105

be a long-lasting condition. Her present state was indeed wretched, and even Edward could not deny that a woman's nerves and sensitiveness might detach her from domestic obligations, might award her time to herself without in any way detracting from her position as angel in the house.

On Being Ill . . .

The art of being ill is no easy one to learn, but is practised to perfection by many of the greatest sufferers.
Julia Duckworth Stephen, in *Notes from Sickrooms,* 1883

A married woman was heard to wish that she could break a limb that she might have a little time to herself. Many take advantage of the fear of 'infection' to do the same.
Florence Nightingale, in *Cassandra,* a fragment unpublished in her lifetime

Wiesbaden was a smart spa town, surrounded by meadows and winelands. Christopher Benson and his English wife Agnes had lived there for some time, taking in boarders and pupils at their house on Elisabether Straße. Barrel-chested and with powerful arms, Christopher had a handsome head much like Edward's, but with an exuberant moustache. A childhood illness had arrested development in his legs, and he moved about in a wheeled chair, or was carried by his valet. At first, Mary found Agnes 'somewhat stiff', but as the weeks went by she warmed to her kindness and intelligence, and grew 'so fond of her that it makes the life very pleasant'.

Mary loved her room, and settled in quickly. Her first morning revealed Wiesbaden crisp and beautiful, 'a most lovely morning to begin this new bit of life on'. Immediately her headaches disappeared and she began to eat well. Within a few days, she was taking exercise in the Walking Room at the Kurhaus, disapproving as she passed 'the fearful low greed on all the faces' of those in the gaming rooms. (Her distress was short-lived, as the new Prussian-led imperial government closed the casino in October.)

The headaches later returned, but did not last as long, nor were they so violent as before. A strict daily routine beginning with prayers at a quarter past eight in the morning through to punctual retirement each night at ten, gave life a structure and rhythm, and Mary began to feel stronger. By October she was well enough to pay a visit to the local synagogue during Rosh Hashanah (where she was shocked by men wearing hats inside and talking during pauses in the ritual), and to go to the opera (where she giggled quietly at the appalling acting). She took German lessons with a Fräulein Bunsen, went for carriage rides in the country, and even on an excursion to Hamburg, nearly three hundred miles away.

During her first days at Elisabether Straße, Mary had noticed 'Miss Hall, a lady boarder . . . a *very* pleasant person—clever and bright and merry'. It was one of her 'My God, what a woman!' moments. In early October, Agnes Benson had 'a very particular friend' to visit, a Miss Abbott, who was 'to be regarded slightly in the light of a nuisance, as she is one of those monopolising friends who wishes to be left alone with the beloved object always and is apt to take offence besides'. Miss Abbott liked nothing better than to sit at the 'Beloved Object's' feet, or with her arms draped around her neck, for hours on end. Agnes was thus much occupied. Mary imagined that she might be seeing more of Miss Hall as a consequence. And indeed she did.

Ellen Hall taught for most of the morning in town, but afterwards she and Mary would read to each other, go for walks in the woods and jaunts around Wiesbaden, then sit up late into the night together. Mary began 'to like her exceedingly'. Soon she was in the hold of a full-blown *Schwärmerei*. 'I began to love Miss Hall,' she later recalled, 'it was a complete fascination ... our exquisite walks ... gradually the bonds drew round—fascination possessed me ... *utter* fascination ... the other fault—thou knowest—I will not even write it—but O God, forgive—*how* near we were to that!'

Back at Wellington, Beth looked after the younger children, and those who could write sent Mary letters about life at home. Martin, who was just eleven but very clever, told her that 'our theatricals went off with a great deal of éclat', and that his reading had put him into 'a fever of excitement about the Peruvian Indians'. Five-year-old Freddie produced a letter that neither he nor anyone else could read, but later managed sweet and loving replies to his mother's accounts of Wiesbaden. Maggie was often quite bossy, and eager to pass on news of her siblings' shortcomings. Evidence of little Hugh is limited to such lines as 'Baby has got two teeth [and] is not that nice'. Martin and Arthur were away at prep school much of the time. The others formed a tight nursery nest with Beth, who took them on outings and bought them little gifts with her own meagre funds. Their father was busy, and often distracted. 'We and papa (for papa is not we) went out yesterday,' wrote Maggie, before going on to relate how much better she was at pony riding than Nellie.

Mary wrote that she missed them all, and separately to Edward saying how letters from him gave her 'a pang when I get them, knowing how your minutes are overflowing with such work of all sorts'. Edward had said he did not want letters too frequently. Mary understood that, but could he perhaps get 'Mama, anyone, to write if you have no time, to tell me how you are'. She had left her household finances at the Lodge in a dismal state, and secret loans from her family had not papered over her debts. Edward's sympathy was thin. He was struggling with his own neuralgic attacks and depression, and soon Mary's expenditure in Wiesbaden became a sore topic. She countered his queries with profusely apologetic explanations of just how she *had* to buy certain gifts, and pay her share of expeditions.

The need for economies became even more of an issue in December, when Bishop Wordsworth offered Edward the Chancellorship of Lincoln Cathedral. This would involve an exact halving of his Wellington salary, which now stood at a handsome £2,000 a year, just at the time when he was having to meet the expenses of the older boys' education—but it would remove Edward from the stress and overwork of a headmaster's role, and take him closer to what he felt was his true calling, among like-minded men in 'the cloistered existence I have always wished for'. He wrote to colleagues, spoke to friends, consulted his absent wife, posting her the Bishop's letter and appending drawings of the Chancery and a plan of the house.

Expenses to November

	Fl.	Kr.
Expedition to Hamburg	6	14
Rooms	15	–
Washing	6	25
Chansee Hans [?]	6	15
Carriages	5	15
Frankfurt	4	45
Nurenbergerhof	4	19
Chemist	9	45
Room end of month	15	–
Tips on leaving	10	30
[illegible]		54
Telegram	1	45
Dr Malcolm	24	00
	Fl. 110.58	
	=£9. 5. 0	

As December wore on, and Mary's friendship with Ellen Hall bloomed, Mary, rather than returning to Wellington, began to ask for warm clothes to be sent her. Agnes, she wrote, had advised a sealskin coat, because it was so warm and light, though Mary made a show of objecting to the expense. Mama could pick out underwear. By mid-December, the people Mary met in Wiesbaden were admiring her 'most delicious' sealskin. Edward made his decision alone, and accepted the position in Lincoln. Servants who had previously addressed Mary as Frau Direktor, now called her Frau Dom Kanzler.

As Christmas approached, Mary lamented the fact that she would not be with her family for 'this last Christmas at the dear old home'. The thought brought on a rush of warmth for her husband.

Ah what a dear home it has been, and how impossible it seems that one will ever be able to look at any other place as home—no other place can be to us what that has been. Our first home—where we first *really* knew each other, and where our love, deep enough always, has grown old and deepened and strengthened year by year, though each year it has seemed impossible to love you more—you have been very patient with me dearest— I was such a child when we married that I am afraid you must have had many sad moments—for it seems to me that I have only grown up of late years, and learnt the fullness and strength of married love, and what *unity* means and only of late years that I have been really a woman.

On Christmas Day, Edward wrote 'but a few lines because it is Christ's birthday', with the wish for Mary that the Lord would 'take away at once the sickness in your head, and the sickness of my heart, which is a much worse evil, though alas! easier to

111

bear'. He reminded her that they had now chosen 'holy poverty for our portion and we must not live as if we were in holy riches, or indulge in all the amiabilities of expenditure'. He also apologized for an earlier, strong, letter that he hoped she would take in good part. Relations were taut. It was 'a bad time', Edward confessed to a friend. 'My dear wife mends so slowly.' 'I *cannot* blame myself,' wrote Mary to her husband, saying there was nothing she could do except try her best to get well, but 'I am afraid you don't think this'.

Whenever talk of Mary's return became definite and a date was set for her departure, she seemed to suffer a relapse—the return of headaches, a debilitating cold. Agnes wrote to Edward suggesting that Mary stay on until Easter, adding that she thought Mary gave 'somewhat too good accounts' of her health in the hope of reassuring him, and that uncertainty about returning 'made her restless, and restlessness of course retards her purposes'. Dr Malcolm, who had originally sanctioned her departure, changed his opinion, saying that he thought when he spoke to her at first that she *had* to go home before Christmas, and that 'it was a question of how well he could make her in the time'. Mary herself sent off volleys of double-edged letters, on the one hand bewailing their separation, while on the other summoning pity for her condition, subtly alluding to another relapse, yet with a great display of bravery promising to overcome it. Clever, yet powerless, Mary had long learned the skills of prodding and tugging at other people's emotions as one of the few means she had to gain some control over her world. She suggested that the continuance of her illness was due to 'the

112

excitement of this great change in our lives', to Edward's accepting the Chancellorship, and hinted that too early a return would lead to an even sorrier situation: 'Sometimes I do feel very low—as if all this time and absence and money were going to be wasted, and I to be a poor incapable creature unfit for life and for you.' She stayed on into the new year.

When, in January, there was again talk of a homeward journey (Edward had not been swayed by the argument for a stay prolonged until Easter), Mary put forward Miss Hall as a travelling companion, even though that would involve paying expenses for her return to Wiesbaden. Her suggestion met with no success. In the end, she made the journey back to Wellington with a Mrs Mackenzie, 'Kenzie', who had also spent some time at Elisabether Straße and had become a firm friend. Kenzie came to stay for a while at the Lodge in Wellington, from where she and Mary sent a teasing letter decorated with drawings to Ellen Hall, asking if she were not filled with envy and hatred at not being with them, and inviting her to be a 'Bad Third', or rather a second, for 'WE are but ONE'. They reminisced about Wiesbaden, made snide remarks about Agnes's dreadful Miss Abbott, and drew a tantalizing picture of how they were constantly entwined in embrace, how they took carriage rides, simply because the carriage was so small that they had to 'sit VERY close to each other'. They ended with a sketch of themselves in each other's arms in Mary's sitting room at the Lodge, with the comment: 'you can *well* imagine how the winged hours go by'.

Ellen Hall came to Wellington. Without Ellen,

Mary had been miserable; passionate letters were exchanged. When she was there, Mary neglected her household duties, she wronged her dear ones, was 'unsympathetic to my boys—how they felt it— Arthur crying'. Mary's love for her children, when it emerged through the heavy mist of the melancholy that descended on her after a birth, was warm and bright. Something of the Minnie of the Blue House in Rugby remained in Mary at the Lodge: the spiritedness, the 'volatility' her mother so despaired of. It helped her to peek through society's curtain of nannies and nurseries, and to join children on the other side. Their tears—and her husband's distress—pained her, yet she seemed unable to check her unsympathetic behaviour. 'I lost my head,' Mary admitted. 'I came to grief.' Ellen's visit was a time of 'tossings, doubts, indecisions, jealousies' that 'grieved E[dward] to the heart'. Edward was moved to speak to Mary about Ellen Hall. Unlike

Sketch in a Letter from Mary Benson to Ellen Hall

Friendship, Thy Name
is { Mengea.
Minnie }

Sketch in a Letter from Mary Benson to Ellen Hall

the earlier occasion, when Emily Edwardes had been the focus of discussion, this talk did not proceed mildly with a blessing and a prayer.

Mary was now a young woman of thirty-two. She had known her husband nearly all her life. 'I first saw him when I was *five*,' Mary once wrote to a friend, 'and *I never* had a time of conscious existence when he wasn't my larger self—The self of myself.' Was love for Ellen Hall a betrayal of Edward? He certainly seemed to think so. 'Ah! my husband's pain,' Mary declared, 'what he bore, and how lovingly, how quickly—*our talk*.' If only, like the Greeks, she could find a different word for each of

115

these loves, words that could somehow keep them separate and explain them.

Edward and Mary found a modus vivendi. Mary had, after all, been schooled her entire life in the virtues of duty, in at least trying to quash her inclination to rebel. Edward loved her, and her behaviour caused him anguish. It appears that Ellen Hall was asked to leave. She did visit again in the summer, but then, Mary writes, 'I *saw* . . . Friendship has its duties like marriage.' Mary was at her husband's side for the final Speech Day at Wellington College, and his emotional leave-taking. She would take her place as wife of the Chancellor of Lincoln Cathedral. And (though whether by design or not is unclear) there would be no more children. Edward went alone with the two elder boys, Beth and baby Hugh to Lincoln to prepare the Chancery for Mary's arrival. Mary took the girls and Fred, her favourite, to her mother's house at Rugby.

Yet Ellen Hall was not the last of Mary's loves. In Lincoln, Mary would meet a woman who would change her life.

Chapter Nine

A Postcard from Edward Benson to his Wife

Sep. 1873

All going well. Boys very industrious and happy. The Precentory a grand refuge. Arrangements are very complete at the Chancery; there is a man to make dust, and a man to burn paint off doors, and a man to make a noise with a hammer, and a man to throw soot at the books, and a man to dig for tobacco pipes in the garden, and a man to splash the paper with paint, and a man to scrape paint off with a knife, and a boy not to fetch or carry, and rods and rings not to fit, and carpets not to fit also, and women to wet floors, and several men to charge. So we shall not be ready for you till Friday, if then. And yet you see what efforts!—and I fell down yesterday and scratched a shilling's worth of skin off my elbow, and to-day made a two-shilling hole in my trouser knee. Baby is splendid and so dirty and so happy. When Beth says she is surprised and asks if he is not he says 'No' in a highly concerned manner, and emphatically repeats 'No.' My best love to Nellie and Maggie and thanks for their letters which were very nice, and to old Fred and Grannie.

Beth seems to like everything.

The Chancery stood in a Close touching the hem of Lincoln's exultantly Gothic cathedral, and was almost as venerable as the church itself. Corbelled arches traversed its ancient flagstone floors; winding stairways led to criss-crossing corridors; light filtered in through mullioned stained glass. Pentacles and holy emblems to ward off evil spirits had been scratched into the stonework by medieval masons; there were Cromwellian bullets embedded in the front door. Haphazardly, over the centuries, a cavernous vestibule, wood-panelled chambers, a subterranean dining hall, curious anterooms and mysterious, poky cabinets had grown together. Ghosts seemed to mutter and rattle from the water pipes, to sidle with the draughts through rows of empty attic rooms; there were dusk-scented cellars, abandoned outbuildings, and a kitchen fit for a castle.

For Mary, Edward brightened up a sitting room, a pleasant half-panelled room with clear windows overlooking the Close, with sprigged wallpaper, white paint and an orange carpet. He threw two bedrooms together to make a study for himself, and assigned the ancient chapel, with its fifteenth-century oak screen, to serve as a schoolroom for the children. Martin and Arthur were considered old enough to have their own sitting room, but were soon to be off to school at Winchester and Eton respectively.

Mary came down from Rugby with Fred and the girls, and the household was further swelled by Rector the blue-eyed tomcat, Watch the border collie, and the parrot that had been bought when Arthur was a baby. Familiar furniture from Wellington took up residence in new surroundings—the grand dining-room sideboard, Mary's sofa, the comfortable ottoman. Along to the Chancery came the keepsakes, the display pieces and well-worn favourites—the dog-eared music for 'Willie We Have Missed You', the epergne with the Arab and camel, the volumes of Sir Walter Scott and Tennyson, even the giant blancmange of a beaded, crimson velvet pincushion that had been placed on a dressing table for the Queen's visit. Just off the drawing room, a narrow chamber with windows depicting Our Lord, the Virgin Mother and St John was fitted up as an oratory for family prayers. An outlay of £5 provided a miniature harmonium with pathetically bleating tremolo, and Mary coaxed hymn tunes from it twice daily. Above the oratory, at the top of a flight of stone stairs, Fred and the girls were given an empty room to do with as they liked. They immediately dubbed it The Museum, stocking it with pretty pebbles and fossils, old bits of glass and pottery, the broken tobacco pipes dug up in the garden, sheep's wool rescued by Maggie from a hedge, an addled swan's egg (soon ejected), a case of their grandfather's butterflies. Here, they would occasionally invite Mama to tea, to which she came, properly and formally attired in her hat.

For the children, the Lincoln Chancery proved an even more exciting place for growing up than Wellington College had been. The large garden came with a Roman sarcophagus and a turreted wall with battlements, once part of the old city fortifications. Inspired by the new fashion for lawn tennis, Edward laid out a somewhat oddly shaped court marked by tape pinned down with hairpins, and the family played with flat wooden bats made

119

Nellie and Maggie at Lincoln in 1876

(in accordance with Edward's characteristic thriftiness) by the cathedral carpenter—line judgements were made easy by an explosion of hairpins. The house itself, with its dark corners and quaint angles, unaccountable spaces and deep, empty cupboards, seemed specifically designed for the delight of children, for terrifying episodes of hide-and-seek and dreadful games of ambush. The children staged boisterous 'sieges', defending the top of a winding stone staircase against each other with some violence. Nellie usually took the lead, was quite up to giving Fred a bloody nose, and could terrify the others by playing dead. Maggie—tall, slim and secretive—and Fred (who became besotted with a chorister in the cathedral, and prayed to be allowed to join the choir), were the quieter ones, most often to be found in The Museum. The others had their more sedate moments too. Arthur, childish for his age, played alone with lead soldiers in the attic, long after he was at Eton. Martin—serious, still with a stammer, precocious beyond his fourteen years and pushed academically by his father—read complicated books and argued abstract questions with both Edward and Mary. Together, the children began the *Saturday Magazine*, a family venture, written by hand. All of them contributed, though Maggie's stories, piling catastrophe upon catastrophe, were thought a little below family par—and, of course, baby Hugh was not yet up to it. An ugly little thing pampered by all, especially Beth, baby Hugh was growing up spoilt and petulant. Yet his elder siblings made a most favourable impact on the Close—the boys clever, energetic and full of promise, the girls 'not a whit behind their brothers in intellect and power'.

Mary 'blew like a spring wind through the calm autumnal Close'. She started a musical society, causing a stir by departing from the usual popular songs and glees into Bach Chorales, singing in a rolling alto as she conducted with a paperknife. Even more shocking, for a clergyman's wife, was her open advocacy of the works of George Eliot, who not only lived in sin with a man and was a dangerous sceptic and free-thinker, but whose *Adam Bede* touched on infanticide and illegitimacy. She even read such novels to her children. Infuriatingly, Mrs Benson could—albeit most calmly and sweetly— effortlessly argue the objections of canons' wives in knots. She was equally adroit when one of her promising, energetic children publicly demanded to know the difference between a bull and an ox, responding without hesitation that the bull was the father and the ox the uncle.

On nights when Edward was not lecturing or giving a bible class, and if Mary was at home and not putting the music club through its paces, the family sat together reading in the drawing room, or played Floral Lotto and card games. Mary often read to the children in her sitting room before they went to bed, though these days it was from Dickens or *The Mill on the Floss* rather than *Ivanhoe* or fairy romances. While she did so, she liked having Fred stand beside her, stroking her hair. Life was quieter than it had been at Wellington, with fewer dinner parties and just a sprinkling of visitors. For the first time, in the children's eyes, their father was no longer the absolute ruler of all he surveyed, the crucial pivot around which the world they observed through the nursery window revolved—though within their family circle he inspired no less trepidation, and still, despite his gestures of affection, even a little fear. Yet to his friend Canon Crowfoot, Edward spoke of his children with love, reverence and 'with awe and trembling, lest his own strong will and that stubborn temper, with which his own life was one perpetual struggle, should do some wrong to them . . . He felt they were his, yet not his, but only lent.'

From E. F. Benson's Our Family Affairs

[My Father] had no idea how blighting his displeasure was to small children, and for fear of incurring it we went delicately like Agag, attending so strictly to our behaviour that all

122

spontaneity withered. Nothing would have pleased him more, had we taken him into our confidence, but we feared his disapproval more than we were drawn to intimacy with him ... he brought too heavy guns to bear on positions so lightly fortified as children's hearts, and for fear of the bombardment we did not dare to make a sortie and go to him ... with him we were careful to be decorous to the verge of woodenness. We had washed hands and neat hair and low voices, because thus we minimized the risks of his society ... We sat on the edge of our chairs, and were glad to be gone.

Edward's tasks as Chancellor were not onerous. All that was legally required of him was to reside in Lincoln for three months of the year, preach once each Sunday and by tradition hold a few lectures in the Chapter House. He had been asked in addition to start a new theological college. The Scholae Cancelarii opened in January 1874 with two students. Yet before Mary arrived with Fred and the girls, Edward was clawed at by depression, dragged into a deep, tearful despondency as he pondered the immensity of the changes he had made in their lives. He was convinced that he was unequal to making a success of the new venture, worried his wife was too ill to play the role he required of her. His drive and vigour soon resurfaced, and Edward threw himself into his work with energy. The Scholae Cancelarii grew rapidly, he founded a temperance society, gave university extension lectures, set up a night school and held weekly bible classes for working men. Unused to having to be answerable to anyone, he clashed with his superior the Dean, who tried to curb his wilder enthusiasms. In response, Edward turned his magnetism and melting, bright-eyed charm to raising independent funds for his schemes, sweeping away such hesitations as those of the elderly ladies who said as they handed over their donations: 'We give this to you, Mr Chancellor, to show our regard for you, but for our parts, Patty and I prefer an ignorant poor.'

Mary, when she arrived in Lincoln, was still beset by periods of melancholy, too, at times prostrated by afflictions that meant long periods away from home to recuperate. Riseholme and the Wordsworths were close at hand, but the ladies of the Close were no match for her Wellington friends, and the life that stretched before her seemed flat and arid. To make matters worse, her heart and mind were dangerously unsettled by 'a time of urgent doubt and mental turmoil'. The certainties of God and Church and Faith had turned fluid and undependable beneath her. Perhaps her brother Henry's scepticism had affected her. She had always been enquiring, even speculative, and had been stimulated by books which Edward found heretical. Certainly her unhappiness, and the quavering of her independent spirit against Edward's rock solidity of character and purpose, had moved her to a crisis. She had in the past been glib in her prayers, a little lackadaisical about church, but the comforts of the old orthodoxy had been there, practised mechanically but supporting of the spirit, accepted without question. Now she was flailing, doubting even that. She had not been swept up by Edward's ardent churchmanship and unswerving belief. Mary looked on God as a Father; for Edward, He was an omnipotent King. As a consequence Edward travelled in His cause on a road of firm granite, and now that she was stumbling along her own uneven path, Mary had no appeal to her husband for help.

The Case of Annie Besant

Annie Besant, née Wood, was born in 1847. Her father died when she was five, and she was raised by a friend of her mother's. At the age of 19 she married the Reverend Frank Besant and had two children by the time she was 23. Annie's independence of spirit brought her into fierce conflict with her clergyman husband. Annie did not concede, and as discord grew she began to question God's goodness. The faith that had hitherto guided her life started to crumble. In 1871, Annie suffered a nervous collapse and 'lay for weeks helpless and prostrate, in raging and unceasing head-pain, unable to bear light . . . indifferent to everything'. When she recovered, she refused to take Holy Communion, and her husband ejected her from the family home. A legal separation ensued, and in 1874 Annie joined the Secular Society. Her later campaigns for birth control, and her publication of a work on this subject dubbed by *The Times* 'an indecent, lewd, filthy, bawdy and obscene book', rendered her husband's humiliation complete.

Intertwined with Mary's spiritual crisis was the issue of the love she felt for women like Ellen Hall, which caused Edward deep heartache and served to widen the gulf between them. Yet it was such a passion that ensured that Mary's commitment to her marriage would remain; a woman who brought Mary firm answers, shoring her up against collapse.

Mrs Mylne was the wife of a student at the theological college, a zealous man who had taken orders late in life. She was middle-aged, motherly, forthright, yet quietly dignified, with a beautiful smile and unaffected charm. Mary called her 'Tan'– when she writes the name it appears sometimes as τ, the Greek letter T, a Christian symbol for the crucifix and for life. Tan called Mary 'Ben'. When she met Tan, in 1875, Mary was in the throes of a *Schwärmerei*, of 'stirrings of the old love—Alice Swan—the old ungoverned desire'. Their meeting was not one of Mary's instant 'My God, what a woman!' moments, but gradually Mary was drawn to Mrs Mylne, began 'to play with my human love for her and hers for me—felt it coming—felt how different places were when she was there . . . so went May and June—and now I loved her indeed—and she was getting *hold*, only humanly as yet.' Tan came with the family for a holiday in Torquay. Mary and Edward were 'terribly apart', in a seeming constant quarrel, saying hard and unloving things to each other. The situation with her husband was the worst Mary could remember, and she had all but given up on God, was 'quite prayerless'.

Tan was a fervent Evangelical. In early 1876, she and her husband were deeply involved in a Mission in Lincoln which Mary attended. Tan and Mary went on long country walks outside Lincoln, sat talking for hours in Mary's sitting room at the Chancery. Tan now had firm hold of Mary, and squeezed any doubt or scepticism from her mind. In the midst of their talks, Mary heard a voice murmur *'Fiat voluntas Tua'*—Thy will be done—and happiness welled and brimmed within her. Mary turned to God. Unlike Mary's earlier loves, Tan was an older woman. She became Mary's 'blessed Mother', her 'Mother in Christ'. This new-found love for God was inextricably bound up with her love for a woman; it was almost the same thing, as if love for God was a development of this earthly love. Mary felt that she would not have known, truly, about divine love—about any true love at all—were it not for the love of a woman. God, Mary wrote in her diary (with her characteristic touch for metaphor), had brought her Tan, had given her 'first human knowledge and human love, and I drank eagerly of both founts—then thou leadest me through human love, and human knowledge, just to the Fountain of both, Thyself—where I lie and drink forever.'

Tan took control of Mary's tottering life. She demanded to know all about Mary's earlier loves. She wanted details. Confessions. She brought Mary to admit that she had never loved, truly loved, Edward. She bombarded Mary with disturbing questions:

'*Why* are you so weak?'

'Why do you fail?'

'Doesn't weakness become guilt?'

She made Mary sit and write it all down—daily for three weeks around her thirty-fifth birthday in March 1876—in a retrospective diary that viewed every part of her life from a new perspective, 'a spirit photograph, whatever its ugliness'. Tan confirmed Mary's sense of sin. The girl who had numbered her *Schwärmereien* with delight, though with occasional twinges of guilt, now wrote of them in terms of 'stain' and 'soil'—words she used again and again, and underlined. Mary wrote her retrospect on the right-hand page of her diary. On the left, she addressed musings to God, wrote out short prayers, pleas to the Lord to burn away her sin, to 'burn truth in, burn this out', to 'burn all that must burn'; an entreaty 'to possess and purify my heart, that this subtle, inward, but indeed alas! *real* fall may be impossible ever again'. Yet still the rebellion remained. Tan knew how to deal with it.

A married woman herself, Tan knew all about the interplay of love and duty. 'Is it not really the same sin in my neglects and my loves?' Mary wrote on the left-hand side of her diary, after she had recorded her neglect of household duties while in the grip of a *Schwärmerei*. 'O Lord, stir my whole nature—rouse, cleanse, fill.' No matter how Mary felt about her passionate friendships, her Christian duty was to her husband—a duty that required even *more* effort on her part 'than if at first our love had been that strong human passion'. 'What, and how far, is the union of two souls in matrimony, and what is individuality?' she asked herself in her diary. It seemed that individuality must take a tumble. Tan was God's messenger. Tan would show her the way. In the same way as she had learned to submit first to her mother, then to her husband, Mary now bent her knee not only to her Lord, but to Tan. More effectively than Mary's real mother had ever managed to do, her 'Mother in Christ' put a damper on her dangerous 'volatility'. To the outside world, Mrs Mylne appeared to produce a stabilizing, calming effect on Mrs Benson.

Mary found it difficult to confide in Edward the power she derived from this charismatic experience, from the personal, mystical religion she was fashioning for herself. He had also attended the Mission, and been affected by it. Some of the ferocity of his old conviction softened, but he was still the orthodox High Churchman, marching ahead on his granite road, with little sympathy for Mary's new Evangelical bent. He did not agree with her that her experience of human love could lead to divine love. At the end of March he wrote her a long letter saying, 'one must, I am certain, *begin* by loving *Him* above all persons and things', yet they were now, he acknowledged, at least facing in the same direction. Edward did offer a form of apology for 'my temper, my pride, my resentment, my self-government . . . my opinion of myself', but, he went on 'a time comes when we must begin to draw to a close our self-analysis'. And he could not resist a few pages of high-minded preaching. After that, Mary was largely silent to her husband on the matter of her personal religious beliefs, but she did begin to participate more in his life at Lincoln, spent more time at home, and became known as a sparkling speaker at ladies' events.

These changes were not easy for Mary. Tan had not quashed her rebelliousness entirely, and assuming the mantle of duty had never come naturally to her. 'I fancied most foolishly that when I became a Christian, [Edward] and I would be more in union,' Mary wrote in her diary, 'I didn't do it *for* this, God knows—but I did think this would come with it . . . I have expected that Christianity would do away with the necessity of my *accommodating myself* to him.' That was not the case, and as rebellion resurfaced, Mary spent whole nights raging, sometimes not against anything in particular, simply with 'a desire for lawlessness as such'. Then Tan would be contacted, and she would come and pray, and duty and God's will prevailed. 'I need *discipline, discipline, discipline,*' Mary commanded herself. '*I must guard myself against unnecessarily opposing.*' She must give up her habit of grumbling about Edward's ways and thoughts (to which she was particularly susceptible in the periods that followed the delights of a visit from any of her brothers); she must become the devoted wife, the 'staff on which he leaned, and the wings that gave him flight'— even if, at times, she reduced that devotion to its bare bones. 'What does a woman owe to her husband and her family?' she asked. 'To herself?' 'Let me see,' she noted in the diary. 'Economy, punctuality, tidiness—these I owe to him and these I will steadily cultivate—I ought to try to *please* him more, and, please God, I will.'

Sometimes Mary's 'falls' involved Tan herself. They would spend too much time together, and Mary would neglect her duties, as with *Schwärmereien* of old. At times, surges of 'the old love . . . the ungoverned desire' might engulf her, as they did one afternoon at the end of May, after she had taken the children on an outing: 'Uneasiness began on Saturday, after the Circus,' she confessed to her diary. 'Somehow, I cannot clearly see how, the suppleness, litheness of the limbs stirred me to an uneasy restlessness, a fierceness, a tingling. I came away and went to Tan and sitting there with her told her all. She helped me as she always does—but the restless desire increased, and I *knew* instinctively wasn't good, and I had a quiet evening quite alone, and sought God here in the oratory—and the consciousness of *stain* came, more than ever before—and it seemed as if the very *core*, the very *ich*, self citadel into which one retired from God before . . . as if *this* was bad and rotten.' When it came to 'the old love', guilt and a besetting consciousness of sin was with Mary to stay. Yet these feelings were at her core, her very *ich* (as on other occasions, Mary retreated into German to express a difficult or intense emotion), and as 'the old love' was associated with neglect of her duty to Edward, this 'self citadel into which one retired' must, corrupted, be pushed deeper and further away.

Mrs Benson Taps into the Zeitgeist and Anticipates Dr Freud's Notion of the Id

I have come to this, then . . . that within the source of all feeling, spring of all action, lies a self, *the* self. What remains undamaged through all the years, from childhood to youth, youth to middle life is not the will, but something further back than that— something by which the will itself is set in motion . . . from this the will is agitated, stirred . . .

Diary, Saturday, 10 June 1876

Edward did not take to Mrs Mylne. Perhaps it was her strong Evangelical belief, of which he disapproved, perhaps it was the intensity of her friendship with his wife, which made him uneasy. He seemed unaware that she had in effect saved his marriage and, by extension, any career he might hope for within the Church.

On the morning of 4 December 1876, Edward was dressing before breakfast in time for the early service at the cathedral. The eccentric layout of the Chancery meant that from his bedroom window he could see, across a small court, into the hall where the morning post was laid out on a table. Through the winter's gloom, Edward glimpsed the white envelopes and, he said later, had an immediate presentiment of momentous news. With the post was a letter from the Prime Minister, Benjamin Disraeli (who had recently been made Earl of Beaconsfield), offering him the newly created See of Truro, in Cornwall. There was another, from Queen Victoria, expressing her personal wish that he would accept. Edward's energies in Lincoln had not gone unnoticed. After just three and a half years in direct service of the Church, he was being invited to ascend from his relatively lowly cathedral position to become a bishop, without having to suffer the inconvenience of any tiresome steps in between.

Chapter Ten

The Great Western Railway had only recently crossed the River Tamar into Cornwall. Much of the county was wild and little travelled. Edward was offered £3,000 a year, substantially more than he had ever earned before. Yet out of that stipend he would, in the absence of good rail connections across his diocese, need to maintain a carriage and pair; he would also have to provide for a house, 'and a sufficient house' at that (he mused in a letter seeking advice from his friend Canon Westcott). In addition, he would be obliged to cover substantial travel costs to London, and make generous subscriptions, as 'Bishops who do not *give* subscriptions are not able to *raise* subscriptions'— there was yet a cathedral to be built.

Mary was horrified at the idea, and said as much. 'The position has *no* attraction for my wife or for me,' Edward told Westcott. Yet such, he felt, was his calling, and he accepted the invitation within days. The Prime Minister was delighted. 'Well, we *have* got a Bishop!' he wrote to a friend. Fred and Maggie were similarly exultant when they were told a few days later, whispering to each other on their morning walk, with secret smiles: 'The Lord Bishop of Truro! The Lord Bishop of Truro!' Nellie read to the others, amidst great hilarity, newspapers that speculated on just what this mysterious new bishop was like. 'A stout and hearty-looking man of the medium height,' said one; another had him at 'above the middle height by a good deal' and admired his 'thin intellectual looking face', and yet another admired him as 'the very model of a handsome Englishman!' The children were particularly delighted by a report that both the Reverend and Mrs Benson desired the well-being of the masses and enjoyed mixing with the working classes. But their mother told Susan Wordsworth that the prospect of life at the very end of England made her feel wretched and rebellious. She knew no one in that part of the world. She would be an impossibly long journey away from Tan, and indeed from everyone and everything else in Lincoln, where she had only just begun to settle and make a life for herself. She would see far less of her brothers Henry and Arthur, in whose company she delighted and found support, and of her mother (who was drifting slowly towards death in a mournful progress from spa to spa, taking cures). Yet Mary had indeed learned to quell her rebelliousness. God led, Edward followed, Mary obeyed.

Once again the Bensons (and Beth) packed up house—the oak sideboard and the comfortable ottoman, the Arabian epergne and blancmange-sized royal pincushion, the books, Floral Lotto, and now also the little harmonium and a set of bronzed dessert dishes, made for Edward with iron from nearby Coleby Mines, by members of his working-men's bible class—a gift that moved him to tears. All were, in the spring of 1877, covered or boxed up and dispatched to Truro. The issue of where to live had been quickly resolved. The parish of Kenwyn had recently been much reduced in size, and its diminished income meant that upkeep of the vicarage—a handsome, stone-built country house which a passing John Wesley had called 'fit for a nobleman'—was proving too expensive. The vicar was happy to take a long vacation until more modest accommodation could be built for him. Edward rented the old vicarage, and had soon raised enough money for it to be acquired by the new See.

Fred awoke exultant on his first morning in Kenwyn. In place of the 'sorry serge of ivy' that had enclosed the Chancery, their new home was a bower of climbing roses and japonica, tree fuchsias and magnolia. The house itself was smaller than both the Lodge at Wellington and the Lincoln Chancery and was initially a tight fit, but as soon as it was purchased, Edward had it substantially extended, naming it 'Lis Escop'—'Bishop's Palace' in Cornish. A governess was enlisted to help Beth look after the younger children, and (now that the family was no longer having to live quite so much 'in holy poverty') Parker, their old butler from Wellington College, returned to them. Ranks below stairs were further increased by Maclean the coachman, Tregunna the gardener, a maid for Mary, a cook, and a host of other local help.

Edward invested in a brougham—a light but tough little enclosed carriage that seated two comfortably—and a larger, more elegant open barouche. Two strong horses were found to pull them, which were also suitable for riding. The new Bishop set out on forays to the farther reaches of his diocese, usually accompanied by a chaplain to take Confirmations. With a billowing black cloak over his purple cassock, his pastoral staff in a special leather case (in one large house it was taken to the gunroom by mistake) and with piles of books, papers and luggage packed into the carriage, he would head off to isolated—sometimes desolate— spots, where he was 'a foreigner from England'. Here were ancient churches, barely attended, lonely priests who struggled with poverty on miserable endowments, who were shunned, even harassed by Dissenters. One priest was so lonely in his unpeopled church that he rented a pew in the Wesleyan chapel, and would go there of a Sunday evening 'to get a little warmth and light, and to see human beings and hear them speak'. Others were more eccentric in their isolation, such as the vicar who did not go into his church at all, but spent Sundays walking in the rectory garden in a flowered dressing gown, smoking a hookah; the one who requested 'white wine for a change' at Communion; or the absent-minded parson whose sister had to secure him to the altar rail with a dog chain and padlock to prevent him from wandering off before the service was over.

At Lis Escop Mary, too, was lonely. 'One gets gradually to accept the fact that we are living here, but at present entirely free from any outside attraction,' she wrote to Susan Wordsworth, a month or two after moving in. 'It is so strange to live so alone, horribly free sometimes it feels.' She felt rage and rebellion welling up inside her again. 'Oh I know how dreadful it is!' she confided to Susan. 'I had thought I was never going to be rebellious again. I wonder if *you* know, to whom I don't think Nature has given a rebellious heart, what an awful inheritance it is—and when a lovely life alters and comes right away, down here where nothing is helpful and all is strange, and one's heart so sore—there comes wilfulness and one doesn't struggle and it lays hold.' Yet the woman whose absence made Mary's 'heart so sore' had implanted such religious purpose within her that she set herself to push these feelings ever deeper. Elizabeth Wordsworth may have dismissed Tan and her milieu as a 'little spiritual hothouse in Minster Yard', but the ecstatic religious atmosphere that prevailed there nurtured hardy seedlings.

The customary round of opening moves and introductions began: the leaving of cards and receiving of cards; the first visits, the returned visits and the non-returned visits, as the elaborate rules of Victorian social intercourse were brought into play, and the whole slow system of making new friends and acquaintances got under way. Of course, Edward's exalted status brought with it a host of visitors—curates and canons, the managers of works and the chairmen of charities, fellow bishops and passing dignitaries—but for many months Mary found it deadening to the heart to be coming home from a drive and for there to be no excitement at the possibility that someone interesting might have called in their absence. Life at Lis Escop reminded her of the early years in the Blue House, when her mother discouraged outside friends. And like the Sidgwicks in Rugby, the Benson children at Kenwyn became self-sufficient—'a close little corporation with clearly defined interests of our own,' Arthur later wrote, 'critical and observant . . . we were rather unduly afraid of life, and thought the mêlée a rougher, harsher less kindly place than it was in reality.' Lis Escop, with its spacious sloping grounds overlooking a glebe of meadows and quiet fields, with a view across the rooftops of Truro to the Fal estuary, offered an idyllic retreat.

Arthur Benson Recalls Lis Escop,
in his Biography of his Father

No sweeter place could well be imagined than Lis Escop. In the soft air trees and shrubs grew with great luxuriance. Camellias flowered and Hydrangeas grew richly out of doors. No severity of winter ever emptied the beds of flowers. The windows commanded a wide view down the green valley in which Truro lies; the spire of St Mary's, soon to be replaced by the new Cathedral, rose from the grey slate roofs amid the smoke of the little city. The valley was crowned by the high airy viaduct of the Great Western Railway, and below lay the wide tidal creek that runs up with its great mud-flats among the steep wooded hills from Falmouth harbour, closed by an elbow of the hills, and looking like an inland lake from Kenwyn.

The calm of the Bensons' life in Cornwall was disrupted just a few months after the family had moved into Lis Escop. In February 1878, Martin died at school in Winchester, at the age of seventeen. He had been showing exceptional promise, was a brilliant scholar, and his death was utterly unexpected. Martin had always been possessed by a passion for learning, taking such intense pleasure in it that Beth once remarked: 'He always worked as if he were not working at all.' He once taught himself enough Italian in a few weeks to take in the literary classics with ease, he read Carlyle's *French Revolution* while still at prep school, and enjoyed exchanging original versions of Latin hymns with his father. At Lincoln, he had spotted an original Dürer woodcut pasted on to the flyleaf of a trifling volume in a penny bookstall, and already at the age of eight, on hearing Edward mention 'idle boys', had asked:

'But *why* are they idle?'

'They don't want to know what they are being taught.'

'Not to *know*? Not to *know*? Not want to *know* things? Oh! No—can't be *that*!'

As he grew a little older, Martin had taken on Edward's intensely serious, fervently religious turn of mind. Of all the children, he was the least afraid of his father, and seemed the only one of them who could talk to him with some ease and frankness. In his eldest son, Edward saw a spiritual heir who might carry on his work on Earth. 'From the time he was six years old,' recalled Edward, 'I always said he was "better company" to me in the diversity of interests which he awoke and pursued than any friend I had except two or three.' Edward drove his son hard, and Martin did not rebel. If the boy faltered in his step, he would be pulled up with such exhortations as: 'Pray pick up directly. Do not flag with the goal in sight.' When he was moved to a higher division at school and bullied by older boys for his diligence (and, to top it all, thought he had lost a railway ticket Edward had given him), Mary commiserated, writing to her 'Dearest of dear old boys', telling him how she missed him, how he would do the 'beasts' who tormented him good, and inserting a line in tiny writing: '(Don't tell anyone, but *I* lost a ticket myself once)'. His father had no sympathy. In response to occasional criticism from masters of Martin's 'dreaminess' or 'inattentiveness', Edward railed: 'What you seem to want intellectually is concentration of mind and body. For Listlessness of Attitude (want of smartness) springs from and then tends to reproduce Listlessness of Attention.' He would swoop on the smallest mistake in otherwise faultless Latin prose with: 'Remember Accuracy is the very soul of a scholar.' The boy had progressed through Winchester College with an ever-burgeoning bag of prizes and honours.

Martin died suddenly, of 'brain fever', later known as meningitis, a condition which many doctors believed was provoked by excessive mental strain. Over the Christmas holidays at Lis Escop, he had been unusually quiet and withdrawn. There was a languor about him, and he did not feel up to reading. He confided in Mary that night after night he was having vivid and alarming dreams. Standing at the front door, saying goodbye to Beth and the family as he left for the new term at Winchester, he had unexpectedly—and uncharacteristically—burst into impassioned tears. There had been no other warning that anything was amiss. On the first Sunday after he was back at school, while Martin was taking tea with a master and his wife, it was noticed that he could not speak. He was taken from the room, and it was discovered he could not write, either. He lost control of his bowels. A telegram was sent to Edward, who arrived the next day. Martin rallied briefly, and by the Wednesday was chatting brightly. That Sunday he relapsed into delirium.

Mary was sent for. She managed to talk quietly with him for a while, then his focus seemed to wander, and he 'gazed with a beautiful expression at a part of the room where nothing visible stood: plainly saw something and exclaimed, "How lovely."' These were the last words he spoke. On the next day he signalled with his fingers that he wanted bread and wine, and his father gave him Holy Communion. Again Martin gazed, wide-eyed and pointing, at a spot where no one else could see anything. Mary whispered hymns into his ear, and said: 'Do not be afraid, darling; you are in the Valley of the Shadow of Death; but do not be afraid; don't fear, darling. God is with you.' Martin died in the night.

Mary's behaviour was saintly. The faith that Tan had delivered still infused her. She comforted Edward, saying that she had never cared for anything but Martin's happiness, and that now it was come. 'Oh, my Martin, how happy you are now, my darling,' she had murmured, the moment after he was gone. For once, Mary was the strong one, walking the straight road, without falter. Only God had the right to Martin, she told Edward, and his going was gain, pure gain. 'I cannot reach to this,' Edward confided to his diary. Mary wrote immediately to Beth, a letter that acknowledged the old nurse's maternal role in her own life as well as that of her children. 'Dearest Friend and Mother Beth', she began, going on to assure her that Martin was now 'in wonderful joy, far happier than we could ever have made him', and asking her to comfort the children at home with the thought that their brother was 'in perfect peace for ever, free from fear, free from pain, from anxiety for evermore', ending her letter: 'Your own child, your fellow-mother, M.B.'. The children at Lis Escop were told of Martin's death by their governess and the Kenwyn curate. Edward wrote to Arthur at Eton, and six-year-old Hugh sent a letter, too, in blue pencil between big lines, reading: 'My dear Arthur, Martain [sic] is dead. Nellie sends you her love. Martin is gone to hefen. Maggie sends you her love. I am so happy that Martin is gone to Jesus Christ. I hope we shall all go to HIM very soon. He is Saint Martin now. Your loving brother, Hugh.'

Edward was stricken. For months he appeared pale and ravaged by grief. In his overpowering way, he had given his firstborn a love such as he afforded no other living creature. Yet his forcing of Martin's abilities, Edward came to believe, his kindling of the boy's intellectual prowess as if he had been an adult, had played a role in over-straining and over-stimulating his brain, provoking the fever. 'It has changed all my views of God's work as it is to be done both in this world and the next,' he wrote in his diary soon after Martin's death. His views on how his children should be educated changed utterly. As a moralist, he was as strict and as nit-picking as ever; as an educationalist, he developed 'a horror of any sort of pressure', giving his surviving offspring a much freer rein, allowing them to take their own particular ways, giving freedom to childlike impulse over adult control. Hugh, in particular, was indulged (by the whole family) to the point of wildness.

Edward visited Martin's grave in Winchester every year on the anniversary of his death. He never fully comprehended why his son had been taken from him, writing in his diary a full decade later that this was the 'inexplicable grief' of his life, and composing a poem in his sorrow.

*Verses Written by Edward Benson
in Memory of his Eldest Boy, on Observing House
Martins Nesting*

The Martin

The Martins are back to cornice and eaves
Fresh from the glassy sea.
The Martin of Martins my soul bereaves
Flying no more to me.

One of them clung to the window-side,
And twittered a note to me.
There's a Martin beyond or wind or tide
Whom you know better than we.

'His nest is hid in a clustered rose
On the Prince's own roof-tree,
When the Prince incomes, when the Prince
outgoes,
The Prince looks up to see.

'Calls him hither or sends him there,
To the Friends of the Holy Three,
With a word of love, or a touch of care.
Why was he sent to thee?'

Martin I know. And when he went home
He carried my heart from me.
Half I remain. Ere Martinmas come
Go with this message from me.

143

Say, 'Thou Prince, he is wholly Thine!
Sent once on a message to me.
Yet suffer me soon, at morning shine,
To see him on Thy roof-tree.'

At Lis Escop, the 'close little corporation' of
children drew even more tightly together. They
developed a coded language, formed secret
societies—some eccentric, such as the club called
'Mr Paido', for which one of the rites was walking
barefoot in the garden; others more formal, such
as 'The Chapter', which had its own seal and
letters patent, as well as graded salaries for
officials, from half-a-crown for the Warden,
Arthur, down to a penny for the Henchman,
Hugh. (They all subscribed to the funds of The
Chapter, although Mary, being an honorary
member, subscribed the most.) One of Edward's
first acts as Bishop was to establish a High School
for Girls in Truro, sending Nellie and Maggie
there as soon as they were old enough, and the
Easter after Martin died, Fred went away to prep
school; but on holidays and after school the
Benson children withdrew into each other's
company at Lis Escop.

Edward liked having his children about him. 'My
dearest love to the dearests,' he wrote to Mary on
one of his trips to London. 'I think I ought always
to have *one* with me here. They could go into a
state of coma when I went out, and *thus* would not
find it *dull*.' In another letter, looking forward to
his return to Lis Escop, he wrote: 'I had rather
teach Hugh Greek, or walk with the girls than
anything else.' Yet the children remained ill at ease
with their father, with his swings of mood, his

144

perfectionist obsession with detail, the enormity of his powers of rebuke and criticism. They adored Mary, who brimmed with fun when they were around her; who (in Arthur's words) 'opened, one by one, the doors of life' to them, and who seemed so close to her own childhood that she 'knew by instinct what we were thinking and caring about'.

'I *did not grow up*,' Mary wrote in one of her diaries, looking back on a girlhood that had come to a sudden, early end when her cousin proposed to her. The little girl thus arrested and contained burst out, in adult company (once she had moved through a barrier of shyness), in brilliant, darting conversation and social effervescence. She could be wickedly witty, enlivening even the most humdrum social events. With her own children, the child still within herself emerged in a 'particular precision of sympathy' and delight in their world. 'She was younger and wiser than anyone else, limpid and bubbling,' said Fred. She had their eye for 'treats'—for the odd conduct of ducks on the pond, for the hilarity of the butcher's quirks of speech, for the overwhelming beauty of a butterfly's wing. Their troubles, their joys, the best of them and the worst of them 'went like homing pigeons' to their mother. There was something 'conveyed in the very atmosphere of her' that let them know that 'she was ready, toeing the mark, so to speak, to run to us when the pistol fired'. When Mary talked with Edward about discipline, she ended up feeling 'just as bad if not worse' than the children, but she could scold when the need arose—there was little sentiment about her. Yet her love was swift and eager, and her forgiveness complete. When Fred, as an errant thirteen-year-old, had been hauled by his father through a 'dreadful interview', his mother gave him a prayer book, saying, 'I shall write in it "Wherewithal shall a young man cleanse his ways?"' Being called a young man at the age of thirteen was quite enough to make Fred realize what an exceedingly tiresome child he had been.

Mary might by now be nearing forty, but she would enthusiastically join in the children's games (tearing a sinew playing 'Three Knights A-riding'). And games there were in plenty at Lis Escop. Most were made up by the children themselves and many were boisterous, such as 'Pirates', a contest of chasing, trophies and tackling that ranged from summerhouse to kitchen garden, from laurel hedge to the beehives. Now that Nellie and Maggie were growing older, they should really have given up vigorous knockabouts with their brothers, and like other young ladies of their class been content with gentle walks and demure carriage drives, especially given the thick, scratchy layers of clothing that enfolded them. (Not that tight collars, high waistcoats and jackets buttoned almost to the neck much bothered the boys, nor—for that matter—did layers of petticoat and bombazine, and the cane and horsehair padding of the 'dress improver' that kept them afloat, deter Mary from running about and taking the odd tumble.) But the girls joined in with glee, be it Pirates or Three Knights A-riding, hide-and-seek or cricket—Nellie, in particular, was a devastating underarm bowler, once vanquishing the entire Redruth High School girls' team with 'lobs that cut daisies from their stalks'.

146

An Excerpt from E. F. (Fred) Benson's
Ghost Story, 'Pirates',
in which Peter Graham pays a visit to his
childhood home of 'Lescop' in Truro, and recalls
an incident with his mother
and sister, Sybil

There was the shop where he had taken his canary to be stuffed (beautiful it looked!): and there was the shop of the 'undertaker and cabinet maker,' still with the same name over the door, where on a memorable birthday, on which his amiable family had given him, by request, the tokens of their good-will in cash, he had ordered a cabinet with five drawers and two trays, varnished and smelling of newly cut wood, for his collection of shells . . . At the end of the street was the bridge over the Fal just below which they used so often to take a boat for a picnic on the river. There was a jolly family party setting off just now from the quay, three boys he noticed, and a couple of girls, and a woman of young middle-age. Quickly they dropped downstream and went forth, and with a half sigh he said to himself, 'Just our number with Mama.' . . . And then Peter gave a gasp of sheer amazement, for he remembered with clear-cut distinctness how on the morning of that memorable birthday, he and Sybil started earlier than the rest from Lescop, he on the adorable errand of ordering his cabinet, she for a dolorous visit to Mr Tuck [the dentist]. The others followed half an hour later for a picnic on the Fal to celebrate the great fact that his age now required two figures (though one was a nought) for expression. 'It'll be ninety years, darling,' his mother had said, 'before you want a third one, so be careful of yourself.'

The Cornish countryside drew the children out of doors—to bathe in the Fal and for picnics at Perran Bay, for walks through meadows of deep grass, among willowherb and loosestrife, following rivers thicketed with reeds, past swamps full of bog myrtle, over low wolds criss-crossed by stone walls and ancient hedgerows. Ferns, marvelled Fred, 'the sort of things not known before to exist in other localities than greenhouses and tables laid for dinner-parties', grew carelessly in the crevices in the lane below the churchyard. Arthur, Fred and Maggie, especially, became fascinated by the natural world. Maggie and Fred went searching for otters, peeked into nests for birds' eggs, built up gardens of native plants and stocked a fish tank from local ponds. Arthur collected moths and butterflies. Nellie objected to killing them, but Fred and Maggie acted as eager anaesthetists each time Arthur returned, perspiring and laden with little boxes, from his expeditions. The contents of the children's 'Museum' now overflowed into all their bedrooms. In addition to her penchant for wildlife, Maggie had a passion for pets. Watch, the border collie brought down from Lincoln, was joined by three more of his kin, together with an adoring nanny goat, a pair of canaries called Thersis and Mummy (later re-christened Buttercup), and a great dynasty of guinea pigs that included Atahualpa, Ixlitchochitl, Mr and Mrs Fenwick, and Edith

Maggie, Aged Seventeen, with some of her Pets

Mitchinson (named after a girl at school).

Indoors, the family played word games—at breakfast they were only passed bread if they phrased the request in an improvised rhyming couplet. A poetry game, curiously called 'American Nouns', involved plucking a written question from a hat, and then another bearing a single word (sometimes one as taxing as 'unconstitutional'), and answering the question in rhyme and good metre, incorporating the word. Mary's contributions to American Nouns were considered generally to be somewhat indifferent, her high point being the occasion when she had to answer the question 'Does the moon draw the sea?' using the word 'artist', and produced a poem ending:

Ask me no more but let me be;
My temper's of the tartest:
For if the moon doth draw the sea,
Why, then she is an artist.

The *Saturday Magazine*, inaugurated one holiday back at Lincoln (and neither confined to Saturdays nor particularly regular in its appearance), was now produced more frequently. Each contributor was required to write at least four pages of prose or one of poetry, on the faintly ruled blue paper Edward used for his sermons. Arthur came up with an essay in the style of *The Spectator*, about how he threw a cake of yellow soap at a serenading cat; Nellie with an imaginary interview with Maclean the coachman on the subject of sore backs; Maggie with a dialogue between two of her guinea pigs; Fred with a poem on the Devil. Little Hugh (by reason of his age allowed to get away with only two pages) made up tales so relentlessly bloody that his readership was reduced to shocked laughter. Their mother's fondness for cheese became the object of wicked satire, and even Papa—in the distance and safety afforded by the written word—appeared in scenarios where he was worsted by his children's superior wit.

Alliances and rivalries tugged the young Bensons this way and that, but there were seldom any severe internecine battles. Fred and Maggie were often together on jaunts into the countryside. The two girls formed a natural alignment, though when Maggie founded an Anti-Slang Society at school (with badges for all carrying the motto 'Manners Maketh Man'), Nellie established a Slang Society, in which members had to vow to say such words as 'awfully' many times a day. Maggie was fond of Societies. Diffident, with a soft, almost breathless voice and unable to roll her *rs*, she liked people to do things *together* and had inherited her father's heart-melting smile, which greatly facilitated such schemes. Nellie, though bookish, was inquisitive, more individual in outlook, and out of all the children now the least cowed by Papa. Arthur was growing into a tall, powerfully built, but wispily blond, good-looking young man. Fred was fine-featured and pretty. Having left his passion for the chorister behind in Lincoln, he immediately lost what he referred to as his 'sloppy heart' to the curate at Kenwyn, the Revd John Reeve. The curate was an engaging young man with 'a mane of yellow hair which he tossed back as he laughed peals of uproarious appreciation of any joke at all', who himself (Arthur noted) 'flung his heart about in handfuls'. He would drop in on Lis Escop on Sunday afternoons and, in a spare room, with his arm round Fred's neck, would read him the sermon he was about to preach at evening service. The Reverend Reeve told Mary that 'that boy was not far from the kingdom of God'.

Little Hugh, who like Martin before him had a stammer, was fast becoming his father's favourite, the son to take Martin's place, on whom Edward's hopes were now centred. Hugh was also 'darlingest of all to Beth's big heart', and able to disarm opposition from anyone else in the family by reducing them to helpless laughter. A large-headed goblin of a child, he was slight in stature, but (Edward noted in his diary) 'the picture of ruddy force, light and strong'. Hugh loved dressing up, had a taste for the *grand guignol*, for blood and violence.

151

During one 'frightful craze for inventing murderous instruments', he came up with a guillotine and various guns made with lead pipes and brass screws, extracting a promise from Mary that if he could create a weapon that lived up to his aim of 'Certain Death if fired', he might shoot it at anybody or anything he liked. He leapt out from behind sideboards with bloodcurdling yells, frightening guests; he wrote insults in a large round hand on pieces of paper which he hurled at the object of his scorn, he tussled with Fred and even with calm Maggie; he insisted on his own way, and generally got it. Only Arthur, who thought him 'petulant, wilful, full of originality, fitful, independent', seemed able to exercise any control over Hugh at all.

Fragment of a Poem by Master Hugh Benson,
Aged Eight, on a Swarm of Gnats

And when they see their comrades laid
In thousands round the garden glade,
They know they were not really made
To live for evermore.

Mary helped give Hugh his lessons, and ran the large household—with greater application and efficiency than she had at Wellington. Her resolve to do her duty to her husband held; she suppressed her rebelliousness. She took her place at his side, supported him in his work, and played hostess to countless visitors, and though none was quite as grand as back in the Wellington days, Mary proved far more adept in her role. In contrast to his fairly

152

The Family at Lis Escop in 1883
Bishop Benson

| Mary Benson | Arthur | Maggie |
| Nellie | Watch | Hugh | Fred |

marginal position in Lincoln, Edward, at Truro, was 'the hero of the whole affair . . . because it was *his* work and *his* responsibility, and everything had as a matter of course to be accommodated to *his* convenience'; but (in Arthur's words) Mary was 'the person who made this all possible, who so attached the servants to herself that they were content to manage anything if only she were pleased, who gave my father at any time the advice, suggestion, help, sympathy and support he needed—for he consulted her about many things, and submitted all difficult and delicate matters to her criticism.' Not only Edward, but her children, friends and sometimes even bare acquaintances opened their hearts to Mary. There was something in the way that she listened without appearing to wish to restrict independence, or exert influence; in the way (in complete antithesis to Edward) that she was 'extraordinarily indifferent and indulgent about small superficial things'; in her ability to convey a complete and separate sympathy and understanding to the person she was talking with, and to give them the feeling that nothing in the world interested her more at that moment than their well-being—qualities that brought the troubles and problems of all those around Mary to her sitting room.

Yet Mary showed no deep interest in Edward's work, and did not involve herself directly with it. She listened and indeed gave him advice when asked, but seldom sought out his company or spent any amount of time alone with him. Arthur thought his mother was afraid of her husband, 'in bondage' to him and to the intensity of his displeasure. On arriving in Truro, Edward had thrown himself immediately into infusing life into his new diocese, into raising money for and starting building work on the new cathedral—the first to be raised in England since the Reformation. He selected figures of Cornish saints to fill its windows, dismissed the design for an episcopal coat of arms proposed by the College of Arms as 'not fit for a public house'. He established the school for girls, made trips to London and toured his See extensively. One year he found time to put together a service for Christmas Eve comprising nine carols interspersed with nine lessons drawn from the Bible that tell the story of the Nativity—the beginnings of the service that, as adapted by the chapel of King's College, Cambridge, has become famous throughout the Protestant world. Yet as at Wellington, and to some extent also in Lincoln, Edward was assailed by fits of dark depression, 'moods of blackness and tortured irritability' that overwhelmed him for days, when he fell into silences that seemed to consume all around him, broken only by his formidable censure of the most innocent or trivial deeds. As he struggled with this 'demoniacal load, longing to be rid of it, yearning to burst out of it, but possessed by it to the point of helplessness', he became entirely unapproachable. Only Mary made the attempt, with some success, though he scorned her. 'Fancy his telling her (as he did),' Arthur commented, 'that she did not enter into his struggles and ideals, and did not give him the background of sympathy *he needed*! He wanted someone much more clinging and admiring.'

155

[His mother] had not, it would seem, been in love with [his father], and she had yielded, rather than known the imperious need of the one man: his tumultuous desire for her had swept her off her feet, even as it had swept him. Anything so strong and so menacingly sure of itself had something of the force of destiny about it, and Margaret Ashton gave him herself, her beauty, her tenderness, the gay charm, the sunshine of her, yet wholly without needing him. Devotion of mind and body, entire self-abandonment she could bring him, and these were his, but it was not till the birth of Rex that love dawned for her. Motherhood was her prime emotional need: all that concerned Rex was her passion, all that concerned her husband was a matter of her watchful and eager duty ... She had never come to him with the white-hot fire, but what was within her power she gave him, warmth and tenderness, and as the years went by the pity that is akin to love.

From time to time, Mary welcomed old friends on visits. They went on evening walks in the garden, were burned by the hot Cornish sun, played ducks and drakes at Falmouth, talked long into the night and, if Edward was up in London or on a visit elsewhere, turned tables and conducted experiments in mesmerism. Her beloved brothers also managed the long journey to Cornwall with some frequency, but old Mrs Sidgwick died in 1879 following a stroke—the force that had so dominated little Minnie long since subdued. 'Her spirit went long before the body ceased its working,' observed Edward. Mary's own children tumbled towards adulthood. Nellie went up to Lady Margaret Hall at Oxford in 1881—her father was a strong believer in higher education for women. At Cambridge her uncle Henry Sidgwick was a renowned champion of the cause, and their family friend Elizabeth Wordsworth had become the founding Principal of Lady Margaret Hall, which offered the first ever opportunity for women to study at Oxford, in 1879. In the same year as Nellie went up, Arthur took his place at King's, Cambridge, and Fred went on from prep school to Marlborough. To Mary's disbelief the following year, even little Hugh was ten and old enough to go away to prep school. Edward delivered him to Walton House in Somerset, while she and Beth sat miserably at home. Beth, especially, who had adored and pampered the youngest of what she saw as her own brood, was as devastated as if she had been widowed, and from the moment Hugh left focused every moment of her life on the advent of the school holidays.

Nurse Beth, Who Loved Being Read
to But Who Struggled to Read or Write Herself,
Takes Pains Over a Postcard

Dearest,
One line to tell you I am sending your Box to-morrow Wednesday. I hope you will get it before tea-time. I know you will like something for tea, you can keep your cake for your

Birthday. I shall think about you on Friday. Everybody has gone away, so I had no one to write for me. I thought you would not mind me writing to you.—Dearest love from your dear

Beth

The family took holidays on the Cornish coast and in Switzerland, where Edward and the children went on energetic walks. Mary, who was growing plumper, found walking a trial and generally stayed behind. Nor did she take any interest in scenery, or accompany Edward and the children as he toured them through cathedrals and other sites of antiquity. Her rebelliousness was taking subtler forms. Firmly but delicately, she placed behind her the days of those energetic marches with Edward over the countryside around Wellington College, and the unbearably tedious trudges around old churches in France. Instead, she 'made excursions into public sitting-rooms, and formed rapid acquaintances with all kinds of surprising and subsequently inconvenient persons'. There was the woman fanatical about the heretical works of Emanuel Swedenborg; the one with violent anti-vaccination theories; the one who collected cowries and glued them on to cards to form religious texts. All these new friends were women, and they invariably ended up in intimate conversations with Mary, confiding their deepest secrets. On the whole, Mary was happiest on visits to country houses, and here, too, would 'attach herself with indissoluble bonds of friendship [to] some member of the hospitable household', not with mere passing cordiality, but in a way that created 'a deep sense, on the part of some girl or woman, that something strong and wise and different had touched her life to finer issues'.

A layer or two deeper than the dutiful Mrs Benson, deeper than the sympathetic and ever-understanding Mary, deeper even than the adored Mama, 'Ben' survived—small and solitary, perhaps, but strong. Edward may have emotionally overpowered her, but there were three areas where he could not intrude—on the private, individual bond she was building with her God, on the world that enclosed her and her children, and on her feelings for other women. The friendship with Tan continued, though fading in intensity. But it was not until the summer of 1879 that anyone came near to rivalling her in Mary's affections.

Charlotte Mary Basset lived in one of the grandest houses in Cornwall—Tehidy, an Italianate pile with four flanking pavilions and a large park, near Camborne, fifteen miles away. Her husband, Gustavus, was head of one of the richest families in the county, and an invalid. The Bassets had made an immense fortune from copper mining in the eighteenth century, and traced their history as lords of the manor of Tehidy back to Norman times. Gustavus had himself added to the family's fortunes, but had been paralysed by a stroke and had lately developed throat and lip cancer. Once kindly and generous, he was becoming known for his greed, alarming irritability and explosive temper. Mrs Basset, who went by her second name, Mary, was vivacious, amusing and adventurous—if at times crushingly haughty. She was undaunted by convention and liked to smoke, keeping a stash of cigarettes in her garden room, in a box with a secret spring lock, disguised to resemble a calf-bound volume of *Hymns of Faith and Love*. Young Arthur was entranced by this remarkable addition to his parents' social circle, thinking Mary Basset 'a woman of great character and charm, upright and handsome, silent, with big dark flashing eyes which seemed to indicate deep reserves of passionate feeling'. Yet he thought he detected an unease about her, 'a certain aversion to life . . . something pent-up and thwarted'. Mary Benson quite lost her heart.

At first, Mary was cautious. 'In some ways letters of this kind are like a game of chess,' she wrote to Mrs Basset, after spending sleepless nights thinking of her, waiting anxiously with each post for a letter. 'I moved my pawn—you know I did—in August. It seemed to me then—was it so?—that yours did not come sharp up to meet it—so now I wanted to make a much more important move—and I was afraid of "check"' [heavy deletion follows]. Eventually, Mrs Basset made her move, too. She invited Mary to call her 'Chat'. Mary was delighted. 'In the greatest friendship of my life,' she replied, 'made in 75, I was "Mrs Benson" until suddenly *"Ben"* was invented, and she always calls me so now. You will have to invent something—what will it be now?' They settled on 'Robin'.

Over the next three years, 'Chat' and 'Robin' exchanged photographs, books, gifts of jewellery. Letters became more passionate. 'I want to know more about you . . . what *makes you*,' Mary began. 'Since last week so much has happened between us. I want you to *talk* to me. In short I want *you*.' Later, she would fill page after page, pouring out feelings she found 'overwhelming'. 'I feel as if I am in a dream,' she wrote, just a few months after they had met. 'I am in the middle of your life and you and I *cannot* come out of it . . . you are in my heart of hearts . . . I don't feel big enough to hold you.' Chat would fall asleep, clutching the last letter Mary had written. After yet another 'restless' day, Mary would spend a night *'restlessly dreaming*—you know what I mean?' So full of Chat did Mary feel that she could scarcely do anything but sit and glow at the thought of her. Even as she kissed and comforted Nellie during her monthly cramps, she wished she were doing so with Chat. Chat paid visits to Truro, and Mary—together with Edward or one or two of the children—would go to Tehidy. Edward approved of Mary Basset, as he had not of Tan and Emily Hall before her. Perhaps he now realized that in his wife's case, such friendships were essential to contentment in marriage. Certainly, Mrs Basset had lifted Mary's spirits, which in the first years of his bishopric had been low, and her being on such intimate terms with the chatelaine of Tehidy could do his position no harm. 'Yes, she is a princess of a woman,' agreed Edward, on a journey one day back from Tehidy to Truro, when Mary simply could not stop talking about her friend.

At Lis Escop, Maggie, now past the age of fifteen, began to shoulder much of the domestic responsibility, as Mary let her attention to her duties slip. 'Did you *possess* me, or I you, my Heart's Beloved, as we sat there together on Thursday and Friday—as we held each other close, as we kissed,' Mary wondered after one of Chat's visits, ending another letter: 'Chat, my true lover, my true love, see, I am your true lover, your true love, Robin.'

Mary was quite aware of the potential

161

sinfulness of physical love, and wrestled with the contradictions this brought. 'When one's heart is fullest, when the physical side of Love asserts itself the most,' she cautioned Chat, 'then one must *love* in mind, that things may be wholesome and well.' Her faith remained strong, but the struggle to keep 'love in mind' never left her, nor could she reconcile how such a holy, sweet gift from God could seem so inseparable from the 'stain' of carnal demands. Yet she was beginning to shape a belief that not only incorporated her passion, but was based on it. 'I love you so, dear,' she wrote to Chat, early in their relationship, 'not one whit less than *all you* will I have, in that mysterious sacramental union where one can have *all*, and yet wrong no other love.' Earthly love made possible an understanding of the true nature of God's glory. What Chat and Mary felt for each other was all part of God's plan, it cleansed them of past sins, was a rebirth of faith. It was in itself a gift of God, as 'none could give two souls to each other so closely so sweetly so holily, except the Lord.' God's love flowed through them, filled them up: 'Besides this new welling of water in you to everlasting life, besides all that God has taught me in this, and through you, our lives have been *welded* here—fused together—united into that union which is both human and divine—human in all the exquisite tender joys of delight in each other, of companionship, of precious intimacy, of our whole nature—divine with that eternal *grounded* strength and lastingness which nothing can ever shake as long as we have each other in the Lord.' Inverting the customary text, Mary declared: *'Love is God.'*

162

On 16 December 1882, the Prime Minister W. E. Gladstone dispatched a letter to the newest and perhaps the least prestigious bishopric in the land, whose incumbent had held his post for barely five years. 'My Dear Bishop of Truro,' the letter began. 'I have to propose to your lordship with the sanction of Her Majesty, that you should accept the succession to the Archbishopric of Canterbury, now vacant through the lamented death of Archbishop Tait.' A telegram followed, from the Queen herself, announcing that she would be writing a letter shortly. Edward replied to the Prime Minister begging 'a few days' interval' in which to consult 'one or two friends who both know my affairs and will counsel me as Christian men'. He asked advice of both friends and colleagues, and wrote a supremely tactful letter to Harold Browne, the Bishop of Winchester, who had been in line for the position, but was considered too old to be offered it. Edward acknowledged that the honour should be Browne's, but wrote that the Queen had 'asked the most unworthy of your young brothers to wear it for you and to *try* to wear it as you would have done,' and he sought the elderly man's counsel, forbearance and encouragement, should he vainly attempt this hopeless task. 'Heard that the Bishop of Truro felt himself overwhelmed at present by the weight of the office I had invited him to accept,' Queen Victoria noted in her diary. 'I shall write to him, to urge him to accept.'

The Queen's letter arrived just before Christmas, expressing her 'earnest hope' that Edward would assume the Primacy, and saying how much both she and her 'dear husband in byegone [*sic*] days', had always had a high opinion of and sincere regard for him. Edward hesitated no longer, and on 23 December wrote letters of acceptance to both Queen Victoria and Mr Gladstone. He planned to make the news known in his diocese on Christmas Day.

On Christmas Eve, Mary sent Chat a letter. It was written, as was her wont, on a sheet of paper, folded in half. In the top left-hand corner of the outer leaf, Mary urged: 'Don't mention this till after 8 o'clock tomorrow morning.' Below that, she wrote: 'My darling, Edward asks me to tell you first of anyone in Cornwall that he has accepted the offer. You will know what we are feeling and what it means. Pray for us ___' To this, Edward added: 'How shall I ever thank you for all you have been to my wife (and will be!). God bless and keep you . . .'. Over the page, came a cry from Mary's heart:

Sweetheart, now a word which won't be seen by anyone. My darling, my love _bless_ you—my poor heart is too full to say _anything_ of all that swells up—and I _daren't_ think of going away from here and _you_ . . . Your sweet and precious gift came last night and I _love_ it so! The two inextricably twined cords, the sweet knot, the dear symbol that will lie so near my heart. The whole mixes in to one dear touch from you to me—so intensely precious and loved—oh my own darling. _How_ I love you!

164

Chapter Eleven

Mary Benson looked about her at Lambeth Palace and despaired. 'Oh my darling I am *quite* as miserable as I ever wish to be!' she wrote to Chat on arriving at her new London home. 'Physically worn, spiritually empty, mentally incapable—and this huge cold Barrack is Disgusting.' The residence seemed 'infinitely long and broad' and she felt as if she had to walk half a mile down bleak corridors simply to get to the laundry—and then, of course, all her fresh white linens would soon be turning grey. London soot was notorious. Dickens described the city's smoke 'lowering down from chimney-pots, making a soft black drizzle with flakes of soot as big as full-grown snow flakes— gone into mourning, one might imagine, for the death of the sun'. The residue of half a million fireplaces seeped under doors and through keyholes. It clogged the ancient corbelling of Lambeth Palace with grime, coated cornices, crept in through cracks to cover unattended objects in a shroud of dark dust, and to discolour anything clean. It even settled on the plants in the garden, so that flowers picked or smelled left nose or fingers smudged black. This was all a far cry from Cornwall.

London fog, as if a living emanation of the soot, followed similar paths, requiring candles to be lit in the middle of the day, submerging the city in a choking ink—sometimes black, sometimes bottle-green, often dingy yellow or dun brown. Stray patches of fog could be found indoors, lurking eerily in corners of rooms. At times, outdoors, it lifted from the ground but still completely blocked the sun. Then people spoke of 'day darkness'. When Mary arrived at Lambeth Palace, fog shrouded London some sixty-two days of the year. It did not improve her mood at all.

Charles Dickens, on a London November Afternoon, from Bleak House

Fog everywhere. Fog up the river, where it flows among green aits and meadows; fog down the river, where it rolls defiled among the tiers of shipping, and the waterside pollutions of a great (and dirty) city. Fog on the Essex Marshes, fog on the Kentish heights. Fog creeping into the cabooses of collier-brigs; fog lying out on the yards, and hovering in the rigging of great ships; fog drooping on the gunwales of barges and small boats. Fog in the eyes and throats of ancient Greenwich pensioners, wheezing by the firesides of their wards; fog in the stem and bowl of the afternoon pipe of the wrathful skipper, down in his close cabin; fog cruelly pinching the toes and fingers of [the] shivering little 'prentice boy on deck. Chance people on the bridges peeping over the parapets into a nether sky of fog, with fog all round them, as if they were up in a balloon, and hanging in the misty clouds.

Edward was not unfamiliar with life in Lambeth Palace. He had been assiduously attentive to the dying Archbishop Tait, visiting him so frequently in his final months that the Primate assigned Edward his own rooms at the palace, in the fifteenth-century Lollards' Tower. One of the old Archbishop's last confidences to his domestic chaplain, the Revd Randall Davidson, was that although the rather too elderly Harold Browne, Bishop of Winchester, was 'a man of peace', the Archbishop had no doubt that the energetic and most heedful Bishop of Truro would 'come forward and do a great work' as head of the Church. The chaplain observed the strong personal link that was being 'forged or strengthened' by 'the visits and the ministry' of the Bishop of Truro to His Grace in his dying days. Others noted Truro's youth and energy, at a time when a strong and vigorous hand was needed at the prow, and the upper echelons of the Church were riven by politicking. The Archbishop of York did not envy 'the man who will be seated in the Chair of Augustine in these times. The winds blow keen round it, and the rains fall heavily just now,' and he thought that 'Truro would perhaps, all things considered, prove best for the Church.' Even Arthur, up at Cambridge, had heard rumours that his father was in the running to succeed Archbishop Tait. So the letter from Mr Gladstone that had arrived at Lis Escop just before Christmas had perhaps not taken Edward too much by surprise.

Whatever his greater strategy for the future of the Church might have been, Edward fell upon the redecoration of Lambeth Palace with the ease and alacrity of a man who had long thought about what he might one day change, and with the flair for interior design he had shown in all the previous homes he and Mary had shared. In the early 1830s, Edward Blore, the architect who took over from John Nash to complete Buckingham Palace, had built a new residential wing at Lambeth. It was an imposing pile of Bath stone in the Gothic Revival style Edward so admired, but inside it did indeed have something of the forbidding atmosphere of a 'huge cold Barrack'. All the rooms ran off a broad central corridor, like a series of offices, offering little privacy. They were charmless, scantily furnished, and though large, there were not enough of them comfortably to accommodate all the functionaries and guests that came with Edward's new role. Despite its magnificence, Lambeth Palace felt curiously cramped, and while seeming impossibly crowded and busy, it was at the same time cavernous and daunting.

During their first weeks at Lambeth, before invitations for dinners and luncheons began to be sent out, with Nellie and Arthur away at university and Fred and Hugh at school, a shrunken family took its place for meals at a table dwarfed by the high vaulted timber roof of the Guard Room—in medieval and Tudor times the Archbishop's audience chamber, turned by Blore into a dining room. Off it ran a gallery—desolate and draughty, lined with dusty, ignored portraits—leading to the old prison (and Edward's former chambers) in the Lollards' Tower. Mary's comfy ottoman, the wheezy harmonium, the beds, books and card games, the bronzed dessert dishes from the working-men's bible class, the butterfly collections, mahogany cabinets, sumptuous sideboard—much that had made the journey from Wellington to Lincoln and then down to Cornwall—

came up to London from Lis Escop, to be sucked almost without trace into Lambeth Palace.

Edward's changes were swift and radical. He had connecting doors knocked through between the rooms of the Blore wing, so that he could walk from bedroom to dressing room to library and sitting room, without having to engage with the constant human traffic in the single corridor. He rooted about in cupboards and garrets, hauling back into the open sofas and chests, chairs and fine tables, many of some antiquity and value, that had drifted into obscurity over the centuries. He personally superintended the re-hanging of pictures, dusting off old paintings in the gallery, and discovering a portrait of Sir Robert Walpole in the process. In one of the towers he came across a bundle of rusty pikes and had them cleaned and displayed in a fan shape in the entrance hall. Joining in the fray, Arthur uncovered—in a box containing bones of old saints—the shell of the pet tortoise that had famously outlived Archbishop Laud (who was beheaded during the Civil War), and had been inadvertently killed at the age of 120, when a gardener dug it up from hibernation. The shell was put on display in the corridor, in a glass case with a curtained recess for the relics.

At first, overwhelmed by the domestic chaos and facing frightening new territory as wife of the Archbishop, Mary hankered for her darling Chat. 'Oh my sweetheart, come soon and help me to laugh at these things that oppress my soul,' she wrote. She had been catapulted from the cosy charms of Cornwall, with its tight circle of family, Chat, and a handful of friends, not only to London, but into the very heart of the Establishment and

Society. Yet gradually a change came over Mary Benson. The shy child-bride who had so quailed at her husband's wrath and crumpled under the demands and complexities of running the household at Wellington; the young woman prostrated by serial childbirth, bored and marginalized in Lincoln; the devoted mother, happier but isolated in rural Cornwall—all these dropped from her like dried husks. Mary took root in her new position, and suddenly blossomed.

Quietly, Mary had been changing the rules. The transformation had begun with the disruption caused by Ellen Hall on Mary's return from Wiesbaden, after which there had been no more children; it had gained force from Tan, and the fervent and very personal religion Mary had fashioned under her direction; it then gathered impetus in Cornwall, as her children grew older and as Chat helped confirm her conviction that 'Love is God'. Mary was still dutifully and devotedly committed to her husband's well-being, yet she had found a way of surviving within these confines. She was no longer scared of Edward.

As the Archbishop's wife, Mary began to exercise this new confidence. The childlike sunniness; the 'volatility' that had never been quite suppressed; the verve and effervescence her children so adored in her; the warmth and empathy that drew admiring young women to her in hotel parlours and country-house sitting rooms, her conversational dexterity as a hostess—qualities previously revealed to just a few—were now on display to a wide and influential world. The wide and influential world relished them, and Mary revelled in the esteem.

Already white-haired at forty-one, and growing rather stout, the new Archbishop's wife did not present a particularly commanding figure, and indeed confessed to Fred that she felt 'shy and inadequate' at her first great social functions. She told Arthur that at one party she had tried to keep her nervousness at bay by thinking of Eternity, 'and how frail a prop Eternity seemed to be'. But her wit and irresistible charm won people over, and soon she 'revelled in the multitude of her engagements' and 'delighted in the froth and bustle and movement' of life both at Lambeth Palace and at the Archbishop's country seat of Addington, near Croydon. Her hapless management of the Lodge at Wellington well behind her, Mary took to the control of two great houses with, in Fred's words, 'a natural and effortless instinct'. Surprising perhaps even herself, she 'took the reins and cracked her whip, and the whole equipage bowled swift and smooth along the road'. Banquets were magicked effortlessly into existence and ran without hiccough; surprise guests were accommodated without fuss or flutter. Mary's neat little victoria would appear with perfect punctuality ('and woe be to the carriage-cleaner if the japanned panels failed to reflect with the unwavering quality of glass') to take her off on a visit, or with young Hugh to the Zoo. Her whip hand could be strong. During an influenza epidemic, when Mary and Maggie had been confined in a room together, 'flecked by depression' and fed on chicken and champagne, Mary emerged to find a fellow-suffering house guest without a fire and drinking medicine from a bottle, because his glass had been taken away. She went on a fierce 'ramp round the household' that soon had the servants back in shape.

As her engagements multiplied, Mary took delight in the delicacies of timing and arrangement, in what she called 'fittings in'. 'Life is roaring on,' she wrote to Maggie, who had gone up to Oxford just a few months after the family moved into Lambeth Palace. 'Dinner of 30 Sat. 55 Junior Clergy yesterday. 40 Bps tonight.' On another occasion: 'My mind is in a whirl with arrangements for parties—one on Saturday, a large one Tuesday, Evg. Party on Thursday, guests all week beginning Sat^y, and a Very August one on the 23rd.' Yet life was not always so grand. 'Such military blokes came to dinner,' she confided once to Maggie. '*Quite* as old as Rural Deans, and I do think duller.' Sometimes, hospitality required immense effort. 'Our party of which I told you went through heavy seas on Tuesday,' Mary confessed about one group of guests. 'It was all such collar work, breakfast talk, slow walking talk, clump driving talk, tea talk, dinner talk—we positively came to shouting proverbs in the evening.'

Mary 'nobly filled and fitted the new sphere', Fred thought, but she remained firmly grounded. After a dinner spent engrossed in the talk of the hour with political notables, followed by a party at the Foreign Office, she might be up before seven the next morning, dressed in her oldest clothes to take a stroll through Covent Garden Market, or down Lambeth Walk, then back home to entertain the family over breakfast with sharp-eyed observations of some 'comic side-show of the streets'. She showed a girlish excitement at meeting certain of the dignitaries she now encountered, but she remained wholly unworldly.

Arthur thought his mother 'so indifferent to the grandeurs and pomps of life that she was neither disconcerted by them nor disdainful of them'. 'Yes,' a worldly and somewhat sour old peeress once remarked, 'poor thing, you see she has *no precedence.*' Nor did she. For although the Archbishop of Canterbury himself ranks immediately below Princes of the Blood Royal, and above non-royal dukes and the Lord Chancellor, as the highest commoner in the land, his wife has no precedence or title at all. The old peeress would have been perplexed to learn that Mary simply did not care, and had too finely developed a sense of 'the infinite comicalities of life' to take such attitudes seriously. Nor was she particularly interested in what Arthur called the 'ecclesiastical machine'—though she did involve herself in some women's charities and committees, and in time gave theological lectures for women. What appealed to Mary about her new sphere was what had always appealed to her—human intimacy and interaction—yet now with a scope she had previously never imagined possible.

'It was the human being beneath that she was in search of,' wrote Arthur, 'and that was all she cared about.' From the pinkest, most tongue-tied curate to the starchiest of aristocrats, Mary could set people at ease, soften social edges, coax out conversation. She was herself a sparkling conversationalist, 'really brilliant' marvelled Arthur. Alas, Mary's flow of talk was 'so fanciful, humorous, suggestive, incisive, and her power of transition so great' that Arthur—like everyone else who knew her and admired her wit and deadly repartee, and

173

to the great loss of posterity—could only throw up his hands and admit that it was utterly impossible to reproduce the quality of her conversation in print.

To Fred, it was Mary, not Edward, who seemed most elevated by their new position in the world. Mary's offspring, like their mother, had scant interest in the 'ecclesiastical machine'. 'Stupendous though my father had become,' declared Fred, 'we knew but little of his work and of its national significance, and it was my mother who to us, far more than he, was exalted into the zenith.' But Mary also happily took the opportunity to puncture any grandeur. It became a ritual after magnificent dinner parties for any of the children then at home to join her 'in a wild war-dance all over the drawing-room in a sort of general jubilation'. (They were thus discovered by the Lord Chancellor, Lord Halsbury, on an occasion when he unexpectedly returned to the palace after having taken his leave.) The young Bensons were then in their late teens or early twenties. Something about them remained rooted in their tight, self-encapsulated childhood. The same was true of their mother. 'I *did not grow up*,' she had written in her diary, looking back on her girlhood betrothal and early marriage. Her letters to the children were strewn with exclamation marks, girlish squeals, breathless capitals, and would burst with such effusions as 'Lor!', 'Oh Lorks!', 'Isn't it Orfle' (a phrase picked up by her green parrot, Joey) and 'O how goluptious!' Yet, in her public role, their mother was the pivot of all that glittered at Lambeth Palace, and infinitely more adept in social situations than their father.

Edward could tell a good story (even if all the accents he employed, from Cornish to American, sounded the same); he had a loud, inspiriting laugh and a dramatic energy in conversation, but he was not inclined to listen, and all too easily went on at length, explaining in minute detail what to his audience was already lucidly clear. He was affable when surrounded by an atmosphere of deference, but was prickly and silent with equals; if opposed, he could be vehement and severe. Arguments with Edward engendered heat rather than light. Mary, on the other hand, had always enjoyed a good argument. She relished the 'intoxication' of frank, friendly discussion, she wrote to a friend. 'Disagreement comes in as a nice little savour ... Yes, intoxication is the best word.' She had most enjoyed the company of those masters at Wellington College who had taken pleasure in conversational cut and thrust, though she had usually remained the reticent, silent headmaster's wife. Now, not only did she join in but became skilled at steering the discussion, and at a level that enthralled her. Though not particularly engaged in politics herself, she delighted in talk about great issues with the people who were making the decisions.

Back in 1881, Mary had written to Chat from Lis Escop with news of a surprise visit:

Fancy, my Beloved, having GLADSTONE'S DAUGHTER in the house! The whole atmosphere is full of it and it is Lovely!

Now she entertained the Grand Old Man (as he was just beginning to be called) himself. It was a full year after Edward's appointment before Mary first met the Prime Minister; she wrote immediately to Fred at Marlborough:

This morning I am a Proud Woman—with the feel still on my fingers of the more than august arm which they pressed going down to dinner last night at Ely House. WHO do you think? Need I say GLADSTONE of course. I was more tired and stupid than usual, still there he was in the flesh and there he talked.

Mary liked the Prime Minister's voice 'immensely', and thought his eyes 'wonderful—so clear and soft, and steady', but found his accent curious, and the man 'so very strong in his expressions and so little polished in his manner' that 'I think if I *did* look upon him as Chat does, as the villain who is ruining this country, I should feel immensely borne out by his manner—but then you see I don't.' On that occasion they talked of St Peter's in Rome, of art and architecture, about everything but politics, as that was territory Mary 'felt too ignorant to touch on and he didn't begin'.

Later encounters made good the omission. The High Tory Archbishop of Canterbury and the Liberal Prime Minister were distant from each other on the political spectrum, especially as regards such issues of the day as the disestablishment of the Welsh Church and Gladstone's consuming political passion, the question of Irish Home Rule. Yet Edward admired the premier's strong sense of religious conviction, and the men developed a robust respect for each other, their cordial relationship outlasting Gladstone's time in office. Gladstone had a great appreciation of Mary's wit,

Fred noticed, of her ability to 'strike a spark out of the most humdrum of happenings'. The man who had reputedly read over 20,000 books by the time he died would engage in deep conversations with the Archbishop's wife, on one occasion detaining her at table long after it was time for the ladies to withdraw, discussing a recent Life of George Eliot, and declaiming: 'It is not a Life at all. It is a Reticence, in three volumes.' Fred was told that once at Hawarden Castle, Gladstone's home in north Wales, in a discussion as to who was the cleverest woman in England, Mrs Benson's name was raised. 'No, you're wrong,' exclaimed the Grand Old Man in impressive voice, reinforcing his opinion with pointed forefinger, 'she's the cleverest woman in Europe.'

Mary 'took an infinity of rapturous trouble' over her dinners. These were usually populated by clerics, though half a dozen times a season the Bensons hosted grand secular affairs where around thirty guests from the worlds of literature and science, art and politics would be magnificently assembled. There were luncheons, seldom *en famille* but more intimate than the dinners, as well as garden parties in the summer—where irreverent behaviour by guests laughing and talking in the chapel, as if it were a public lounge, once drove Mary to complaint, and the Archbishop to suggest that they raise two large boards under the East window, reading: 'Keep thy Foot' and 'Hold thy Tongue'. On one occasion, in 1888, when Mary and Edward were called away, Maggie and Nellie had to officiate. Maggie wrote to Hugh (then on a scholarship at Eton): 'We had a Queen at our last garden-party we had, and as Mar and Par were

177

both ordered down to Windsor to dine with the other Queen (of England I mean)—we are so sought after by the Royal Family—Nellie and I had to entertain the first Queen, who was from Hawaii. She had an interpreter, who told her Wiclif [*sic*] was the first Archbishop—and stopped her by a nod when she wanted to put a sponge cake in her tea.'

Maggie's flip remark about being sought after by the Royal Family was not too far from the truth. The Queen relied heavily on the Archbishop, at times disclosing confidences to him that she kept from her ministers—'my excuse is my great loneliness,' she told him, 'my many heavy trials and troubles and the great need I have during my declining years.' Edward was associated with the happiness of the time before she became a widow, when her beloved Albert had so admired the young headmaster of Wellington College. He was a support to her during her Golden Jubilee celebrations in 1887, an ordeal the Queen dreaded, but which marked the beginning of her re-emergence from decades of a seclusion that had become increasingly unpopular with the public. On the day itself, that support very nearly fell away most inopportunely, when Edward became close to being excluded from Westminster Abbey. He had forgotten to give his coachman the carriage pass for transit through the surrounding cordon of troops and police officers, and had to lean out and assure an obdurate inspector that 'They can't begin till I get there.'

As Archbishop, Edward also officiated at royal marriages and christenings. In doing so he became, at moments of import, part of the family life of a

178

most family-oriented woman, growing over time to be, as the Queen remarked to her grandson the Duke of York, 'such a friend of ours'. Quite extraordinarily, the monarch sometimes wrote to Edward using 'I' (rather than referring to herself as 'the Queen' or in the first-person plural, as was her usual practice), ending letters 'yours affectionately'. Her affection extended to the Archbishop's family, who were all invited to Balmoral one summer towards the end of the eighties. Fred, who had not been born when the Queen visited Wellington College—when Beth had called her 'My Majesty' and little Martin had told her she had a very funny bonnet, and received a kiss in reply—was bewitched (as Mary had been at Wellington) by her beautiful voice and prominent blue eyes. Fred and Arthur both later moved in royal circles, and Arthur would be invited to edit Queen Victoria's letters.

From Queen Victoria to the
Archbishop of Canterbury

Osborne, Dec. 21, 1891

My Dear Archbishop,

I must thank you very much for your kind letter, and congratulations on the engagement of my dear grandson Albert Victor to Princess Victoria Mary of Teck, which promises to be a happy union. 'May' is a charming girl, with much sense and amiability and very *un*frivolous, so that I have every hope the young people will set an example of a steady, quiet life, which, alas, is not the fashion in these days. The wedding is to be at St George's

179

Chapel, on the 27th February. I hope you will perform the ceremony.

In conclusion, let me ask you to accept the accompanying card with best wishes for Christmas and New Year for yourself and family.

I am,
Ever yours affly,
Victoria R. & I. [Regina et
Imperatrix]

The reticent and notoriously brusque Lord Tennyson—Poet Laureate since 1850, and to Fred 'antique and imperishable'—having been prevailed upon through a number of invitations, eventually relented and came to dine at Lambeth Palace. It was a sombre occasion, with the poet plunged into deeper silence than usual as a consequence of being disallowed his tobacco. Edward, whose loathing of smoking had by no means diminished over the years, did not permit the foul habit after dinner at either Lambeth or at the country seat, Addington, even though the practice of cigarettes after the ladies had withdrawn had taken hold in most houses by the 1880s. Only one exception was ever made, for the Duke of York. A Poet Laureate did not warrant such a bending of the rules. The mood of Tennyson's visit was by no means enlivened when, after a single round of port and brief joining of the ladies in the drawing room, the entire company trooped off for evensong in the chapel, which at Lambeth was sometimes held late in the evening, following dinner. 'After this long devotional interlude,' said Fred, 'it was frankly impossible to resume a festive sociability.' Later, Tennyson walked with the Archbishop, and at a loss for conversation offered to tell him a bawdy story (the great poet was inordinately fond of limericks). Edward related that he declined, but according to the man of letters Sir Edmund Gosse (a close friend of Arthur's), His Grace later admitted that the story 'wasn't so very bad after all'.

Robert Browning, one of Mary's favourite poets, was, by contrast, an ebullient guest, 'immensely genial'; he 'ate and drank and talked with a juvenile pleasure'. He provoked much speculation in the family when, on hearing that Edward most liked his lyrics, he remarked: 'Lyrics? I've got deskfuls of them.' (Browning was to publish no further volumes of poetry apart from the slim *Asolando* which came out on the day of his death, a few years later, and no great hoard of unknown lyrics came posthumously to light.)

Henry James, who had immediately taken to the tall and dreamily handsome twenty-two-year-old Arthur at a Cambridge luncheon party in 1884, was invited to Addington for the first of what became a number of visits both there and to Lambeth Palace. His *Roderick Hudson* and more recent *Portrait of a Lady* had won him multitudes of admirers, and he had not yet embarked on his more confounding later works, which (Fred thought) raised 'armies of new readers, who took the place of the old brigades who fell stark and staring beneath the stroke of the *Wings of the Dove*'. Mary delighted in James as 'full of talk, though lengthy', and she, too, was surprised that 'he thinks his writing now much better than *Roderick Hudson*. Fancy that! And wouldn't hear our praise and said his former work was

181

subaqueous, and this time his head was above water!'

One winter's night at Addington, James seems to have drawn out the Archbishop more than most guests managed to, and roused memories of the Ghost Club at Trinity. The two men sat by the fire in the drawing room, 'talking a little, in the spirit of recreation' of things 'ghostly and ghastly', when (James later wrote to Arthur):

[The Archbishop] repeated to me the few meagre elements of a small and gruesome spectral story that had been told *him* years before and that he could only give the dimmest account of—partly because he had forgotten details and partly—and much more—because there had *been* no details and no coherency in the tale as he received it, from a person who also but half knew it. The vaguest essence only was there—some dead servants and some children. The essence *struck* me and I made a note of it (of a most scrappy kind) on going home.

An Entry (of a Most Scrappy Kind) in Henry James's Notebook

. . . the story of the young children (indefinite in number and age) left to the care of servants in an old country house, through the death, presumably, of parents. The servants, wicked and depraved, corrupt and deprave the children; the children are bad, full of evil, to a sinister degree. The servants *die* (the story vague about the way of it) and the apparitions, figures, return to haunt the house *and*

182

children, to whom they seem to beckon, whom they invite and solicit, from across dangerous places, the deep ditch of a sunk fence etc.—so that the children may destroy themselves, lose themselves, by responding, getting in to their power.

The tale the Archbishop gave to Henry James became the chilling *The Turn of the Screw*. Some years later, Mary—with the sort of motherly well-meaning that has caused acute embarrassment to offspring down the ages—sent the grand novelist, on Fred's behalf but without his knowledge, a draft of his lengthy first novel. Entitled *Dodo*, it was not even typed but scrawled on hundreds of sheets of blue foolscap, 'written in a furious hurry and covered with erasures, that exploded into illegible interpolations'. After some months, James emitted a polite note to Fred apologizing for his tardiness in response, saying that when consenting to Mary's request he had 'rather overestimated the attention I should be able to give to a production in manuscript of such substantial length. We live in such a world of type-copy to-day that I had taken for granted your story would come to me in that form . . .' A rather delicately expressed judgement followed:

I am such a fanatic myself on the subject of form, style, the evidence of intention and meditation, of chiselling and hammering out in literary things that I am afraid I am rather a cold-blooded judge, rather likely to be offensive to a young story-teller on the question of quality. I am not sure that yours strikes me as quite so ferociously literary as my

Fred Benson in 1886

ideal . . . Only remember that a story is, essentially a form, and that if it fails of that, it fails of its mission . . . For the rest, make yourself a style. It is by style we are saved.

It was an extremely measured response to a work whose chief literary merit was the first recorded use of the word 'diddums' in the English language.

Mary mixed easily with the literary greats, but also

enjoyed a jolly camaraderie with the various young men who came one by one to the palace as domestic chaplains, and were encouraged to join in family discussions and amusements. She 'delighted in their arguments, called them by familiar names, and was repaid with a loyal and chivalrous affection'. Over the years, the glittering company at Lambeth somewhat eclipsed Chat Basset back in Cornwall. Mary's fervour for the Truro friendship grew less intense, though the pair kept in touch, and even speculated together a little in shares, losing money.

Mary now had a circle of intimates in London, who increasingly addressed her as 'Ben'. Two particular friends were the imperiously beautiful Marchioness of Tavistock, later Adeline, Duchess of Bedford (whom Fred thought could on occasion be rather over-conscious of her rank, trailing 'clouds of glory from the abodes of light'), and the Marchioness's rather unfortunate sister, Lady Henry Somerset. A torrid scandal at the end of the seventies had resulted in Lady Henry being debarred from the best houses in Society. She had not only separated from her husband, but had made public her reasons for doing so—his infatuation with a seventeen-year-old boy. In doing this she had broken an inviolable code of propriety—that all may very well be known, but nothing should be spoken—and had outraged the principle of feminine reticence. 'Dire was the wrath of the silent ones,' Fred noted. Society showed 'when defied, of what savagery it was capable'. Shunned and scorned, Lady Henry had thrown herself into good works, opening a refuge for alcoholic women, and becoming deeply involved in the temperance movement. These activities provided her with an entrée to Lambeth Palace, but even so, Mary's further friendship showed social courage, or at least a willingness to ignore the 'wrath of the silent ones'. Yet Lady Henry's very presence was a cold warning to Mary of the consequences of too much being said. Certain issues could more effectively simply have a lid closed on them, and be left quietly in a place of tacit acknowledgement, so as not to release their dangerous destructive forces.

Mary's ability to lend a sympathetic ear, to console, counsel and elicit confidences had by no means diminished. 'Sometimes she tried to shake herself up into an interest in politics, national

Ethel Smyth by John Singer Sargent

affairs, and burning questions of the day,' wrote Fred, 'but no question concerning collective interests and the affairs of the masses burned so bright for her as those of individuals.' In Mary's sitting room at Lambeth, the by now famous comfortable ottoman saw admirable service, as she sat a new intimate down with a 'Now tell me exactly why you think that,' or an 'I don't agree at all. Let's have it out,' or, 'Quite so: I see that, yes I feel that . . . but how about this? Let me see if I can put it to you.' Her energy for participation in others' feelings seemed boundless. 'O what an awful year has been yours,' she once wrote to a friend. '*Yes, do, do* let us have a talk abt *bad pain*—I shd love it.'

One recipient of such sympathy and advice, a young composer named Ethel Smyth, referred to Mary as a 'physician of souls', and spoke of her 'magic intuition' in discerning the emotional needs of others. 'Her master passion was undoubtedly the cure of souls,' Ethel observed. 'A great part of her life was consecrated to her patients, as I used to call them, who when bereft of her physical presence were kept going by words of counsel and comfort written on letter-paper so diminutive that it inevitably suggested a prescription.'

A strapping, tomboyish creature with a loud laugh, a strong jaw-line and a penchant for older women, Ethel Smyth was twenty-seven when she met Mary in 1885, and already enjoying some success in her field, as a composer of string quartets, sonatas and Lieder at the ready. They were introduced by family friends, as Ethel was in sore need of the 'physician of souls'. Her emotionally entangled relationship with Lisl von Herzogenberg—an Austrian aristocrat eleven years her senior—had come to an acrimonious and abrupt end. Lisl was the wife of Ethel's composition teacher, and for seven years Ethel had lived in the couple's house in Leipzig as a sort of surrogate daughter, passionately in love with Lisl, with a fervour that was fully reciprocated. But in early 1885, Ethel became embroiled in a complicated flirtation with Lisl's brother-in-law Henry Brewster, and Lisl suddenly and completely severed relations. Heartbroken and convinced she was no longer able to compose, Ethel limped back to England, to the comfort of Mrs Benson's ottoman. 'I would give anything to be any good to you,' Mary told her, 'but I leave that in God's hands—only if patient listening and eager desire *really* to *see* and understand tenderly and truly is any use I think I dare promise that.'

Edith Staines, a Character Based on Miss Ethel Smyth, Returns from an Enjoyable Morning Out Shooting, in Fred Benson's Novel Dodo

Edith had gone up to her room after insisting on having two of Dodo's bottles of eau de cologne in her hot bath. 'There is nothing so refreshing,' she said, 'and you come out feeling like a goddess.' Certainly Edith looked anything but a goddess just now. Her hat was pushed rakishly onto the side of her head, there was a suggestion of missing hairpins about her hair; she wafted with her about the room a fine odour of tobacco and gunpowder; she had burned her dress with a fusee head that had fallen off; her boots were large and unlaced, and curiously dirty, and her hands were black with smoke and oil, and had a sort of trimming in the way of small feathers and little patches of blood . . . But she insisted she had never enjoyed herself so much, she talked, and screamed, and laughed as if nothing serious had occurred since breakfast.

For the forty-four-year-old Mary, meeting Ethel was one of her 'My God, what a woman!' moments (it is Ethel who records Mary's use of the phrase); for Ethel's part, the now somewhat matronly Mary soon became 'the mainstay of my life', offering succour in the 'long cold night of the spirit that fell upon me'. Mary provided in abundance the nurturing love Ethel demanded, and the younger woman adored the attention. Soon, Ethel was calling Mary by that 'so intensely appropriate monosyllable adopted by some of your inner circle', Ben.

'The reasons for which I love you are unshakeable,' Ethel wrote to Ben, 'here are some of them; your truth, your fire, your intensity, your power of sustained effort, your extraordinary grip over other souls, your intellect, and above all, in the words of a prayer I like, your "unconquerable heart".' Ethel appreciated another side of the Archbishop's wife. She enjoyed the 'particular look of devilment one knew so well on her face', her delight in a little social wickedness, her acute sensibility to absurdities. On a more fundamental level, Ethel discerned the dexterity of spirit Mary needed to sustain herself as dutiful wife, effervescent hostess and sympathetic friend. When Ethel said that Mary Benson was 'as good as God,

189

and as clever as the Devil', the remark struck such resonance among those who knew her well, that it did the rounds of their friends.

Ethel played up to the more adventurous aspects of Mary's spirit. She was more outspoken and deliciously frank than any of Mary's other correspondents. In 1891, Ethel was on holiday with the Empress Eugénie, the former consort of Napoleon III, when a spider ran up the imperial leg. Ethel had developed an infatuation for the Empress, although (Ethel wrote to Ben) she felt that one 'might as well be in love with the Rock of Gibraltar', despite the fact that Eugénie had admitted to 'likings'. With characteristic heartiness, Ethel had pooh-poohed the fuss caused by the spider, and dismissed any notions of danger. That night, the sixty-five-year-old Empress summoned Ethel to her room, and appearing in her nightdress . . .

> . . .showed me her beautiful leg bared absolutely (but decently) up to the hilt . . . absorbed as she was in proving her point about the venom of spiders. Ben! You never saw such a leg! Not one hair on it—absolutely white and firm and modulated like—a nocturne of Chopin (would that you were musician enough to appreciate that comparison) and a foot and ankle like the Venus of Medici. The same is true of her shoulders—Form—Form!

'I think Ethel would like to call herself a "woman of the flesh",' observed Mary one day, after hearing a sermon on how a 'man of the world' is really but a 'man of the flesh'.

Ethel blew into Lambeth Palace like a wicked wind sprite. She visited bearing golf clubs and musical scores, attacked anything she did with vitality and verve, talked volubly and peppered her conversation with slang. The corridors echoed with: 'Congratters!', 'Oh, hang it!' and *awfully*. She was the living embodiment of a new generation. She took up the daring new pastime of bicycling, and wobbled in style along the gravel sweep in front of the palace, later giving instruction to the Dean of Windsor. Off she hauled Nellie (of the devastating underarm bowling), when a cricket mania possessed young women of their acquaintance in 1889, to the celebrated White Heather Club to join the team of Meriel Talbot, the W. G. Grace of the ladies' game. Ethel was boisterous, spirited and argumentative, and her relations with the Benson siblings were tempestuous, 'most of us being more or less aggressive and cocksure'.

Nellie had a maxim (which Maggie acknowledged held for all of them) of 'Contradict while you are thinking what to say'. The resultant wrangles made Ethel long for a pocket gramophone recorder. She had never known a family in whose existence humour played so great a part, and her prevailing concern when with the Bensons was: 'What made you so awfully clever?' They enthralled her (except Hugh, for whom she had an 'instinctive un-liking'). Yet Maggie, especially, could infuriate her with religious pomposity and a supreme conviction of her own rightness. Arguments at Addington and Lambeth raged late into the night. Mary once wryly sent Ethel a 'Thanksgiving to be used irregularly' that read: 'I thank thee, O Art, that I am not as other women are—strait-laced, narrow-minded,

191

dogmatic—or even as those Bensons.' With Arthur and Fred, Ethel made friends for life.

Fred Benson Depicts Miss Ethel Smyth as Edith Staines, in his Novel Dodo

The door was half open, and there came from within the sounds of vigorous piano-playing, and now and then a bar of music sung in a rich, alto voice. These tokens seemed to indicate that Miss Edith Staines was taking her breakfast at the piano . . . Edith Staines talked in a loud, determined voice, and emphasised her points with little dashes and flourishes of the dish of poached eggs . . . Edith went back to the drawing-room, whistling in a particularly shrill manner.

'Oh, did you ever!' said Dodo, who was laughing feebly in her chair. 'Edith is really splendid. She is so dreadfully sure of herself. And she does talk so loud—it goes right through your head like a chirping canary . . .' [. . .]

'The worst of it is,' said Edith, 'I care for such a lot of things. There's my music, and then there's any sort of game—have you ever seen me play tennis?—and then there isn't time for everything. I am a musician, and a good shot, and an excellent rider, and a woman, and heaps of other things. It isn't a conceit to say so—I simply know it.'

Dodo laughed.

'Well, you know, Edith, you're not modest. Your worst enemies don't accuse you of that . . .'

Inasmuch as the Primate of All England may be permitted such feelings, Edward loathed Ethel Smyth. So deep was his antipathy that it was soon considered expedient to smuggle her into Lambeth by back entrances and usher her into side rooms. The mere sight of Ethel from his study window, strolling with Mary in the garden (beside the long, dreary border of spiky flowers Mary had nicknamed 'the Apostolic Succession'), would 'infallibly wreck whatever work the Archbishop might happen to be engaged on at the moment'. Some of the boys' young male friends had the same effect. When Edward overheard Ethel playing parts of her Mass on the piano at Addington, he remarked that it appeared the Lord was being commanded rather than implored to have mercy, that the music sounded 'like orders issued in an extremely peremptory manner'. (In this instance, the Archbishop might have found an ally in George Bernard Shaw, who thought the Mass belonged to 'the light literature of Church music', and when reviewing it wrote: 'It repeatedly spurts ahead in the briskest fashion, so that one or two of the drum flourishes reminded me, not of anything so vulgar as the Salvation Army, but of a crack cavalry band.')

Ethel, for her part, 'stood in deadlier awe [of the Archbishop] than of anyone I ever met in the whole course of my life'. His disconcerting physical beauty, the weight of his office, his own prickly social unease, crippled her with nervousness. 'The sight of his majestic form approaching the tea-table scattered my wits as an advancing elephant might scatter a flock of sheep,' she confessed. With no one else did she say quite such stupid things, 'raking up scraps of schoolboy slang' in her disorder. On one occasion,

193

when Ethel had blurted out that Handel's music reminded her of a Mothers' Meeting, the Archbishop (in whose opinion this great 'English' composer's work was the only music worth listening to, other than church psalms) demanded with some hauteur that she justify her statement. He listened in silence, until her halting explanation spluttered to an end, then retorted: 'Are you aware that you have used the words "that sort of thing" seven times running?'

Mary, in her devilish way, rather enjoyed the progress of these run-ins, and would afterwards declare that 'the mouse-like voice which replied to the Archbishop's remarks was a very beautiful thing to listen to'. After one particularly acid encounter, she told Ethel cheerily: 'We all realise that you and the Head of the Church are *not* two dewdrops destined to roll into one.' The rare instances on which Ethel encountered any archiepiscopalian goodwill somehow made matters worse. After a memorable cricket match at Lambeth Palace, with a team made up entirely of the cricket-mad Talbot family playing against another raised by Nellie, the home team (in which Ethel took a leading part) quite unexpectedly won. The Archbishop's delight in the victory was almost boyish, and enveloped Ethel, too. And yet, she pointed out, 'it was just these human rays, shooting out unexpectedly from behind clouds of awfulness, that made him such a nerve-shaking acquaintance.'

Despite her rumbustiousness, and her gaucheness with the Archbishop, as a musician Ethel was sensitive and talented. The writer Maurice Baring, an acquaintance of Arthur's, heard her singing Brahms and Schubert for a group of friends, and 'knew at once that I had opened a window on a new

194

and marvellous province'. Ethel's interpretation was so intimate, so penetrating and revealing, that it seemed as if the composers themselves were singing their own work. Baring was moved by 'the rare and exquisite quality and delicacy of her voice, the strange thrill and wail, the distinction and distinct clear utterance, where every word and every note told without effort, and the whirlwind of passion and feeling she evoked.'

Music was all to Ethel, and formed the one serious sticking point in her friendship not only with Mary, but with the family as a whole. The Bensons were indeed an 'unpermissibly gifted family', she wrote, but 'the women of that family had not an ounce of artistic blood between them'. Maggie had gone so far as to give her reasons for not going to hear a *Passion* one day as 'I don't like Bach because he is so very ugly'. Ethel saw this as a 'difference of breed' between them, and it was the source of many of those late-night discussions. 'People who only admit one view of moral law—that of the Church,' observed Ethel, 'can hardly mix at bottom with those who see life through an artist's eyes; not at least unless artistic kinship is there to bridge the gulf between them.'

When Ethel first met Mary, in the tumult of the collapse of her relations with Lisl von Herzogenberg, 'the artist was in abeyance'. Although Ethel was not a committed Christian—at least, apart from a short 'phase of intense belief', not with Mary's fervour— she had a High Church upbringing, and their outlook was 'more or less the same; but even then the dissimilarity of grain made itself felt'. Ultimately Ethel needed someone who could understand what was most important to her, her art, and Mary was not 'musician enough' for that. Apart from the occasional gathering round a piano after dinner, music played little part in Mary's life. Without it, there was a gulf between her and Ethel which meant that on Ethel's part at least, the intensity of their initial feelings could not be sustained. She and Mary, Ethel later recalled, were 'like two trees whose upper branches occasionally mingling gave the illusion of one tree, whereas their roots were far, far apart'.

Something else intervened between Ethel and Mary—some*one* else. Ethel and Nellie fell in love. They were closer in age—Nellie was five years younger than Ethel—and although Nellie, like her mother and sister, had not 'an ounce of artistic blood in her', she shared with Ethel a devotion to games and adventure, unmatched (Ethel wrote) by anyone she had ever met. The two could also make each other erupt with laughter. The spirit that had impelled Nellie to found a Slang Society, in opposition to the more severe Maggie's Anti-Slang Society at school in Truro, appealed to Ethel. She was also secretly impressed by the fact that, of all the Benson siblings, Nellie was the only one at ease with their father. As she grew older, Nellie had no awe of Edward. Not only could she hold her own in conversation with him, but she could allow him the affection he craved from his other children, and which they were unable or unwilling to give.

Nellie had been recalled from Oxford when Maggie went up in 1883, as it was felt that at least one daughter was needed at home, to help with hospitalities at Lambeth and Addington. Short and rather dumpy, like her mother, Nellie also shared Mary's sunniness and self-deleting interest in others.

196

She was always delighted to fall in with other people's plans, skilled at reflecting their moods, and ever willing to give people their own head—a characteristic that endeared her both to Edward and to Ethel. 'What shall we do?' was Nellie's favourite question. She was outgoing, caring, and often 'uncommonly jolly'. 'No one could be morbid or haunted or unduly fanciful in Nelly's company,' wrote Arthur (who persistently spelled his sister's name thus), 'her humour and common-sense and a power of almost complimentary ridicule, swept cobwebs away very quickly'. Back from Oxford, she had flung herself into life at Lambeth and Addington, her sincere caring overflowing the palace boundaries into engaged and effective work among London's poor.

Like Mary, Nellie formed her most intense friendships with women. Both at school and at Oxford she was an object of adoration, a recipient of impassioned billets-doux (as their friendship deepened, Ethel wrote her over 150 letters in a single year). As Ethel drew closer to Nellie, she began to push Mary away, causing anguish on Mary's part. 'I am just yearning over you,' Mary wrote to Ethel. 'The past *is* and will always be, for me as well as for you ... you say I "must be a factor or nothing". I can never be "nothing" now. The past makes that impossible—why reject a factor even if small. You see 8 x 2 = 16—why can't you give me the place of 2?' Ethel was also on the verge of an affair with Henry Brewster, Lisl's brother-in-law. That was easier for Mary to deal with, as it could be condemned as adultery.

The triangle of tension between her, Ethel and Nellie presented far more difficulty. It meant Mary had to confront the conflict between her Christianity and her physical desires that had so troubled her in the past, and to accept the blowing away of the mist that comfortably clouded the borders between sympathetic counselling and erotic desire. She exercised her old arguments with Ethel—that she had come to God through understanding human love, but that impulses of desire needed to be controlled. But Ethel was of a new generation, one for whom such reasoning lacked the power it held for Mary—and, as her behaviour over Henry Brewster, Lisl and Lisl's sister had shown, she was uncomprehending, if not uncaring, of any heartache the pursuit of her own passions caused others. Mary had to cope not only with being an older woman rejected by a younger; not only with being in a position which seemed to require she give her blessing to the new friendship that excluded her; not only with being a mother whose daughter was embarking on a journey she feared for; but with the tortured, tangled knot in which these strands came together.

At first, Mary seemed willing to stand aside. She wrote to Ethel from Switzerland, where the family was on holiday in September 1889, admitting that the situation was one that would cause 'any amount of wear and tear and confusion on all sides', but:

> As far as I can help it there shant be. I have always claimed both for myself and others, that when a new friendship began to blossom there should be freedom given to form it . . . I know personally I cant form two relations worth having at once. Therefore I wanted and want you to know how free I leave you about Nellie.

But later in the long letter Mary's hurt, and a little of her confusion, emerges:

> Now as to the 'position you assign me'. Heaven forbid that I should deprive you of the old joke of General Physician, or any other joke ... *Only*, let it *be* a joke. Don't you see, when you speak of my *'function'* towards you and my possible feeling that it could be discharged equally well by my daughter, there you go awfully wrong. The bond that knots you and me is no *function*.

A month later, Mary was less assured about giving any blessing to Ethel and Nellie, and seemed compelled by circumstance, rather than magnanimity. 'I feel now that I must stand aside in the matter and leave you two alone,' she wrote. 'Ethel, I *do* wish you knew human nature a little more! you would then understand my inarticulateness—I am *here* yet must be quiet. The relation between you and me is a very tender plant, and of slow and delicate growth ... It is superfluous to say that I accuse you of nothing. But I must keep these delicate tendrils free from tangles—and you will admit that in this case tangles are very difficult to avoid.'

Tangles were indeed unavoidable, as Mary tried to align her role as a mother, her concern for Nellie's happiness, and fears that she may be hurt by Ethel, with her own role in the affair, her sense of loss and her awareness of age. Nellie appeared infatuated. She had refused to show Mary a letter Ethel had written her, and when Mary asked if there was anything private in it had said 'yes'; asked if she had 'any feeling of indecency' in showing it to her mother, she had said 'yes' again—though admitting that Ethel might not see it thus. 'I have been pained to think that Nellie was desiring something fuller than you spoke of in your first [letter],' Mary wrote to Ethel in October. 'But I realise now that more is developping [*sic*] in you, and feel more satisfied . . . I think Nellie is very happy now. You must have foreseen that from the first. Your nearness in ages, and her possibilities etc. made it so certain—and you did it with your eyes open. I feel that this time is emphatically *hers*, and I do long for her to have it good.' Having lost none of her deft touch with metaphor, Mary added a note of caution: 'She is a bivalve you see, and you *do* want both her shells . . .'

At times Mary's resolve crumpled, and her heartache and anger exploded: 'Quiet!! and you really think I can get a "letter" like that from you, and be *quiet*—Ethel!' Mary began a letter in November, without any salutation. 'I call it a "letter", because I scarcely ever saw so short a thing contain so much pain . . . Ethel, I mustn't get too tragic—it is always my tendency—but answer you I *will*.' Then she went on, slightly calmed by her outburst, to summarize the situation:

Think over the past—we meet first, you and I—we sound depths together—and out of that there grows of itself a relation—a deep relation . . . Then there comes this new drawing of you and Nellie—I don't understand it at first . . . all this means on either side. But soon it dawns on me. You speak of 'confusion and wear and tear on all sides'—and by Allah, it *comes*. *But*—and here we come to our present crux, your way out of it I cannot make mine. The play of nature between Nellie and me—The awful inner tie of mother and daughter—and if you will, *my own limitations* speak all together in clear tones, and a most deep inner instinct bids me be still—bids *me*, so to speak 'get out of the way' while this relation, which is evidently increasing more than either of you knew it would, developes [*sic*] itself . . . You say we speak too different languages ever to understand each other. Are there no dictionaries? No grammars? Must we give up the moment we make a poor translation, or a false construction? *I cannot* give it up. I will bungle on. I _will_ know you.

Ethel Smyth may well in time have discovered that the gulf that separated her from Mary, also, in the end, lay between her and the unartistic, similarly devout Nellie; or tensions between all three may eventually have torn through the fabric of the Benson family—but neither scenario was given the chance to play itself out. Within a year of Mary's writing that letter, Nellie was dead.

Chapter Twelve

In October of 1890, just over a fortnight after her twenty-seventh birthday, Nellie developed a sore throat while at Addington. The doctor diagnosed diphtheria, which Nellie had probably caught through contact with children in the village schoolroom, on her usual round of good works. Within days she could not speak at all, and was communicating only through shakily written notes, which were dowsed in disinfectant before being delivered. Nellie deteriorated rapidly. Her final note was to Mary, who was by her bed, and read: 'I wonder what it will be like. Give them all my love.' Mary began to say the words of 'Jesu, Lover of my soul', and as she was doing so, Nellie died.

A Hymn by Charles Wesley

Jesu, Lover of my soul,
let me to Thy bosom fly,
While the nearer waters roll,
while the tempest still is high.
Hide me, O my Saviour, hide,
till the storm of life is past;
Safe into the haven guide;
O receive my soul at last.

Other refuge have I none,
hangs my helpless soul on Thee;
Leave, ah! leave me not alone,
still support and comfort me.
All my trust on Thee is stayed,
all my help from Thee I bring;
Cover my defenceless head
with the shadow of Thy wing.

Wilt Thou not regard my call?
Wilt Thou not accept my prayer?
Lo! I sink, I faint, I fall
– Lo! on Thee I cast my care;
Reach me out Thy gracious hand!
While I of Thy strength receive,
Hoping against hope I stand,
dying, and behold, I live . . .

Mary sent telegrams to Arthur, who after taking a First in Classics had become a master at Eton, to Fred at King's, Cambridge, and to Hugh, who had just that month gone up to his father's old college at the same university, Trinity. Maggie was at Addington. Her studies at Oxford—at a time when women were not permitted to hold degrees or sit the official examinations—had led to a First in the Women's Honour School of Philosophy, with by far the highest mark of her year. 'If only it had been Greats [the official examination],' her tutor wrote. 'No one will realise how brilliantly she has done.' Mary also wrote to Ethel.

The boys came to Addington, but stayed in a nearby hotel for fear of infection. It was golden October weather, wrote Fred, 'with frosts at night and windless days, and the chestnut leaves peeling

203

off trees and falling in a heap of yellow below them, each leaf twirling in the air as it fell'. Nellie had been 'the best of us', Arthur lamented, 'gay, adventurous, brave'. Each of the Benson siblings felt they had a special bond with her. It was Nellie (a talented actress) who had organized theatricals every Christmas, who was the driving force behind the magazine they had produced together, whose childlike spirit had kept alive all manner of quaint family usages and games. Only a few weeks previously, Fred and she had larked about, playing at being children with Beth. (The old nurse had her own rooms at Addington.) In many ways, Nellie had bound them all together. Her death marked 'the closing of the old days of childhood for all of us', felt Arthur; with her passing, 'some unrecapturable moment was lost,' wrote Fred. At the funeral, Maggie, who had always been more reticent than Nellie, and much in her shadow, looked pale but brave, 'as if she had vowed to herself to fill so far as possible, Nellie's place as daughter and sister'. A friend later remarked that it was as if Maggie passed from childhood to womanhood without any intervening phase of 'young ladyhood'.

Shortly after the funeral, Mary wrote to Ethel Smyth: 'All is well here; our three sons have been so infinitely beautiful and have grasped the further communion of death (which you speak of) so wonderfully. 'It is expedient for you that I go away' is a human truth, I verily believe ... Only selfishness or dreariness or repining would really separate us. Maggie is wonderful. I could break my heart about her, but loving is better—and God knows, as he does ... all.' Ethel remained a friend of Mary's (and of Arthur and Fred, in particular), though the intensity of their earlier intimacy was gone. Another woman had entirely engaged Mary's heart, and as she had admitted to Ethel, she could not 'form two relations worth having at once'. Just weeks after Nellie's death, Lucy Tait came to live at Lambeth Palace.

Fifteen years younger than Mary, Lucy was the daughter of Edward's predecessor, Archbishop Tait. Full-faced and statuesque, she was a determined young woman, with a firm set to her mouth and small, assessing eyes. Edward liked Lucy. He respected her commitment to charitable works, and admired her as a woman who 'not only thinks how she may serve her friends but if there is one way more thorough than another does it'. It was Edward who had invited Lucy to live at the palace, in a seemingly well-meaning but heavy-handed attempt after Nellie's death to provide a substitute daughter for Mary and an older sister for Maggie (who was nine years Lucy's junior). 'She will come live with us for our Nellie,' he said. Perhaps Edward was also aware that in return for the support and devotion he desired of Mary, he would have to admit Lucy as her prop.

In the very hot summer of 1882, when Edward was paying such scrupulous attention to the ailing Archbishop Tait, he had once brought Lucy back with him from London for a visit to Lis Escop. Mary had taken to her immediately. Walks in the garden and long talks about God, fulfilment, and love consumed the ensuing days, with Mary worrying 'am I boring her?'. On Edward's next journey to London, Mary went along, too, noting in her diary when it was time to return home: 'Leave Addington. *BOTHER*.' Arthur, who accompanied them, noted that Miss Tait was 'greatly attached to my mother'.

Moving back into Lambeth Palace—which, after all, had once been her home too—Lucy behaved as a full-fledged member of the family. She helped entertain guests, she went riding with Edward, and to religious gatherings with Maggie. She impressed Ethel Smyth at a prayer meeting led by a particularly saccharine woman—who wound up her address with a saintly: 'Do you think dear friends, we shall smile in Heaven? ... *I* ... *do*!'—by muttering 'low and thunderously: "If people are going to smile like that in Heaven, I don't think I want to go there."' She took Mary to hear Tom Mann (a leader of the great London dock strike of a few years previous, and soon to be Secretary of the new Independent Labour Party) lecture on 'The Religious Basis of the Socialist Movement'. They were struck by his eloquence, and horrified Edward by returning home fired with (albeit fleeting) enthusiasm for Mann's ideas. The summer following Nellie's death the family holidayed together in Switzerland, and at the end of December 1891 Lucy joined Edward, Mary, Fred and Maggie on a trip to Algiers and Tunis.

The journey was undertaken very much at Mary's urging. Edward had for years been working on a Life of the third-century theologian and martyr St Cyprian of Carthage, and she finally convinced him to take a pilgrimage to 'the places where in thought he had so often dwelt'. A month in north Africa also deeply appealed to her own sense of adventure. On an earlier journey through the Holy Land with Edward, she had been exhilarated by the 'colour and handsomeness of the people', their brightness and variety of dress, and was entranced by the scenery: 'The mountains of Moab blue and bright—[and] like a green enamel below [,] the valley of the Jordan—a dark treelined groove along it the Jordan itself—running into a pushed-out yellow line of mud into the white-blue of the Dead Sea.' She had watched Arab children sitting on mats at their lessons, girls filling washpots at fountains, and mounting winding stairs with wrung-out washing on their heads; she had even visited a Bedouin camp and tasted camel's milk, some 'very sweet and good' cheese churned with a stick, and coffee roasted before her eyes. Now she looked forward to similar exploits, and Lucy was equally intrepid.

The journey did not begin well, with Edward in pain from neuralgia at Marseilles, and suffering from one of the depressions that had been afflicting him with increasing severity since he became Archbishop. Fred read aloud everyone's favourite part of *In Memoriam*, but unknown to the others, this only darkened Edward's mood, as it reminded him both of his inability to express his love for his children and that this love was not reciprocated. To his diary he confided:

In Memoriam was inexpressibly dear to me for the best part of my life ... There was nothing I so longed for in early life as to lead my children along those ways and kindred ways in other poets. It had been done, and yet they were quite unconscious of my having any keen, deep interest in it ... I could not but be silent throughout. It was strange to *be* in, and not be in the least felt to be in, my children's tender thinkings.

207

But soon Edward was propelling the party with the same furious energy he had shown on his honeymoon—travelling fifteen hours to see the ruins and basilica at the one-time Carthaginian outpost of Tébessa, and after just a day there, making a seventeen-hour journey back; or arriving at Sétif after dark, having travelled since four o'clock that morning and aiming to set off again at seven o'clock on the next, scorning those who did not accompany him to peer through the ramparts after dinner. Yet this time, Mary did not always permit herself to be bullied into exhaustion. Rather, she left Edward to his vigorous sightseeing and went off on her own adventures with Lucy—boiling eggs in hot springs, shopping for necklaces in the souks (with Lucy doing the bargaining), feasting on lamb and couscous beneath an aqueduct, even dropping in on an 'Arab cottage'. Here they encountered a 'handsome smiling man and a handsomely decked out woman [with] magnificent earrings and silver clasps in her breast'. The young couple did not speak French, so they all communicated in sign language and, amidst much hilarity, Lucy sang.

The trip was almost brought to an abrupt and early end when news arrived of the death of the Prince of Wales's eldest son, Albert Victor, Duke of Clarence, during an influenza pandemic. Edward was preparing his return to officiate at the funeral, when a telegram arrived from the Prince of Wales himself, saying that on no account was he to curtail his holiday. A letter followed, in which the Prince expressed his sorrow that Edward would now no longer officiate at the late Prince's wedding; Albert Victor's 'Bride has become his Widow without ever having been his Wife'. (The charming 'May' of whom Queen Victoria had noted that she was very *un*frivolous and had much sense, was also resourceful. The following year, she married the next in line of succession, Prince Albert Victor's younger brother George, Duke of York.)

The party resumed its original schedule, as Edward went on to spend many hours among the ruins of Carthage, while Mary, Lucy, Maggie and Fred remained in Tunis, visiting the souks, befriending a young Frenchman who was going to London to stay in 'Cheeseweek Park' and learn English, and engrossing themselves in local street life—including a musician who was so delighted by the half-franc Mary dropped into his tambourine that 'in gratitude he brought down—from heaven— two large nails into his nose'. One Sunday they encountered a snake charmer, a hideous man with matted hair who teased and irritated a large cobra in a bag until it reared, spreading its hood and flicking its tongue at him. 'A curious contrast, I thought,' wrote Mary, in the beige school exercise book in which she had improvised a travel diary, 'to an Addington Sunday afternoon.'

Fred Remembers Sunday Afternoons at Addington, in Our Family Affairs

There was early communion in the chapel ... [then] morning service in the church was succeeded by lunch, lunch by a slow family walk during which my father read George Herbert to us; the walk was succeeded by a Bible reading with him, and then came tea.

After tea was evening service in the church, and after Sunday supper, he read the *Pilgrim's Progress* aloud until we had compline in the chapel . . . No shoal of relaxation emerged from the roaring devotional flood; if at meals the conversation became too secular, it was brought back into appropriate channels . . . No games of any sort or kind were played, not even those which like lawn-tennis or golf entailed no labour on the part of the servants . . . The Day of Rest in fact, owing chiefly to this prohibition on reasonable relaxation, became a day of pitiless fatigue . . . To my father, I make no doubt, with his intensely devotional mind, this strenuous Sunday was a time of refreshment . . . What he did not allow for was that on other temperaments, that which so aptly fulfilled the desires of his own produced a totally different impression. That day, for us, was one of crushing boredom and unutterable fatigue.

On very hot Sundays at Addington, the customary leisurely afternoon walk might be replaced by a gathering under the enormous cedar in the grounds, at which each member of the family read in turn from 'some saintly chronicle', while the others surreptitiously dozed. One somnolent Sunday afternoon, with 'the serene sunlight outside the shade of the cedar positively gilding the tennis court' and the croquet lawn 'starving for crack of balls', the spirit of 'Satan, or at least Puck' entered Fred, and he began to read at random from the *Lives of the Saints*—a few lines from a page already read, a paragraph about an entirely different saint a hundred pages later, a sentence or two from the introduction to the whole volume, a fragment from the life of St Catherine, another from the life of St Francis—all in the same reverential drone. Then he suddenly stopped. The silence roused his sister.

'Oh, how interesting!' she said. Her voice woke the Archbishop.

'Wonderful!' said he. "Is that all, Fred?'

'Yes that's all,' said Fred.

Later, Fred discovered to his great delight—in a book given to him to read by his father—that for many centuries following patristic times, no idea of such a dull Sunday had ever entered a Christian head, that the Sabbath was (once a suitable act of worship was out of the way) a time of village sports, general hospitality and *festa*. Barely suppressing his giggles, he ran up to his mother's room to tell her. Mary 'steered a course so wonderful that not even then could I chart it,' observed Fred. 'Her sympathetic amusement I knew was all mine, but somehow she abandoned no whit of her loyalty to my father's purpose in giving me the book.' With a consummate stroke of what Nurse Beth referred to as her 'tac', and that godly goodness combined with devilish cunning that Ethel Smyth so admired, Mary deftly placed Fred's plan to pronounce sentence on boring Sundays right out of the question. 'How she did it I have no idea,' Fred admitted, 'but surely the very test of tact lies in the fact that you don't know how it is done.'

As Mary's children grew into clever and idiosyncratic young adults, even though they were less frequently at home, her skills of 'tac' in mediating between them and their father, without compromising her devotion to either, became ever more necessary. The young Bensons were growing more assertive, each carving a most individual space in the world. 'That's one comfort about all of you,' the explorer Gertrude Bell ('uglier than ever, all points and peaks and moustached') said to Arthur once, 'You are not the least like the children of Archbishops.' Another friend told Mary that 'her children might cause her pain and vexation, but she *would never be dull.*'

Initially, it was Arthur who was most likely to arouse her concern. Self-absorbed and introspective, Arthur appeared to have inherited his father's tendency to dark depression. Just prior to Nellie's death, having injured his knee, Arthur found that stopping regular exercise led to insomnia, and that soon 'the curse was on me'. During the 'horrible dreary time' around her funeral he turned his focus upon himself, one night 'being seized by faintness, and creeping up to my room convinced I was going to die'. Arthur found some comfort in writing poetry. His first volume was published in 1893, when he was thirty-one—he had already had a collection privately printed a year earlier, and had a novel and a couple of biographical works behind him.

In his diaries, Arthur indicates a possible trigger to his depressions, an event that occurred in 1882 while he was at Cambridge. He refers to it as 'my great misfortune', as 'the greatest and most sudden blow that ever befell me—which influenced my life incomparably more than anything before or since', and which he marked every year on the ninth of November as 'my great anniversary', which 'made its mark like nothing else in my whole life'. On 9 November 1882, Arthur attended a Revivalist meeting at the Cambridge Corn Exchange. Strong winds of scepticism were blowing through Cambridge at the time. Arthur's uncle, Henry Sidgwick, a university lecturer in moral philosophy, was an influential sceptic. Edward appears, with some success, to have discouraged contact between the two at Cambridge, but Arthur could not help but feel the influence of the agnostic atmosphere. He had gone to the meeting originally in a spirit of mockery, but appears to have been dealt a soul-shaking blow. Alongside this religious experience came an emotional crisis, the ruinous collapse of an intense romantic friendship with an unnamed man, that arguably left Arthur unable to be truly intimate with anyone ever again. In his diary he later observed of those months: 'I have often thought I was nearly out of my mind—and have certainly never quite recovered it.' Arthur plunged into self-hatred and depression, and even wrote to the august Roman Catholic Cardinal Newman for advice—but he could not approach his father. Whatever Arthur might have confided to Mary within the seclusion of her sitting room, with the family at large, especially in front of Papa, no such disturbing sentiments surfaced. At least, not in conversation.

From A. C. Benson's Novel
The House of Quiet
The unnamed hero, 'a distant cousin', remembers
'how strangely and secretly the crucial moment, the
most agonising crisis of my life, drifted upon me'

The [Revivalist] meeting was held in a hall in a side street; we went smiling and talking, and took our places in a crowded room . . . [The preacher] had not spoken half-a-dozen words before I felt as though he and I were alone in the world . . . Every word he said burnt into my soul. He seemed to probe the secrets of my innermost heart; to be analysing, as it were, before the Judge of the world, the arid and pitiful constituents of my most secret thought . . . his words fell on me like the stabs of a knife . . . Even as he spoke, pierced as I was to the heart by contrition and anguish, I knew that this was not for me . . . He invited all who would be Christ's to wait and plead with him . . . but I went out into the night, like one dizzied with a sudden blow . . . I felt like a wounded creature, who must crawl into solitude . . . every nervous misery known to man beset me—intolerable depression, spectral remorse, nocturnal terrors . . . For some weeks this lasted, and I think I was nearly mad.

He writes for advice to 'an eminent Roman Catholic, in whose sermons I had found some encouragement', and receives an 'irritated, and bewildered' reply

[M]y only way was to submit myself to true direction, and he did not see that I had any intention of doing this; that it was obvious that I was being plagued by some sin which I had not ventured to open to him.

From A. C. Benson's First Novel,
Memoirs of Arthur Hamilton
Christopher Carr researches the life of his friend Arthur Hamilton, and concludes that a 'baptism

214

of fire' that occurred at Cambridge was not the result of a Revivalist meeting, but of 'some emotional failure, some moral wound'

The exact day was November 8, 1872. It is engraved in a small silver locket that hung on his watch chain, where he was accustomed to have important days of his life marked . . . He had formed, in his last year at school, a very devoted friendship with a younger boy; such friendships . . . when they are truly chivalrous and absolutely pure, are above all other loves, noble, refining, true; passion at white heat without taint, confidence of so intimate a kind as can not even exist between husband and wife . . . This friend, a weak but singularly attractive boy [came to Cambridge] and fell in with a thoroughly bad set there . . . my belief is that disclosures were made on November 8 which revealed to Arthur the state of the case . . . I can hardly picture to myself the agony, disgust, and rage . . . loyalty fighting with a sense of repulsion, pity struggling with honour, which must have convulsed him when he discovered that his friend was not yielding, but deliberately impure.

The other's was an unworthy and brutal nature, utterly corrupted at bottom.

Fred was as flighty as Arthur was grave. He remained quite Mary's favourite. For Fred, Lambeth Palace became a springboard for an entry into the very heart of fashionable London society. He was ideally equipped to become its darling—an insouciant wit, brilliant conversation and an easy style. More than any of his siblings, he strove to ignore the fact that he was the child of an archbishop; he was eager to take part in the daring social metamorphosis of the 1890s, as elements of society began to push against the chrysalis of late-Victorian stolidity. He even aspired to join the colourful group that fluttered around Oscar Wilde at the Café Royal. For Fred, this was the moment when 'the long-retarded spring burst into fullest summer . . . I confess that I was then tipsy with the joy of life and the horns of Elfland were continually blowing.' Arthur thought him facile and shallow.

Like Arthur, Fred had taken a First at Cambridge (in his case after very little effort), but had then stayed on for a second Tripos, in archaeology. The Greeks, thought Fred, were 'the supreme race of all who have inhabited this earth'. After the family holiday in Algiers and Tunis, Fred left for Athens, to take a course at the British School of Archaeology and work on a dig at Megalopolis. He missed the first night of *Lady Windermere's Fan*, Oscar Wilde's first notable success, but went with Mary as soon as he was back in town. Both loved the play, but then, as Mary remarked in a letter to Maggie, she could sit through anything with Fred anyway. 'He is the *dearest* person and so delicious to have in the house.' Yet she sensed that Fred was frustrated in London, found living at Lambeth stifling. He stalked the corridors, seemed unfulfilled, restless, demoralized, 'for he can't settle and doesn't take enough exercise. Bless the darling!' That was soon to change.

The spark for Fred's sudden trajectory beyond the confines of Lambeth Palace was the publication of his first novel, *Dodo*. He had reworked the manuscript that (to his acute embarrassment) Mary had sent to Henry James. Methuen accepted the book for publication and it came out in May 1893, while he was on a second visit to Athens. *'Dodo is out!'* Mary wrote to him, adding—with even greater surprise, given the novel's Wildean frothiness: 'Your father had the first copy and has positively read some of it!'

Dodo was an enormous success. It drew a wicked picture of a rich, aristocratic, brilliant and witty London set known as 'The Souls', delivering just the degree of delicate birching as to be found bracing even by those it satirized. The first printing sold out within a month. By October, it was into its ninth edition. Fred returned from Athens to find that he had become a sensation, his book a fad. The brittle, extravagant conversation of The Souls that Fred had so perfectly captured, was in turn affected at fashionable London parties, in repartee 'à la Dodo'. Fred himself came to be nicknamed 'Dodo' after the book's heroine, and the Archbishop had to suffer the ignominy of being referred to as 'Dodo's Papa'.

Though Fred denied it, it was clear to most that he had based his rather appalling 'beautiful, unscrupulous, dramatic, warm-hearted, cold-blooded' leading character on the vivacious, acerbically witty Margot Tennant, whom Arthur had introduced to the family. The Prince of Wales once even addressed her as 'Miss Dodo' at a ball. Arthur travelled all the way from Eton to offer her a personal apology for his brother's book, and she wrote him a most gracious reply, though could not resist a slight sally of her own: 'If the book had had more intellectual merit I should get less tired of being talked to about it.' To Fred, who had somewhat disingenuously sent a note apologizing for the unexpected publicity the book had caused her (or so the gossip went), she wrote: 'Dear Mr Benson, have you written a novel? How clever of you.'

There were those (Margot's soon-to-be husband, the future Prime Minister Herbert Asquith among them) who agreed with Lady Emily Lutyens that young Fred Benson deserved 'a good kicking', and thought he had 'let the side down', but the book ran into twelve editions before the year was out. On rereading her son's first major literary effort, Mary judged: 'I think it cleverer than I even thought, I also am afraid the blots are more crude than I thought too.' Later, she confided privately that she felt the characters did not develop and did not always ring true. The Archbishop was bemused by such fuss over so frivolous a trifle, but considered the character of Edith Staines to be so clearly based on Ethel Smyth that he was moved to break with all previous personal precedent and be effusively pleasant to her one dinner-time, sure that she must be offended by his son's effrontery. Ethel was nonplussed by such civil behaviour on the Archbishop's part—and, in any case, considered Edith Staines to be the one decent character in the book.

Mary was delighted to have Fred back from Athens and living at home, even if he was pursuing a hectic social life. She fretted that such popularity and financial success were not good for him, that he needed some sort of steady employment to tether him, even though he continued to produce the occasional learned archaeological paper. Fred was

218

now welcomed at the more flamboyant tables at the Café Royal. He fell in with the pretty young poet Lord Alfred Douglas, 'Bosie' as he was known, and in 1894 Bosie introduced him to Oscar Wilde.

Young Fred Benson has his Wildean Moments
Extracts from Dodo

He is devoted to her, and she is clever and stimulating. Personally I shouldn't like a stimulating wife. I don't like stimulating people, I don't think they wear well.

Dodo had a deep-rooted dislike for ugly things, unless they amused her very much. She could not bear babies. Babies had no profiles, which seemed to her a very lamentable deficiency . . .

Mrs Vane was a large, high-coloured woman of about middle age, whose dress seemed to indicate that she would rather not, but that, of course, may only have been the fault of the dressmaker.

'They sleep like hogs,' she said, 'and they are very cheerful in the morning . . . It is very plebeian to be cheerful in the morning.'

With one son a reclusive schoolmaster, and another a frivolous scribbler and social gadabout, Edward pinned his hopes on Hugh to follow him into holy orders. Wilful, argumentative and petulant, young Hugh did not show much promise in that direction either, though he had always enjoyed dressing up and shared his father's fondness for ritual. While still at

Eton, Hugh decided he wanted to go into the Indian Civil Service—a popular recourse among young men wishing to flee the constrictions of home life. It took the combined forces of the entire family to dissuade him. 'He certainly takes a manly tone and listens to none of us in the way of defection,' wrote Edward in his diary. While Edward was pleased (in answer to many prayers, and in gratification of his firm Arnoldian principles of Muscular Christianity) that a 'new power of manliness' seemed at last to have come over Hugh, he was concerned that the boy had yet to see himself as God's servant, and to 'live as to the Lord and not as to men'. Mary was not of the same mind, as Edward noted, resignedly: ' "Our little sheltered boy!" his mother says—and breaks my heart. I always reckoned on this one to be my great friend as I grew old.'

In the end, Hugh was rejected for the Civil Service. Some desultory years at Cambridge followed, which fizzled into a Third. He was ordained in 1895, and went on to work with boys' clubs in Hackney Wick, and serve occasionally as his father's chaplain. In this capacity he doubly irritated Ethel Smyth (who had never liked him much), as he would 'flit up and down the corridors of Lambeth in coats the skirts of which almost swept the floor—a common foible of short men'. Lucy Tait, also, did not take to Hugh, and thought him 'odd', and his position on ecclesiastical matters 'dangerous'. Hugh quarrelled fiercely with Lucy (but then he did with almost everyone).

Lucy's presence at Lambeth presented Mary with the greatest demand yet on her powers of 'tac', and for once they seemed not quite up to the mark. 'Lucy came bustling in to give me a kiss,' she wrote to Maggie, 'and finding me dolorous . . . said "I'll be

Maggie, Aged Twenty-Eight, in 1893

Maggie to you".' Far from welcoming Lucy as a new elder sibling, Maggie resented her presence. She grew peevish, and began to demand more of her mother's attention. Maggie could be proud, fierce and cross, as she herself admitted, 'not about anything particular, but in the sort of condition where one feels it would be very undesirable to be contradicted'. She was scathing about Lucy's intellectual capacities, and demolished her in argument. A note of acidity crept into letters when Maggie referred to herself as Lucy's 'little sister', and she tried to create rifts between her mother and the interloper, subtle and razor-thin: 'I have just got a *lovely* new French hat,' she wrote to Mary, while on a visit to Aix-en-Provence, 'which you will like and Lucy may think vulgar.' In another letter she expostulated: 'Please thank Lucy very much for her letter—but say I shall just wear whichever hat I like—and if her thoughts of her little sister in a strange land centre upon *hats*—no climax strong enough occurs to me.'

Now nearly thirty, Maggie was girlish-looking for her age, with a pale, fresh complexion. Tall, straight-backed and slender, her hair pulled tightly back from a marble dome of a forehead and with earnest blue-grey eyes, she could seem stern and aloof. Like her father, she had little small talk. Nellie had once said rather impatiently of her that 'if Maggie would only have an intimate relationship even with a *cat*, it would be a relief', and Arthur noted that 'her friendships were seldom leisurely or refreshing things'. Clearly brilliant, Maggie was quick and devastatingly incisive in argument, cutting through sophistry with what her Oxford tutor marvelled was 'absolute remorselessness'. 'I never met anyone else

222

so quick to notice a flaw in an argument as she was,' noted one clever but somewhat intimidated young male acquaintance.

It was clear to Mary that Maggie needed some sort of distraction from life at Lambeth Palace, something to occupy her busy mind, and to divert her attention away from Lucy. Maggie's health was also a cause for concern. She developed pains in the temples, suffered from passionate outbursts of temper, and was later diagnosed in succession with rheumatism, heart problems, and that hold-all of the time for almost any woman's woe, a gynaecological upset—in Maggie's case described vaguely as 'congestion, dilation, displacement'. Foreign travel seemed an attractive solution. On his next archaeological expedition to Greece, at the end of 1893, Fred took his elder sister along.

From Athens, Maggie wrote to Mary that she felt 'for the first time almost' that she had 'a little taste of the world'. Edward was strict to the point of being old-fashioned and excessively restraining with his children. Alone among her contemporaries at Oxford, Maggie had had to be accompanied by a chaperone at reading parties, and was completely forbidden from joining a group where Browning's ever so slightly racy drama *A Blot in the 'Scutcheon* was read. Even Arthur, in his undergraduate days, when he let slip that he had been invited to dinner to meet the actor Henry Irving, received a letter from his father stating: 'he would not think of forbidding me to go, but he spoke of it as if it were a parting of the ways, and that if I went to such an entertainment, I might easily be drawn into an attractive current of the world, with much superficial charm and interest masking a vague sort of morality and dubious

223

standards.' Arthur declined the invitation. In Athens, Maggie, though excited by this first taste of the world, hastened to reassure her mother that home was so much nicer, and that she would rather that too much of the world not intrude on it. Yet she and Fred were soon at the centre of Athenian social life, 'quite hand in glove' with the Greek Royal Family (Maggie boasted in a letter home), with Fred having to restrain himself during audiences with King George of Greece from imitating the monarch's habit—'as infectious as yawning'—of standing with feet close together, rising on to tiptoe and dropping back again. Momentary loss of concentration would mean that king and visitor became locked in a gentle seesaw as they conversed. Maggie, for her part, had to accustom herself to Queen Olga's habit of grabbing women she was speaking to by the shoulders and shoving them back into their seats, causing a descent both sudden and drained of any decorum.

Together, brother and sister wrote, staged and starred in a farce they titled *The Duchess of Bayswater*. The piece was originally intended to entertain local English governesses, but *Dodo*'s fame had spread. Soon word of the farce was out, and 'the entire host of royalties' announced their intention to attend. *The Duchess of Bayswater* premiered before 'a row of Kings and Queens and ten rows of English governesses, and a swarm of English sailors'.

Maggie's emotional outbursts were contained, though she did have periods of 'fussed depression', and one rather dramatic 'attack' after someone told her she was a disagreeable sort of person. It was up to Fred to take Mary's role of easing his sister back into some sort of self-control. From Lambeth, Mary sent upbeat letters in the perky, school-girlish style she often employed with Maggie. 'Oh *do* be *normal*,' she wrote, and *'PUL-EASE* do what is best', reassuring Maggie that such snubs were nothing to distress her 'blessed little mind' over—Mama wasn't fussed: 'I larf, I dew.'

Quite apart from looking after his sister and working on archaeological excavations, Fred was having his own fun. Lord Alfred Douglas visited and shared his room at the Grand Hotel for a week, and Fred later became inseparable from Reggie Lister, a diplomat at the British Legation. Two years older than Fred, Reggie had an irresistible charm, an exuberance and infectious enthusiasm for almost anything he did and anyone he met, and was pleasingly lacking in the grit of 'manliness' that the Archbishop so valued. His friendship with Fred 'dispensed with all the preliminaries of acquaintanceship: there was no gradual drawing together about it, it leaped into being, and there it remained, poised and effortless'—for life.

In January 1894, Fred and Maggie went on to Egypt to follow Fred's archaeological pursuits, and again mixed with the grandest of British society, this time at the Luxor Hotel. Lord Alfred Douglas was again there, and Fred took a steamer with him up the Nile, together with the novelist Robert Hichens, a member of the Café Royal set, whose book *The Green Carnation*, clearly based on the lives of Oscar Wilde and Bosie, played a part in the scandal that descended on Wilde the following year. Hichens rather envied 'Dodo' Benson his beauty and success, thought him gloriously tanned, 'a thorough outdoor man', and was impressed by how 'he and Lord Alfred got on marvellously together,

225

the wit of the one seeming to call out and polish the wit of the other'.

At the large communal dining table at the Luxor, Maggie 'was as clever in conversation as her brother', and thoroughly enjoyed having company of her own age. To her mother she confessed that while she would want only the 'smallest possible driblets' of this exciting new world to be allowed to colour life back home: 'The only thing I should like more of—it will amuse you but I feel quite capable of saying it out loud—is the society of young men. I have had much more of that than of girls since I came out [to Egypt]—naturally with Fred.' Ultimately, though, Maggie would observe that she could never conceive of meeting anyone who was 'man enough to marry and yet woman enough to love'.

Brother and sister returned to London. Delighted, as ever, to have Fred home, Mary found him to be 'in magnificent health', declared by a doctor to be '"like an Apollo" . . . in the perfection of his muscles. Lor!' Maggie had been bitten, but by an entirely metaphorical bug. 'This place grows on one extraordinarily,' she had declared back in Luxor. 'Bas-reliefs of kings in chariots are only now beginning to look individual instead of being made on a pattern, and the immensity of the whole thing is beginning to dawn—and the colours, oh my *goodness*! You get to see them more every day.' She had worked on Arabic and turned her considerable mind to deciphering hieroglyphics, and before returning home had taken up Egyptology and done some excavating of her own. In the winter of 1895–6, Maggie returned to Egypt, this time to

226

work on the excavation of the Temple of Mut at Karnak.

'I am really immensely happy,' Maggie wrote to her mother, just days after arriving. 'Instead of idling as a pursuit, one has pursuits and idles for pleasure.' Maggie was given the role of overseer, and a local workforce quailed before this tall, imperious Englishwoman. A family friend, Lady Jane Lindsay, was most impressed visiting the dig on the first day to see 'Maggie the centre of a howling mob with a copy-book in one hand and a courbash [buffalo-hide whip] in the other—some score of individuals beyond the number she desired, being determined to get their names inscribed as labourers'. 'Hurling small boys' from her position atop an elevated stone, Maggie appointed her assistants, and soon set to work. Over the following weeks she made a number of rare and significant finds, among them a rose-granite seated statue of Rameses II, which the Government Excavator later permitted her to take home.

So energetic was Maggie in her archaeological work that Mary began to worry about her health in such a hot climate, and persuaded Fred to join her. He reported that Maggie was well, and so lively in company at dinner 'that you wouldn't have known your own daughter'. But a deeper concern troubled Mary. Maggie had written to her of a Miss Reed, who had become passionately attached to her and was growing most importunate. Mary wrote instantly to warn her daughter not to 'allow any parleyings', to distance herself from Miss Reed, and to be wary of any growing 'morbidity' (a term commonly used at the time when speaking of same-sex attraction). She followed it with another letter a few days later, advising: 'I don't want you not to be kind, goodness knows, but do be *very* firm—and don't sit with her more than you ought ... *don't ever yield one tittle* to her morbidity—her letter, poor little blue-eyed child, is very bad.'

Mary need not have concerned herself over-much about Miss Reed. Maggie's heart was elsewhere. Helping her on the dig was a demure, introverted young woman

Maggie with Nettie Gourlay

named Nettie Gourlay, who was somewhat in awe of Maggie's ferocious energy and incisive mind. Nettie and Maggie shared many sentiments, and enjoyed discussing metaphysics. 'I like her extremely,' Maggie wrote to Mary, at the same time assuring her that there was 'not the slightest touch of *Schwärmerei* but thorough interested liking'. As the weeks went on, Maggie wrote: 'I like her more and more—I haven't liked anyone so well in years. She is so much more free than almost any woman I know from anything small or cheap or common or coarse.' And then:

> *Nettie*—how can I keep you up
> in this, for it changes every day
> —oh, I *hope* you'll like her—
> you can't help it if you know her,
> but she is so horribly shy ... Oh, Mother, it's
> so odd to me to make a friendship like this—

generally there has been something in the way—mostly I've not been sure of the other person, and generally I've had a radical element of distrust . . . I don't think her perfect—preserve me from it! but there's nothing small nor hard about her. There—I wanted you to know. Do you remember my saying you didn't like my friends? and there was a truth in that—but I think I'm ceasing to be attracted by the brute. You know what I mean.

On her way back to England in May, bringing Nettie with her to meet the family, Maggie told her mother: 'You can't think how new this sort of thing is to me. Except you and Tan, I don't know any one in the world I admire so much.' Even without the reminder of her own past passions, Mary had already recognized that this was a friendship that needed to be accommodated within what was already a family of unconventional shape.

Lucy Tait's arrival at Lambeth Palace had led Mary once again on to the tricky terrain where she had so frequently tripped in the past. 'I feel nearer her now than I have done these 6 years,' Mary wrote in her diary in the summer of 1896. 'O God draw us together more and more—if I might—if I might! but this is as it shall please thee.' Once again Mary struggled with 'carnal affection' and its place in a loving friendship so intense that the union seemed to her a gift of God. She writes of her shame, of how 'last night I fell again', and sometimes more esoterically: 'I must put away forever the red failing.' Mary owned a leather-bound copy of

Thomas à Kempis's *The Imitation of Christ*, which Edward had given her for her fiftieth birthday in 1891, soon after Lucy's arrival. Underlined in pencil are passages that portray religious life as a constant struggle against a powerful enemy, lines which uphold temptation as an offering from God that encourages us to fight sin and emerge triumphant, together with such texts as:

> And, save you act with violence,
> You will not crush your sin.

Mary Benson Records a Private Prayer in her Diary, in August 1896

O merciful God, grant that the Old Adam in me may be so buried that a new man may be raised up in me.

Grant that all carnal affections may die in me and that all things belonging to the Spirit may live and grow in me.

Grant that I may have power and strength to have victory and to triumph against the devil, the world and the Flesh.

Lucy seemed reluctant to bend to Mary's arguments. 'Look here Ben—I've been having rather a time of it in Chapel,' she wrote, while on a short trip from home. She felt spurned, sent back in upon herself, 'rather like a sea anemone when its feelers are touched', and she explained why: 'it's no earthly good you and me having anything together except just the very thing we have always wanted from the beginning, and no other relationship is the *slightest* good, not even only as a temporary arrangement for a few days.' She dismissed some compromise solution Mary had offered (possibly of abstinence and reward) as 'a Sunday-school prize-giving arrangement', and would have none of it. 'I claim,' Lucy went on, 'to have you yourself and every bit of you.' Later, she edged a little closer to Mary's point of view: 'Nasty to me Ben? No I should think not my own darling. If there's any nastiness it's not with you. The difficulty is to know how to "totally abstain" but what you said particularly about keeping one's desire true is the thing to begin with and I'm at that.' In her diary, in the early autumn of 1896, Mary wrote a prayer for them both:

Once more with shame O Lord grant that all carnal affections might die in me, and that all things belonging to the spirit may live and grow in me—Lord look down on Lucy and me, and bring to pass the union we have both so [illegible] and so blindly, each in our own region of mistake, continuously desired. The Devil has been fading lately, though despair is back, in our own way—and despair is very near me still as I write and pray. I ask from thee O Lord, strong and unconquerable love of the spirit, a flame of fusing, an eternal fire that the desire which came from thee may be accomplished by thee in us, forever.

Tormented by this struggle, Mary began to eat, comforting herself with oysters and cutlets, game pies, roast goose, rich steamed puddings and rum-soaked cake. She had always been plump, and enjoyed her food. She loved cheese and jam and

231

peaches especially, and the banquets at Lambeth offered untold temptations. Soon, the short Mrs Benson was edging towards twelve stone. To others she made light of this, recounting with amusement the denting of her dignity when, tagging along behind the royal procession to the opening of Tower Bridge in 1894, and feeling rather pleased with herself in her smart landau with its pair of black horses and bewigged coachman, she had heard a voice from the crowd cry out: ''Ullo! 'Ere comes the Queen's cook!'

Privately, Mary's intake of food began to distress her. 'I am prone to *excess*,' she confided to her diary, 'it isn't delicate flavour or exquisite cooking, but it is *quantity*.' She tried remedies of her own, such as cutting out biscuits (which led to binges of eight at a time), forswearing sweet fruits and eating meat instead, a vow in her diary *not* to eat more than two dishes at dinner, nor take sugar—followed by an entry, 'Soup, fish, pheasant and soufflé. What a Pig I am!' She tried Dr Nathaniel Yorke-Davies's new Stationary Diet, designed to keep patients at a steady weight, which was 'Again a hideous failure. I gave way at dinner, late too, just before cheese, and eat cheese and butter and reckless dessert, with my eyes open.'

Day after day, entry after entry, her 1896 diary records her shame and frustration: 'Bad, bad, and so I shall weigh this morning. I know I shall find my weight gone up, and I shall see my shame with my eyes.' She began to see her appetite as conjoined with other 'carnal affections', until the whole became a lumpen mass of guilt and self-reproach, compounded by further remorse at being obsessed by something as base and fleshly as mere food—

'this attraction of the flesh the garment I have to cast away—the carnal affection which must die in me—or must I put this away and let it go—this present state of things is just too grovelling—thinking abt food eternally, and breaking my resolutions'. On occasion, a solution presented itself. 'Today my sins have found me out and I am altogether livery bad,' Mary recorded one October morning, '*glad* to be puked up.' In other diary entries she refers more elliptically to, 'P. again, both last night and this morning,' or 'and P. too later on. This awful weakness makes me so ashamed and fearful.'

Some Symptoms of Bulimia

Bingeing that may alternate with fasting.
Purgative vomiting.
Constant preoccupation with food and dieting.
Self-disgust when too much has been eaten.
Mood-shifts including depression, self-hate and guilt.
Severe self criticism.
From twenty-first-century medical sources

Increasingly, Ben relied on Lucy for support—and felt guilty about that, too. She felt she lacked courage, she was fearful and constantly anxious. Anxiety was her 'deadliest and most constant foe . . . a sort of demon of fright', and 'I lean so much on Lucy—*how* to counteract this?' Yet of Lucy she writes: 'It remains for her to be strong and continuous in spirit, for me to be yielding and dependent.' For her part, Lucy could be just as ruling of Ben as Edward was—and just as with Edward in the early years of her marriage, Ben responded with petulance. 'She was didactic and I was unkind and hufty,' noted Ben, after one contretemps. Lucy could be searingly critical. The impetus behind Ben's starting her 1896 diary was to draw up a series of rules and resolutions for self-improvement. It was rather like the confessional journal she had written for Tan, with daily entries on the right-hand page, and corresponding prayers and missives to the Lord on the left. Within the first pages, under the heading 'Things to think of' she mournfully lists 'Lucy's complaints'. Among these are that Ben has no sympathy with the poor, or with Lucy's work among them; that she puts inconveniences to the family before the good of others; that she sets faults of temper too high and those of selfishness and extravagance too low; that she is contradictory and wants humility; and—in an eerie echo of those days at Wellington—that she lacks energy, reads too many novels, is self-indulgent and over-loving of comfort. The list goes on.

'Anxiety' featured prominently among Lucy's complaints, apparently caused by Mary's 'selfish dislike to *be* anxious and fear of personal discomforts'. Mary began to fret about being anxious. Fred was more sympathetic to his mother than was Lucy. He saw that there were 'times when the lights were low, times when the whirling wheels slowed down and halted', when Mary succumbed to the 'arch-enemy of her soul', a gripping, almost random dread: 'that ghostly enemy of hers, whom she was always trying to throttle, and who kept raising spectres for her, the grimness and unreality of which were truly surprising even to herself.' Sometimes her worries were so exaggerated as to be comic. She expected dreadful accidents, her loved-ones' corpses delivered to the door; she became convinced that she herself was going to die—on one occasion even setting a date, which resulted in the family initiating a daily countdown at teatime, intoning 'Nine days now', 'Eight days now' in sepulchral voices, until finally 'Today!' burst out amidst general hilarity.

Yet when really heavy blows fell, as on the deaths of Martin and Nellie, Mary remained clear, composed and strong, as if the succession of minor panics had merely been practice for the true trial. It was the day-to-day fears that crippled her, and through the summer of 1896, Fred noted, they became more chronic, the demon 'couched in the shadow . . . ever ready to pounce on her with claw and teeth'. Mary worried about Maggie's health and Arthur's depressions, about Fred's fecklessness and that Hugh was so rash, but most of all she was anxious about Edward. The depressions that had plagued him throughout their married life would infect her, too, and she would fret about him long after he had recovered his spring and vigour. She bore the brunt of his severity and dark moods, but for Mary self-denial had become a way of life. As Fred noticed, 'the primary desire of her heart was to give love', and that went for her children, for Lucy, and to an all-consuming extent for her husband, too.

Arthur and Fred Benson, in their own Middle Age, Reflect upon their Parents' Marriage

Arthur

I have been present at talks at Addington when Papa's hard displeasure about some trifle was intolerable. On the other hand I used to think at the Addington meals, that Mama was dextrous in reverting to subjects which always rubbed Papa up the wrong way. It was a case of real, natural incompatibility. Mama was an instinctive pagan, hence her charm. Papa was an instinctive puritan with a rebellious love of art. Papa on the whole hated and distrusted the people he didn't wholly approve of. Mama saw their faults and loved them. How very few friends Papa ever had. Some old ones like Bradshaw—sort of tradition, but how he drifted away from Bishop Wordsworth and John Wordsworth and Wilkinson. He disliked feeling people's superiority. His mind was better and stronger than his heart and his heart didn't keep his mind in check. It was a fine character, not a beautiful one. He certainly had a tendency to bully people as he believed from good motives. Mama never wanted to direct or interfere with people and I think was the most generous and disinterested character I have ever known. But her diary is very painful to me because it shows how little in common they had and how cruel he was.

Papa was a very difficult person to deal with, because he was terrifying, and remembered things, not very accurately, because he remembered the points which were in his favour and forgot the points which were not. Mama forgot everything, or if she remembered, forgot the sense of resentment. Then he wanted, as you say, obedience and enthusiasm. Mama never claimed either exactly, but got both. Then Papa cared intensely about details, and details never interested Mama; and one must remember, as you say, the other side— and Papa's affection, when it rose to the surface, was very revealing indeed.

From correspondence between the two
brothers in 1925

Edward wrote of the 'fearful blackness and whiteness and hardness and coldness' that curbed and checked him. He suffered from insomnia, sometimes sleeping only four hours or so each night. He worked ferociously hard at Lambeth, hankering after retreats to Addington—but his depressions once there, without work to occupy him, lasted longer and were more severe. At times, doctors confined him to bed, and he would lie, Arthur wrote, 'revolving many things and reviewing his own inadequacy, and the consequent downfall of the Church and the wreck of religion, till he was in complete despair'. Arthur felt that his father was unsuited to the role of Archbishop, that in accepting it he had yielded 'to what had always been a temptation of his, the love of ruling'. A successful archbishop should not only tolerate compromise, but embrace it enthusiastically. 'The note of the Primacy is sympathetic caution, and that was not by any means my father's ideal.' Edward's dissonance with the demands of his calling, Arthur thought, lay behind the bouts of neurasthenia that so paralysed him.

In America, neurasthenia was accepted as a condition that affected both men and women, but most British doctors considered it largely an affliction of the weaker sex. Whatever opinion his own physicians might have held, for Edward such debilitating nervous exhaustion took on moral overtones, going against every element of his belief in Muscular Christianity and manliness of spirit. Overwork and grief were more acceptable causes of nervous collapse, and both certainly held in Edward's case. In 1890, as Nellie lay dying, he was working on the most difficult single decision of his entire career: writing his judgement for the Lincoln Trial, the result of a bitter doctrinal conflict within the Church, centred on rituals practised by the Bishop of Lincoln which inclined to Catholicism. And just weeks after the judgement and Nellie's funeral, Edward's younger brother Christopher died in Wiesbaden.

Whereas Mary took her fears inward, or relied on her faith for strength, Edward's 'moods of depression and dark discouragement' fell like night on all about him, and 'required a buoyant vitality in his immediate circle'. His wife, especially, was expected to deliver unbounded adoration, cheer and support. Yet implore though Mary might, Edward would simply not listen, would not slow down or rest. At the end of July 1896, she persuaded him to see a doctor, in preparation for a visit to the Anglican Church of Ireland. The doctor diagnosed that the Archbishop's heart was 'weak and wanting in power', and advised rest before and after meals. 'He is furious and won't,' wrote Mary in her diary. He also refused to cut down on work or abandon the Irish tour.

Lucy did not come to Ireland. For some reason Mary did not want her to, and for once stood her ground against her friend. Alone with Edward, on an uncomfortable journey and with far too many daily appointments (Mary thought the Archbishop of Dublin a 'slave-driver') her day-to-day anxieties multiplied. Simply hearing him blow his nose would cause 'the cold hands to clutch'; the slightest hint of rain and she raised her own umbrella to protect him. Yet, at the age of sixty-seven, Edward seemed—despite a passing cold—not to have lost any of his drive. He relished the time in Ireland, met every part of his packed schedule, and remained full of vigour.

From Mrs Benson's Diary, Ireland,
September 1896

. . . this has been a dreadful time—my own shrinking from the nights has been terrible to me. There was no giving way on the other side, and with the help of God I must think it out— Soundly and in proportion . . . I have taken my resolve for this time—not, unless illness of any kind comes, to make any moan or any difficulty—*but for the future* what? God show me . . .

The Archbishop and Mrs Benson returned to England on 10 October, and travelled directly to Hawarden Castle, near Chester, to visit the Gladstones—something Edward had eagerly been looking forward to. As he sat working in the railway carriage on the way to Chester, Edward was so engrossed that he did not answer Mary when she asked if he wanted lunch. She did not ask a second time and remained hungry. They continued to Hawarden through gales and torrents of rain. Edward got his comeuppance when they arrived. They sat down immediately to tea, and Mr Gladstone, by now well into his eighties, held forth on the subject of a recent Papal Bull, which had denied the validity of Anglican holy orders, for a solid three-quarters of an hour, while the Archbishop (as was so often the case when in the presence of men of equal or superior intellectual stature) remained silent. He sat, teacup in hand, poised ready to take the first sip.

At dinner, Mrs Gladstone was dressed rather curiously 'as a bride, in a long white lace veil and a flowing lace robe'. The Archbishop sat between her and the Gladstones' daughter, Mary Drew, who was 'struck by his *wellness*', and they talked of Ireland, the Armenian massacres, and the Queen. Stimulated by the visit, Edward was still 'very bright and full of talk', when he went up to bed, keeping Mary awake until past midnight.

Next morning, the tempest had abated and Hawarden was blanketed in snow. Mary went with Edward and Mary Drew to early Communion. That day, down in Truro, the last service in the large wooden building that had been Edward's temporary cathedral was in progress. The new church was ready, and the big shed that had stood in for it was to be demolished. Over breakfast at Hawarden Castle, talk again turned to the Papal Bull, and before morning service, Edward slipped off to his dressing room to work, not noticing when Mary came up to check on him, and having to be hurried along so as not to be late. Mary and Mrs Gladstone walked on ahead. Mr Gladstone had a cold, and stayed at home. The Archbishop walked slowly with Mary Drew, resting frequently along the way. In church, he took the former Prime Minister's place alongside Mrs Gladstone. Standing for the Exhortation, he raised a hand to his eyes, looking up towards a window as if testing his sight. Kneeling for the Confession, he sunk, his head falling on his prayer book. During the Absolution several people came to his aid and carried him unconscious from the church. They laid his body on the sofa in the rectory library. Edward died before the service was over.

PART III

BEN

Chapter Thirteen

All day, Mrs Benson stayed at the Hawarden Rectory, as if she could not believe what had happened, nor could she pull herself away. Again and again she went into the library. Hawarden lay still under its blanket of new-fallen snow, but the sky was a hazy blue. The library blinds had not been closed, and sun soaked in through the windows. At last, in the evening, she went back up to the Castle. 'It was a soldier's death,' said Mr Gladstone to her. Mrs Gladstone offered a magnificently embroidered white pall for the coffin. Two years later, it would be used for the same purpose at the lying-in-state and funeral of her own husband.

At Addington, on Sunday afternoon, Fred was having tea with Beth. He had thought of joining his parents at Hawarden, but his old nurse had said: 'Nay, don't you go away today, you be here for when your Papa and Mama get back. Have a quiet Sunday, you and me.' A telegram arrived from Mrs Gladstone. It read: 'Your father passed over quite peacefully this morning. Can you come with Maggie?' At first, Fred thought Mrs Gladstone was merely telegraphing that his parents had arrived after a comfortable crossing from Ireland, but then the import of 'Can you come with Maggie' dawned on him. He could not get through to Chester that day, but spent the night in London and went up with his sister by an early train on Monday morning.

On receiving his telegram at Eton, Arthur, characteristically, turned his attention to himself and feared he was about to have a nervous breakdown. The fact that his presence was required to agree to funeral arrangements forced him to rally, and he, too, set off for Hawarden, meeting Hugh at Euston Station. Hugh said he felt 'as if the roof were gone'.

The Archbishop's body was taken in procession to the nearest station on Wednesday morning, and on to Canterbury to be buried. His funeral was held that Friday. In his will, which ran to a full 4,000 words, Edward showed his customary obsession with detail as he dispensed his worldly goods, down to the last silver cup, miniature, manuscript or print. His children were left £5,750 each, though Fred's sum was reduced by an amount equivalent to the value of objects he already made use of, and a codicil deprived Arthur of £1,000 for money his father had advanced him. Maggie received £500 more than her brothers. Any of Edward's effects or household items the children chose to keep, were to be valued and deducted from their share—except for Maggie, whose choices were to be her absolute property. Various relations and friends were rewarded with an engraving, a book, or some item of personal remembrance. Lucy Tait was among them—yet some of Edward's oldest and closest friends were ignored. The bulk of his books were to be divided between the Archbishop's Library at Lambeth Palace and any son who took holy orders. To his wife, Edward left £500 payable immediately upon his death, his clothes (customarily left to a butler or valet), wines and housekeeping provisions, and the residue of his estate after various gifts, bequests, and small legacies to servants had been made. At almost every mention of her name, he added the stipulation 'so long as she remains my widow', as if unable to relinquish control over her, even in death. To Wellington College, Truro Cathedral and the poor of Lambeth, the Archbishop left nothing at all.

Telegram from Her Majesty
Queen Victoria to Mrs Benson

I am stunned by the awful news. My heart bleeds for you; but my own sorrow is great, for I was so fond of the dear, kind, excellent Archbishop. A terrible loss to us all.

In an instant, the world in which Mary Benson had shone so brilliantly existed for her no longer. The 'necklace for glory & beauty' that had been her life at Lambeth had its string cut, and the beads were scattered, rolling far from reach. It was as if she had never imagined this moment, never prepared for it. The child-bride who had gradually forged a role and a meaning from her lot was, in the end, the Archbishop's wife, without precedence. All that had appeared to be hers, she had because of Edward. 'All the beauty of the past life together, the home we made, the dignity and glory of it, the fellowship and the humour, the conspiracies, the discussions, the beating keen pulsating life, the splendid web . . . All this is over, with one touch,' she wrote in her diary in November, and a few weeks later: 'All over—all over—rings in my ears.' 'The ship of my mother's purposes and activities in life slipped its moorings,' wrote Fred. 'It slid away from the busy quay-side and, as if grounding on some remote and barren shore, left her to disembark on an emptiness, a nothingness.'

The Archbishop's widow was also homeless. Back at Lambeth Palace, Lucy came to share the big carved wooden bed in which Ben had given birth to all her children, an arrangement that would last for the rest of Ben's life. Around them, the past was being put into packing cases. Ever since Ben and Edward married, they had lived in houses that were not their own, and Edward had never bought any property that might one day serve as a home. Yet the furniture and possessions had accumulated. The paintings and plate, the porcelain and engravings, the mahogany wardrobes and heavy carved tables had built up over the decades into a wealth of chattels sufficient to fill a palace. To fill two palaces. There were magnificent showpieces as well as much-loved stalwarts—the altar-panel sideboard from Wellington College, the comfortable ottoman, the bronzed dessert dishes from the working-men's bible class in Lincoln, the wheezy harmonium. All had to be removed within weeks, and the welfare of some thirty servants attended to.

Arthur retreated to Eton, still concerned for his state of mind. Hugh, now twenty-five, suffered a severe attack of rheumatism, and Maggie was expected at an archaeological dig in Egypt, long since arranged. It fell to Fred to dismantle the 'huge mournful house so lately humming' room by room until it 'lay moribund, with the last drops of its life-blood, as far as our family affairs went, dripping from it'. His mother, he wrote, was blank, numbed, as if in a trance—'Everything was over, and nothing new had yet begun.' Ben found her twenty-nine-year-old son 'as tender as a child, as loving and as strong as a husband, and as sensitive as a woman,' and was deeply touched when 'he told me one evening he could never marry he loved me too much'. Yet she remained strained and dislocated, unable to bring herself to dispose of furniture or even the smallest objects with associations of the past. It was decided that she and Lucy should go with Maggie to Egypt.

The party set off towards the end of November. Hugh, whose rheumatism made a winter in England inadvisable, followed shortly afterwards. Fred remained for a month to wind up family affairs, and then he joined them.

The women, with Hugh at their heels, crossed to Paris, then meandered down through Venice and on to Luxor. Maggie, who had bridled at the 'older sister' role her father had assigned to Lucy when Nellie died, was sourly jealous of Lucy's status as Ben's intimate and bedmate—but Egypt was *her* territory. There, Maggie was in her element, and with the other women feeling unsure of themselves in such a foreign country, she could assert a certain dominance. At the dig at the Temple of Mut, from the back of her large white donkey, jingling the piastres in her moneybags and with her faithful sidekick Mohammed panting along behind with a flywhisk, Maggie ruled over her workforce with the buffalo-hide whip and a few phrases of Arabic. She was already acquainted with regular visitors to Luxor and commanded a bemused respect among the male archaeologists. Back at Pagnon's Hotel she continued to play the priestess. She would dismiss

249

Ben's attempts at buying a scarab with a contemptuous: 'Forgery: mafish mish-mash', or urge the family into playing their old word games, while Lucy, not as quick as the others and unable to think of rhymes, fell asleep. Obediently, Ben and Lucy would follow to watch Maggie work the dig, or she would lead them on expeditions across the Nile and into the desert. Fred lost himself in his own archaeological projects. Hugh distressed his mother

Sketches from Hugh's Egyptian Diary: The Benson Family Caravan *and* Disembarking from the Steamer

by being 'curious & difficult & rude', or cheerfully went out shooting, returning with the occasional spoils of quail or a jackal. December unfolded into January.

Under her parasol at the dig, or in the hotel garden at Luxor, Ben pondered her life. For forty years she had devoted herself to Edward, abnegated her own desires to what Arthur called his father's 'ardent and emphatic personality', to 'his depressions, his impatience, his insistence on small details, his easily provoked discontent, the crushing character of his displeasure'. Edward had always been the centre and focus of all life about him. Ben's attention was concentrated on reassuring him, contriving for him, placating him, pleasing him. 'I had to originate nothing,' she noted in her diary in Luxor. 'I seem to have been only a series of respondings—and no core—but there *must* be a core . . .' Fred remarked of his mother that her devotion had been given solely to his father's convenience, and not to his work itself, that 'she had absolutely no individual life of her own: she had neither artistic nor literary taste that absorbed any part of her . . . All her enthusiasm and energy was at the service of others.' She had played the role of dutiful wife to extremity, and allowed her self to be pared away to nothing. 'There is nothing within, Good Lord,' Ben wrote, 'no power, no love, no desire—no initiative—he had it all and his life entirely dominated mine. Good Lord, Good Lord— give me a personality—break the cords a little . . . let me *live*.'

Yet what, Ben asked herself, was the next step? Something was required of her, but 'what is it? . . . What can I do? . . . this personality established,

251

this freedom given—what then? . . . *I have never had time to be responsible for my own life.* In a way I feel more grown up now than I ever have before—strange, when for the first time in my 55 years I am *answerable to nobody.* No-one has the right to censure my actions, and I can do what I like. What a tremendous choice!'

In capitals in her diary, Ben noted that she had lived all her life 'in FEAR', and that now she wanted to replace it 'with LOVE'. She even wondered whether she might not in this moment draw closer to Edward, as if the union that had not entirely worked on Earth might be repaired now that he was in Heaven. Ben had many a long talk with Lucy, who was often hard on her—as critical as Edward might have been—or would offer such maxims as 'Live from salvation not for it'. On some days she would feel uplifted by 'this sun, this air, these sunsets and glories of the sky', exclaiming 'Lord I want to live' or 'I desire *love & life*'. Yet on others the quest seemed hopeless, and she would feel 'all knocked to pieces', or 'entirely routed & defeated & undone'. She was over-eating, and began once again to worry about her diet. Soon, there were further troubles to concern her, and anxiety—that 'arch-enemy of her soul'—resumed its grip. In mid-February Hugh caught a slight chill. He recovered, and set off for Palestine alone. It then seemed that he had passed his cold on to Maggie, but she did not rally as quickly, and succumbed to an infection of the lungs. Her condition worsened, and the doctor diagnosed pleurisy.

After Maggie's lungs were drained, she began gradually to recover, but a few days later, on a Sunday morning, she was found in a faint, her face and hands tinged blue. She had suffered a heart attack. The doctor said bluntly that there was no hope. He had not reckoned on Maggie's steely will. As Ben and Fred sat at her bedside, Maggie drifted back into consciousness muttering 'Father, make me better,' and after a few minutes, 'I'm a little better,' and ten minutes later, quietly: 'I'm better, I'm better.' Within days she was well enough to be placed—bed and all—on a paddle steamer for Cairo. Luxor was growing too hot, and the family decided that a move to the genteel oasis of Helouan, near the capital, would aid Maggie's convalescence.

Fred went ahead on a faster boat to prepare the way, but when Ben arrived with Lucy and Maggie on the steamer, she was met by a messenger with the news that Mr Fred had been taken from his boat on a stretcher, directly to Helouan. He had caught typhoid, swimming in the Nile at Luxor while

Her Majesty Queen Victoria Celebrates Her Diamond Jubilee,
20 June 1897

Maggie was ill. To Ben it appeared that not only her husband, but two more of her children were to be taken from her, and then, just as Fred began to edge out of danger, Lucy fell ill with typhoid, too. She was so close to death that her sister Edith, wife of Randall Davidson (a Benson family friend, now Bishop of Winchester), was sent for. On 23 February, Ben wrote in her diary: 'Worse and worse—all is gone.' She scored a diagonal cross through the rest of the blank page, and did not pick up the diary again for months.

Lucy did recover, as did Fred, but Maggie, though much improved, was left with aggravated rheumatism. It was late April 1897 before Ben could at last leave Egypt. Any sense of the visit as a period of rest and renewal after the shock of Edward's death had long since crumbled. Fred went to Athens, then on to visit his ebullient bachelor friend John Ellingham Brooks on Capri; in the wake of the Oscar Wilde trial two years earlier the island had become a refuge for similar young Englishmen appreciative of the handsome and remarkably compliant populace, and eager to take advantage of Italian laws under which sodomy was not a crime. Maggie departed to soothe her aching joints in the waters of Aix. Ben and Lucy returned to England, to find somewhere to live.

Queen Victoria—to whom white-haired Ben was beginning to bear an uncanny resemblance—was concerned for the widow of her 'dear, kind, excellent' Archbishop. She discreetly enquired of the Bishop of Winchester, Randall Davidson (also quite a favourite of hers), whether Mrs Benson was

254

sufficiently provided for. After leaving Egypt, Ben and Lucy had gone to stay with the Davidsons at the Bishop's palace, Farnham Castle. The Bishop replied that though 'certainly not rich', Mrs Benson was reasonably comfortable, would continue to live with Lucy Tait, 'but where the home will be is not yet settled'. The Queen promptly offered the pair the use of the Royal Lodge in Windsor Park, and Princess Christian wrote to Ben to encourage her to accept, pointing out how convenient it would be to have Arthur so close at hand, at Eton. Arthur examined the Lodge, but pronounced it unsuitable—possibly because it needed modernizing and renovation, having been long unoccupied. Fred said that his mother baulked at the 'formidable dependence' that such a tenancy would imply. Ben respectfully declined the offer, and instead she and Lucy took a house in Winchester—a spacious early Georgian mansion, large enough for all the family at holiday-time, which Fred, when he arrived from Capri, found 'quite adorable'.

Winchester, an eager local lady told Ben, was so very varied in its society: 'There is the Close, Mrs Benson; there is the County; there is the College; there is the Military. It is quite a centre!' This was clearly no Lambeth. In Egypt, Ben had realized that she was now at liberty to do as she liked, and had foreseen tremendous choices, wanting to break the bonds and live. She relished the sense of 'affairs swiftly and ardently a-stir' around her. Instead, she found herself in a charming but essentially provincial town 'mediaeval in its setting and middle-aged in its actors', not juggling exciting new possibilities at all, rather mourning 'the cessation of magnificent stimulus'. The house on St Thomas Street, backing on to the Cathedral Close, was expensive, and although Lucy made a considerable financial contribution (further fanning Maggie's resentment of her), the cost precluded frequent trips up to London, or excessively lavish entertaining at home.

Fred returned to England to help with the move. During a particularly hot week in August, van after van brought furniture out of storage to Winchester, until at last—long after the house seemed as full as it could possibly be—a billiard table, the organ from the chapel at Addington, Maggie's statue of Rameses the Great, and a line of immense mahogany wardrobes, stood in a queue down St Thomas Street, as if awaiting admittance. Ben's grey parrot, Matilda, made the sounds of corks popping, as if to remind everyone of how thirsty they all were, while the green parrot, Joey, with his squawk of 'Isn't it Orfle!', and his fiendish hatred for people's fingers, punished the foreman severely for saying 'Poor Polly!' and giving him a friendly poke through the bars of his cage. Taffy, the Welsh collie, guarded the hallway and growled, and Maggie's big black Persian cat, Ra, stalked testily. The household's first visitor, a canon of the cathedral, arrived in the midst of this, unannounced and unheard, to be nipped on the ankle by Taffy, mauled for his friendly advances to Ra, and after negotiating a drawing room made almost impenetrable by excess furniture, to find Fred playing loudly on the piano, with Joey squawking on his shoulder. The Bensons were perhaps not made for Winchester.

Arthur, now in his mid-thirties, remained a master at Eton, where he was popular among boys in his house for the stories he made up for them. The father of one of his pupils told Ben that 'Arthur goes round every night and *tickles* all the boys, and shows them too how strong he is'. 'Doesn't it sound funny?' Ben observed. Arthur entertained literary ambitions, and was nurturing his friendship with Henry James. Hugh was curate in a village in Kent, but had some surprises in store for his mother as far as his religious inclinations went. Fred had published four more books after *Dodo*, with varying degrees of success, and his income from these together with his inheritance meant that he did not have to look for other employment. He came to St Thomas Street to live with Ben, Lucy and Maggie—and Nurse Beth, now nearly eighty and still devotedly part of the household; as well, at times, as Nettie Gourlay, whose passionate friendship with Maggie had continued since the first Egyptian trip. Although not initially sold on the idea of living in Winchester, Fred soon came to enjoy it, spending most of his time playing golf at the Country Club, or scooting up to London to revel with the smart set he knew there. Arthur, who was at first benignly admiring of his younger brother's ability to fit in with other people's plans and make the best of everything, began to mutter that Fred was too frivolous, and ought to 'go away and rough it for a year' in some job that would put a bit of fibre into him, such as being a newspaper correspondent.

A Letter from Henry James to Arthur Benson, Prior to a Visit to Eton

34 De Vere Gardens, W.

Thursday (Jan. 16, 1896)

My dear Arthur,

I am divided between 2 sensations—panting for tomorrow p.m. and blushing for all the hours of all the past days. I ought to have acknowledged your beautiful letter (after your last being here,) about—about everything. But I have been so taken up with living in the future and in the idea of answering you with impassioned lips ... [You] are not to worry in the faintest degree about the question of my conveyance to-morrow, meeting me, causing me to be met, or getting me over at all. I can with utter ease procure myself to be transported. I shall *come*—'that is all you know—and all you need to know.' *Voilà*. I shall in the meantime weave spells over your house and its inmates.

Yours almost uncontrollably
Henry James

A few of Ben's old circle—most notably the imperious Duchess of Bedford, and her sister Lady Henry Somerset—did visit, but life in Winchester went on in a low key. The Christmas of 1897 was largely a family occasion, although the vicar of

Addington was of the party (praying constantly that Arthur be ordained), as was a certain Miss Bramston. Ben had lost none of her abilities at forming rapid and devoted acquaintances, and the besotted Miss Bramston irritated everyone, Arthur in particular, sitting 'four square at tea like a penguin: she slops her tea about, grabs food, gazes at M.B. and takes no notice of anyone else. She walked with us to Cath. on Xmas Day, in ugly black clothes rudely cut with a large grey woollen shawl around her neck. She is shapeless and walks like a swan.'

At first, Ben found the sleepiness of Winchester calming. 'I seemed to *find myself*,' she noted in her diary, but occasional visits to London made her long for her old world, that 'beating keen pulsating life, the splendid web' which had once surrounded her. The sight of a woman riding in a carriage, splendid by comparison with her shoddy hired brougham; the talk from Court and Westminster now filtered to her through newspapers rather than directly conveyed; all helped to emphasize that she had fallen on the far side of the barrier that excludes the general public from the heart of things—but at least they were echoes of the past. When she returned to Winchester, Ben was doubly cast down by the staleness and mundanity of her life there, at the wittering chat of Close and County and College, or the supposedly thrilling occasion of a carriage ride across the Downs, of pinch-and-scrape dinners for four rather than banquets for dozens of the great and good. 'I sicken at all this everyday life, at the setting of it,' she exploded in her diary. 'Oh, the awful backwater this is!'

Ben set herself to read through Edward's letters and diaries, including the one dating from the year he proposed to her, which revealed 'that he chose me deliberately, as a child who was very fond of him and whom he might educate—he even wanted to preserve himself from errant fallings-in-love'. 'Oh God thou knowest how this has pierced,' wrote Ben in a despairing diary prayer. Not only was she forced to relive that 'terrible, difficult, amazing Rugby time', when as a child desperate to please she had been propelled into a situation where she 'could scarcely be said to have a choice of my own', but she began to question the forty-three years that followed it. Ben sank into deep, miserable introspection. A moment at William Gladstone's funeral, on 28 May 1898, drove the point home even more painfully. As Mrs Gladstone entered Westminster Abbey, supported by her sons, the entire congregation rose to its feet. That had not happened for Ben at Edward's service, and now she realized with a shock that '*I was not associated with him in people's minds*'. Apart from a very few, most of the old circle seemed indifferent to her after Edward's death, as if she, too, had died. '*His* friends did not and do not seek me,' she wrote. 'I think I had imagined they would take me as a *relic of him*.' All she had ever been, it seemed to Ben, was a pleasant hostess, yet though she had toiled to make herself agreeable to everyone around Edward, they had not wanted her '2d. agreeableness'; instead they wanted 'his massiveness, his large ideas, his power. *And I was never associated with these*.' She doubted that, after all these decades, she had 'any life of my own at the back' at all, was sickened by the thought that she was merely 'a ghost in a phantom world'.

Edward, Ben opined, had had *aims*—so many that there hadn't seemed any room for hers. Her role had merely been to make life pleasant for him. She thought, too, that she had 'no *honour*' from her children: '*They have aims, all* and have for so long regarded me as a person who kept things pleasantly going.' Now, they no longer took her seriously. And indeed what was she, after all these years? 'What can I do now? at 57 not very vigorous—having spent all my life in scrappy interruptions—small means— fat and ugly.'

Ben turned to Lucy for help, but Lucy often compounded Ben's feelings of self-doubt and worthlessness with harsh criticism. At times, it was as if with Lucy Ben was recreating another version of her marriage to Edward. Lucy even took Edward's side, criticizing Ben for want of sympathy, for not having entered into Edward's life, not caring for the things he loved. 'She says I have a way of disassociating people from their life and caring for them apart from it. She has often felt this and thinks that he did and that the *cause was the same.*' Lucy went on: it was the same with Nellie, too. Ben's failings as wife, mother, intimate were laid flatly before her. Later, she confided to a friend: 'I never really knew what depression was till '96.' In her diary she wrote: 'This flat dull leaden depression—what is right about it? It feels like a slow finding of one's level—and such a level!'

Adapting to widowhood, for Ben, also meant having to learn to economize—and she had never been much good at that. In at least one moment of economic crisis, she consulted Fred, 'who has taken it in a good masculine way' (which probably means he bailed her out). But Fred also contributed to the problem, as his lavish social life brought to St Thomas Street a stream of house guests with high expectations. At one point Ben, Lucy and Maggie (in a rare moment of unity) together demanded a dam to the flow, much to Fred's annoyance. 'I am *awfully* sorry about having made Fred low,' wrote Ben, 'I *hate* not falling in with any plan of his, but it's *economy* that sits beside me at bed and board—and so I fear our staff couldn't do it (and perhaps a secret thought that we can scarcely afford more guests than the ordinary spare room).' Ben began increasingly to find Fred 'captious' and 'contradictious', and he spent longer periods away from home, visiting friends or on the golf course. In her diary, she writes of him almost as a lover, regretting how detached from each other they are becoming, and asking God for 'insight and love and *attractiveness* and patience. How is it that we are so far apart! And yet Fred loves—and I love.' Ben thought her son was growing a little too uppity for his own good, too full of his success as a writer, but then she acknowledged that, as with her, life in Winchester was the problem.

It is all on so small a scale. He is awfully nice to me but we run dry in a few minutes, and in the drouth I hear my own silly words ringing in my own sad ear. I think the only thing would be to live with him, *alone*, for two or three months. I can't do it, and if I tried I shouldn't last out . . . Clearly this points to WIFE. Will it be?

Arthur was also on his mother's mind. He had written to Fred urging him to wed, as 'he is the only one of us four likely to. We are the only Bensons of our line left . . . we have struggled into a certain position and it would be pathetic if we died out just now.' Of Hugh, Arthur wrote that he did not have 'the slightest touch of sexual passion', that he liked his friends and loved children but 'shrank from women', a description Arthur might well have applied to himself. A decade or so earlier, Arthur had briefly wondered whether he might be able to fall in love with a certain Miss Erna Thomas. There had been rare, fleeting and largely theoretical thoughts of marriage at other times in his life, but he was happier developing robust friendships with his boys at Eton, or experiencing the 'indescribable thrill of romance and desire' of watching naked young men diving and playing in the river, or, while walking, glimpsing a favourite pupil through a window undressing by candlelight for bed. Such matters clearly remained unspoken between the brothers, or at least locked firmly in the rapidly filling cabinet containing aspects of Benson behaviour that were allowed their place in family life simply by being ignored. And Fred's heart, unfortunately for the Benson line, also lay elsewhere. By the spring of 1898 he was on an extended trip to Capri and Athens, where, Ben remarked, 'he found a little boy to play with—a nice young officer'.

Far more of a cause of anxiety to Ben than Fred's

contrariness was Maggie's behaviour—and Maggie was acting very strangely indeed. If Winchester was frustrating for Ben and Fred, it was crushing to Maggie, offering little to stimulate her formidable mind. With her rheumatism and weak heart confining her much of the time to the house in St Thomas Street and its small walled garden, Maggie set herself to writing an account of her Egyptian excavations, as well as a philosophical work, eventually to become *The Venture of Rational Faith*. Progress was slow. She also began to prepare for publication a treatise of her father's on the Book of Revelation, to which he had been putting finishing touches just before his death, and editing some addresses he had delivered at Lambeth. At the same time, she entered into intense correspondence with Arthur, who was writing the Archbishop's Life. The family noticed that the oddest change was coming over her, as if she were being possessed by Edward's spirit. As Maggie soaked herself in Edward's works, Fred observed, 'they gripped her mind. With the effect that his very personality, dominating and masterful, and his sense of responsibility for the spiritual strenuousness of those round him began to take possession of her.' It was, he thought, as if 'some masculine fibre had begun to assert itself in her'. Maggie attempted to exert strict rule over her mother, wanting to run the household herself, and, Fred noticed, 'into her nature there passed as well something of [Edward's] severity and of those moods of dark depression which sometimes obsessed him'.

Ben's liberation from the fetters of the previous forty years was sharply checked. 'There is in her displeasure,' Ben wrote in her diary of this force

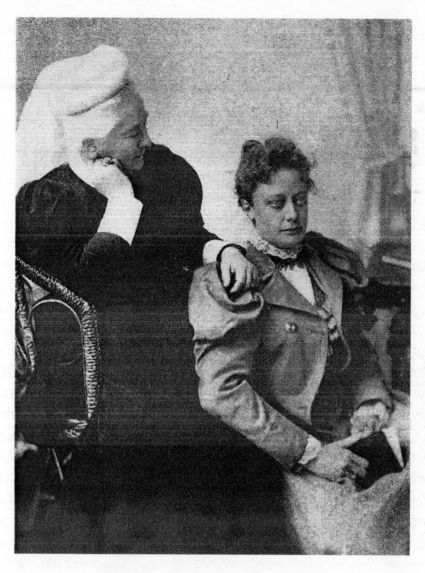

Mary Benson with Maggie in 1898

that had taken over her daughter, 'as there was in
her father's, a power of bringing one into
bondage—a dreadful fear—fear that one should be
displeasing her . . . that lapses or neglects . . . are
being added up against the cloudy and dark days'.
Ben could recognize this bondage, but found herself
unable to escape: 'O God what to do . . . how, O

Lord, to get a personality—the old cry. *Freedom* is so gone. . .' She caught herself once again acting 'in a sort of dull slave spirit', and saw life before her with 'a fettered sense of a long vista of slavery'.

Maggie's jealousy and resentment of Lucy now grew ferocious. Time and again in her diary, Ben writes of Maggie's fury, or gloom, or of her complaining of tiredness for days on end and then lapsing 'into silent depression only broken by some sharp sparring with Lucy'. Maggie complained of Lucy's role and influence in household affairs, insisting that Lucy occupied too much of Ben's time— *'day and night*, first thing in the morning last thing at night'— and that Lucy held too much sway over her. She picked fights with Lucy, and cornered Ben in 'horrible' or 'terrible' talks, accusing her of mouthing Lucy's opinions, of the two of them excluding her, of Ben's growing distant from her. Maggie became sulky and suspicious that Ben and Lucy were conspiring against her, complaining that her life was dull in comparison with theirs. She said she felt neglected, and that she hated Winchester. Most of all, she said she wanted *change*—and when Ben suggested she might find it by spending a week with Nettie Gourlay, Maggie interpreted the suggestion as a desire to get rid of her.

No shrinking violet, Lucy could spar quite as fiercely as Maggie, and even initiate her own skirmishes. Ben, ever the conciliator, tried a gentler approach. 'I thought that this time I would try to meet the attack cheerfully, I mean on my side,' she wrote after one outburst. 'I set before me this plan: To give no ground of offence by anything—not to be betrayed into a cross word . . . and to try and steady her conditions with my mind instead of feeling them with my nerves and heart.' The collapse of this plan left Ben flailing pathetically, during a dismally silent carriage ride with Maggie: 'O what a drive! She scarcely spoke and was most curt—I tried many subjects ... I asked her whether she was interested in Church Reform. "No," she said, "I'm not" so that ended it.' Ben found herself not mentioning letters she had received if Maggie wasn't mentioned in them, fearing an outburst, or not going to visit Hugh because Maggie wouldn't like it. Rarely did she retaliate in kind, although after one of Maggie's tirades on change, she was 'goaded into a most unwise word' and suggested that perhaps what Maggie wanted was change from Nettie Gourlay, but she 'took it back at once'. Into these toxic waters came Tan, Ben's old inamorata and mentor from Lincoln, though only for the briefest of visits. Perhaps Ben was seeking spiritual advice. The day was not a success. Maggie sat sullenly silent throughout a drive with Tan and Beth, too, and in the afternoon Lucy quite rudely insisted that Ben sit down with her to do the household accounts, leaving their guest to fend for herself.

By the beginning of 1898, the situation with Maggie had grown so fraught that Ben had called in the family doctor, Ross Todd (whom she affectionately nicknamed 'Toddles'). He advised a move to the country, to a house with large grounds so that Maggie need not feel cooped up by the restrictions placed on her by her weak heart— somewhere, given her inability to walk much, where she could stroll in more diverting surroundings than the walled-in garden at St Thomas Street. Ben's attitude to the countryside, according to Fred, inclined to Dr Johnson's view that one green field was much like another green field, and that a walk down Fleet Street was infinitely preferable. She regarded the prospect of exclusive country life 'with sheer blank dismay'. They had lived barely a year in Winchester, and Fred himself deeply disliked the idea of leaving.

As was so often the case with Benson family affairs, the question was not openly discussed, but 'began to ooze into the water-supply of domestic life, somehow hardening it and producing reticences and changes of subject'. Yet Ben's inclination to self-sacrifice was deeply ingrained. 'In the country she can have her sphere,' she said of Maggie. 'Something to look after. A sphere.' Once Ben had a catchword, ideas became more definite; a label made difficulties seem somehow more soluble. It was at this point that Fred fled to Athens. 'At the crucial moment EFB flies to Greece,' harrumphed Arthur to his diary, adding—unfairly, given his own disengagement from any family difficulties: 'His motto is anything to save trouble . . . Fred by golf and avoidance of all responsibility prolongs insouciance of youth longer than most people.' Ben and Lucy began to look for somewhere else to live. Arthur was furious: 'The entire decision has really been made by a hasty doctor humouring Maggie in a nervous and fanciful mood. And the painful sense remains in everybody's mind that all their wishes have been sacrificed to this. Either MB could have averted this by decision, or M herself by consideration.' Arthur even felt a twinge of sympathy for Fred, who although he had not liked the idea of Winchester at first had graciously gone along with it, and now 'just when he has got rooted, it is all pulled up and he has to start again'.

Money was once again an issue, especially as an idea had formed to take a little house in London in addition to a place in the country. It was put to Arthur that he might contribute financially and make the new country house his home. 'I fear I don't really want it,' he wrote in his diary, contemplating the idea of forsaking cosy Eton life to live with his family. 'I don't think I should do to live at home; we are all too much alike—too critical—too clever—all see what everyone is going to say before they open their mouths—I always get depressed there.' Fred was far more adapted to such a life, thought Arthur, as he 'can give way in trifles, is very companionable, easily amused, seldom depressed' and what was more, 'he understands women which I don't do'.

Houses were viewed, and rejected, in Basingstoke and Haslemere. Half-hearted efforts dragged on through the summer and autumn, though Lucy did find a London pied-à-terre, a little Queen Anne house at 5 Barton Street, just within the precincts of Westminster Abbey. By Christmas even Henry James had come to hear that all was not well with Ben and that she 'had some need of change of residence'. It was Lucy who, paging through *Country Life* one afternoon, finally found the house—largely Jacobean, part Carolean, with manageable acreage, a bowling green and cherry orchard, reached down an avenue of Scots pines, near the village of Horsted Keynes in Sussex. It was called Tremans.

In the spring of 1899, the removal men once again arrived at the house in St Thomas Street, to load

up Ben and Lucy's bed, the mahogany wardrobes, the comfortable ottoman and Addington chapel organ, the statue of Rameses the Great. Ben had just turned fifty-eight. She was moving into her final home. The twentieth century was about to begin.

Chapter Fourteen

Tremans—or Treemans, Tremaines or Treemaynes, as it had been known at various times in its history—was not thirty miles from London yet seemed remote from the world, like a spellbound house in a fairy tale. The countryside around it was furrowed into ridges, threaded by quiet streams, darkened by pine forest that melted into pasture and dipped into lonely valleys. A dusty road ran the mile or so from Horsted Keynes to the avenue of Scots pines that formed the approach, but the house itself was screened behind an immense and ancient yew hedge.

To one side of the firs, a bank of rosemary bushes, broom and peonies reached up to the bowling green, tussocky and long untended, but in the spring a ray of daffodils. Below it, at the end of the avenue, an iron gate between two high posts crowned with stone balls opened to a lawn, surrounded by beds that in their season bore begonias and scarlet salvias, pools of blue gentians and forget-me-nots. A pink rambler and purple clematis fought for supremacy over the pilasters of the gateway, and ivy crept between bricks of the old stone wall that protected the kitchen garden from chill north winds. Over the wall, beyond knots of fragrant herbs, meadowy grassland ran down to a cherry orchard and a chain of little fish-ponds.

271

Tremans

Woodpeckers nested in the orchard, pheasants on the bowling green; great tits pecked about the stone walls, robins peeped from the hedges, at night owls hooted, it seemed, from every copse and crevice.

The house itself was a tumble of styles— Elizabethan brickwork, Jacobean outgrowths, a dignified Carolean façade that rose through three storeys of expansive windows, topped by a little cupola. A fantastical array of mismatched chimneys sprouted from roofs at different levels. Tremans was ample, impressive, and possessed of extraordinary allure. 'It doesn't seem like a place to live in, but a place to go and see,' said Beth.

Three curved stone steps climbed from the front lawn to a large door, but by the time Ben and Lucy took Tremans, the main entrance had been moved to a more convenient door, around the corner of a

Tremans

little Elizabethan promontory, flanked by a stone-walled wing with mullioned windows. Inside, the house was low-ceilinged with wood-panelled parlours, its rooms faintly fragrant of woodsmoke in winter and lilac in summer, most with big tiled fireplaces bearing Tudor mouldings. The wide oak staircase was so seasoned that no creak ever betrayed a passing foot; smaller stairways ran hither and thither, to airy attics, turning odd corners, rising and dipping, some ending almost where they had begun. There were sitting rooms and anterooms, recesses, cupboards and bedrooms a-plenty; it was a house 'full of lobbies and useless spaces and little mysteries, strange lofts and obscure passages'. Yet even here, the family furniture of four decades and the *objets* that Edward had accumulated filled the place to the brim.

273

8 July 1899

The monument to Archbishop Benson was unveiled today by HRH The Duchess of Albany at Canterbury Cathedral. The fine Gothic design is by Mr T. G. Jackson R.A. and the figure by Mr Thomas Brock R.A. It was a day of sweltering heat, made even more intense by flashes of magnesium from photographers' flares. The station was lined with red carpeting and an escort of lancers met Her Royal Highness, who was representing Her Majesty The Queen. Thirty bishops were present. During the ceremony, thunder boomed and rumbled like a bourdon pedal. Hailstones fell, as big as eggs. There were addresses by the Lord Chancellor and Lord Mount Edgcombe. Mrs Benson prayed alone on the steps of the monument, and was then presented to Her Royal Highness, who held both her hands in hers and talked quietly for some moments. Then the Archbishop of York read a lesson, and while he was so doing there came a terrific peal of thunder and a great rumbling in the roof, followed by a cataract of water. The Cathedral had been struck by lightning.

Arthur, who had absented himself from the fuss and difficulties of both house-hunting and the move, came down to Tremans from Eton in July, and was plunged at his first sight of it into 'speechless delight'. He was captivated, he wrote in his diary, by its very *Englishness*. There was something in its manor-house grandeur that made Tremans an appropriate seat for a family of the status he felt the Bensons had attained—though the socially conscious Arthur admitted sorrowfully to himself: 'We have got a middle-class taint about us. We are none of us aristocrats in any way.'

The house was large and expensive to run. Lucy helped Ben bear the cost of the lease, and Arthur and Fred also augmented her funds, financial support that grew burdensome as time went on—their mother never having quite gained the knack of economical living. Lucy adored Tremans from the start, and she was 'invigorated by village life and country people'. Hugh also took to the house immediately, though his early engagement with local life, while on a visit with a fellow clergyman (also in his thirties), went no further than buying pea-shooters and peas at the village shop, and spending the evening shooting down corks on the lawn. Beth was installed in a room in the attic furnished with remnants from the Wellington College nursery and hung with pictures of her boys, Master Arthur, Master Fred and especially Master Hugh (they were never 'Mr' to Beth). From here she made occasional forays to supervise the folding of the linen, or—with no babies to nurse—to carry Maggie's Persian cat Persis, like an infant on one arm. Children who visited Tremans, often taken by Maggie to see if there were fairies near the fish-ponds, marvelled also at 'a visit to that realest fairy of all—old Beth the fairy nurse, with her snow-white hair and twinkling black eyes which saw everything, old Beth who lived in a room upstairs, and . . . who was of fabulous age'.

For Ben, moving to Tremans was indeed an act of self-sacrifice. Life was even quieter than it had been in Winchester; she longed for the city and, unlike Lucy, was neither invigorated nor revivified by what the countryside had to offer. Even Hugh noticed. 'The world is divided into two classes,' he wrote in a letter to a friend, 'those who like people and those who like things. It has come to us as a good classification at home. My mother yearns continually for town, and loves eleven hundred people; and all the rest of us love the country, and cocks and hens, and small events on the lawn like the dog digging a hole, and discuss them as if they were the pivots on which the world moved.' When Ben told one friend that she had settled at Horsted Keynes, she received a shocked response: 'What have you *done*?'

Ben far preferred the little London house that Lucy had rented in Barton Street. It was tiny—the whole of it would have gone into one tower at Lambeth Palace, but, 'I feel at home in it,' she wrote to Maggie, while up in town. 'I *LOVE* the surroundings. I feel we are in exactly the spot—in the heart of *real* London . . . The Abbey has become our Chapel.' The move to Tremans had been made entirely for Maggie's sake but she was determined to 'throw myself into Tremaines [*sic*]' and to make it a success. 'I am full of hope and heart, and please God we will have a dear time there and love the place well,' she said to Maggie, before they moved. Even stronger than her own disaffection with country life, Ben knew, was

Fred's. On the day she signed the lease for Tremans, she confessed in her diary: 'I feel deeply heavy hearted for down at bottom lies the deep sadness that Fred is not with us in all this.' After Edward died, Fred had promised to live with her, but he would not be happy, she felt, with 'no-one about and no amusement and no employment'.

She was right. Fred was miserable at Tremans. The nearest golf course was a seven-mile cycle ride away, life at home proceeded with somnambulant routine, entirely in the company of women. As Fred put it: 'I wanted golf and games and ease and casual intercourse with those of my own sex.' 'Fred hates it,' Ben exclaimed. 'One day's loneliness makes him capricious.' Fred raged and moped in his room. He lasted four weeks. Finally, Ben wrote, 'Fred's depression, culminating in such awful gloom . . . gave me the courage of despair to write him an exhaustive letter setting him free, body and spirit and financially.' As was so often the case, a family difficulty was tackled avoiding face-to-face confrontation. Ben released Fred from his promise to live with her. He promptly rented a flat in Oxford Street, coming to Tremans at weekends. Once the pressure was off, and Fred could—as his mother put it—spend time 'playing with his Earls and Countesses', he, too, became better disposed towards Tremans, and far more than the house on St Thomas Street had ever been, Tremans took on the mantle of a family home. 'I never knew a house with so friendly an air,' wrote Arthur. 'It seemed like a joyful mother of children, glad to enfold us.'

The Hero of A. C. Benson's Novel
The House of Quiet *Describes his Family Home,*
Golden End
An ancient manor reached down an avenue of
great Scots pines

The house seen, as I love best to see it, from the avenue on a winter evening, rises a dark irregular pile, crowned with a cupola and the massive chimneys against a green and liquid sky, in which trembles a single star . . . Within all is dark and low . . . There are wide, meaningless corridors with steps up and down that connect the wings with the central building . . . my father was a great collector of books, china and pictures, which, with the furniture of a large London house, were put hurriedly in, with little attempt at order; and no one has since troubled to arrange them . . . below the stairs is a tiny oratory, with an altar and some seats, where the household assemble every morning for a few prayers, and together sing an artless hymn.

The Narrator of R. H. (Hugh) Benson's
Novel The Necromancers *Describes the*
Large House with Twisted Chimneys at
the Heart of the Tale
It is occupied by an elderly widow, her son
and her daughter Maggie

The house, in fact, was one of those that have a personality as marked and as mysterious as of a human character. It affected people in

278

quite an extraordinary way. It took charge of the casual guest, entertained and soothed and sometimes silenced him; and it cast upon all who lived in it an enchantment at once inexplicable and delightful ... Maggie had fallen in love with the place from the instant that she had entered it ... There was here a sense of peace and sheltered security that she had hardly known even at school; and little by little she had settled down here ... with the leisurely, tender life of this place, where it was so easy to read and pray and possess her soul in peace.

Maggie blossomed at Tremans. She had a beautiful room on the first floor, panelled at one end, with a huge cupboard behind the panelling and with quaint recesses in the walls, but she spent most of her time in the garden. 'That invincible mind of hers, which had barely dragged itself along under the weight of infirmities and depressions at Winchester, shook off the dust and soared,' wrote Fred. 'The keen, kind air which in the heat was bracing, and brisk in the cold, was exactly what her body needed.' Just as Ben had forecast, Maggie prospered once she had a 'sphere'. She had in no way lost the aura of being possessed by Edward's spirit, but her drive to dominate and control found an outlet—at least in the beginning—in organizing life outdoors, and Ben was happy to let her take the reins. Maggie mapped flowerbeds and planted bulbs, designed a sundial as well as a rotating summerhouse that could be turned from wind and sun; she painted a shield for the iron gate and had an oak pediment built to shelter the front door.

Always fond of animals, she established hens and cinnamon turkeys, pigeons and peafowl, and wrote a series of musings about her charges, published as *The Soul of a Cat, and Other Stories* in 1901. She took holidays with Nettie Gourlay—whom Fred found 'one of the most silent of human beings and quite imperturbable'—and Nettie in turn spent weeks on end at Tremans.

Taking her new energies further afield, Maggie established—with the help of another close friend, Gladys Bevan—the St Paul's Association, a bible-study society for women, in London, and together with the authorities at King's College there arranged theological lectures for women. She turned to her writing with renewed enthusiasm, working again on *The Venture of Rational Faith*. While she was doing so, she kept all her other activities in hand by (Ben observed) becoming 'very good at using help . . . she could keep several people employed—it was like the Japanese plate trick—as many as seven volunteers could be kept going, and each revived with a smart touch when flagging'. In the winter of 1900–1, Maggie was thought sufficiently recovered to be able to return for some weeks to Egypt, together with Nettie and her Aunt Henry Sidgwick. She relaxed her antagonism to Lucy, sharing her love for Tremans and the countryside, and she became more easy-going with Ben.

A Scrap, on Tremans Writing Paper,
Dated 10 January 1900

I, Margaret Benson, in full possession of my faculties do hereby declare that for the future, I will go to bed at an Earlier Stage of a really bad cold, especially if Influenza is about—and this I acknowledge to my wise and doting Mother and in conjunction with her

Signed
Margaret Benson

In the midst of her Winchester depression, Ben had written in her diary that the previous forty years of her life were a completed tapestry, and of her determination to fashion the new length put into her hands 'into a garment of praise, not into a cowl of heaviness'. At Tremans she set about doing that, becoming—in Fred's words—'the whole spirit and inspiration of the place'. Yet her impact was a subtle one. As her children progressed through adulthood, making their very individual marks on the world, she took a quiet role in the background. As Arthur put it, his mother had always 'evoked rather than dazzled', and nowhere was that more true than at Tremans.

Ben's instinct for spiritual survival was strong. The outward Christian conventions were there—family prayers with the servants, twice daily in the little downstairs oratory off the hall (curiously, also sanctuary to the statue of Rameses the Great)—but it was the idiosyncratic faith she had begun to fashion for herself in Lincoln, her conviction that 'Love is God', that sustained her. To a friend she once wrote: 'Faith is not a bundle of mere spiritual truths, but a *condition of the soul* which I should describe as eternal life.' Elizabeth Wordsworth, who had been so irritated by the young Mary Benson, thought that 'it was not perhaps till after her widowhood that the full beauty of her character came out'.

Ben's own sitting room at Tremans was a low-panelled one near the front door, with two windows overlooking the lawn, decorated with some of her favourite pictures. She had a bookcase of her most-loved works, and the well-worn comfortable ottoman—two seats of which were by now entirely unapproachable—against one wall. Behind her own writing chair was an armchair for a visitor, and in one corner stood 'a sort of blasted tree' for Joey, the vicious green parrot, who perched on her shoulder whistling his only tune ('Pop Goes the Weasel') or laughing hoarsely in her ear as she saw to her letters, and pulled out her hairpins. Joey adored Ben blindly, attacking invaders of her bower in insane rage—Beth did not like him at all, as he was 'not kind and loving', a description, observed Fred 'which but faintly expressed his satanic nature'.

Ben and Lucy's bedroom, over the dining room, boasted an enormous fireplace, its fireback representing a chariot and horses, the charioteer in a flying robe. Each morning at seven o'clock, Lucy read to Ben from the Bible, in such a voice that every vowel could be heard at the other side of the house. Such mighty resonance was possibly employed because Ben was going deaf, though Arthur noted that even in church Lucy responded as though she were talking into a telephone (he had first seen one being used at Windsor Castle: 'it is *very* funny to hear this done'). Ben, by contrast, had two tones in prayer, one as if she were telling a ghost story, the other as if she were wheedling with a cat. A little later in the morning, it was Ben's voice that filtered through the corridors, as she sang a hymn accompanied by the old Addington chapel organ, at household prayers in the downstairs oratory—a good octave lower than the pure contralto she had once been—while half-muffled stentorian tones came from above, as those sons too sluggish of spirit to join her, carolled from their beds.

Arthur was the most reluctant to join in, not through laziness but from a growing antagonism to the rituals and paraphernalia of orthodox Christianity. Ben's insistence on compline—communal prayers before bed—riled him the most, 'the discomfort, the silly idiotic responses, the false sociability of it all'. He baulked, too, at matins in the village church: 'I get no good out of such a service, I fear; no good at all . . . To sit in silent rows, like sheep in pens, and to cry out suddenly at once, words that we are not thinking about, like ducks in a pool. How very odd it must seem to God that we should think that we please him so.' Ben, whose own rocky religious path gave her every sympathy for scepticism, had lost none of her motherly 'tac'.

'Are you coming to church, Arthur?' she asked one Sunday, noticing he wasn't quite dressed for the purpose.

'Would you like me to go?'

'I should like you to like to go, but I don't want you to go because you think I should like you to go.'

Breakfast, when the 'boys' were at Tremans, was a staggered affair, as they wandered down at all hours of the morning. Ben breakfasted early, then saw to her correspondence, sorting it into piles on little black leather boards with legends embossed in gold letters, *Unanswered, Secretary, Destroy*.

Arthur suggested there should be one for *Unreceived Letters*, for those that were difficult or dangerous to answer. Next, she fell to a detailed reading of the newspapers, but all this was interspersed with many short walks, usually with Lucy, and in all weathers, even though her joints were beginning to ache. Undeterred when local gamekeepers put a wattle fence across a track that led through some exceptionally good woodland cover, Ben bought a small tool-chest with saw, mallet and chisel, and together with Lucy reasserted her right of way by destroying the barrier. Repeatedly. She made one or two overtures towards joining local committees, gave bible-classes in Horsted Keynes, and visited distressed families, but charity and good works in the village were more Lucy's realm. However, Ben did once serve single-handedly as the 'Orchestra' when Lucy held a tea dance on the lawn.

London was closer than it had been from Winchester, with a railway station easily reached at Horsted Keynes. There were numerous trips to the little house on Barton Street, and—after Lucy's brother-in-law Randall Davidson was himself elevated from Bishop of Winchester to become Archbishop of Canterbury in 1903—nights spent, once again, at Lambeth Palace. The Davidsons came down every summer for long stays in the country. Visitors arrived at Tremans in droves—in 1901 alone, sixty people signed the visitors' book, and that was by no means a remarkable year. Ben's old friends the Duchess of Bedford and Lady Henry Somerset were there frequently, and Ethel Smyth dropped by. Tan came down from Lincoln to stay from time to time. Ben's favourite brother, Henry Sidgwick, died in 1900, but Ben was close friends with his widow Eleanor ('Aunt Nora', the sister of A. J. Balfour, who became Prime Minister in 1902). She, too, was a regular visitor. She had been Principal of Newnham College at Cambridge, and played a leading role in the Society for Psychical Research, which Henry had helped found. Freed from Edward's disapproval (at least in a corporeal sense) Ben renewed her interest in the occult—to the clear disapproval of Randall Davidson. A visiting medium determined that Tremans was haunted, and saw dwarfish figures dressed in brown running nimbly around table legs in the upstairs parlour. Ben took to visiting a spiritualist in Croydon, who after one séance walked back with her to the station and described Edward walking to one side (apparently indulgent of Ben's dabbling), Hugh's spirit guide—a French abbé, wearing his name and the date 1732 on a label— between them, and Zola, the French writer, in front.

Cousins of Lucy's came to Tremans, too—tall, effusive, and a touch vulgar. They called her 'Loo' and showed their uvulas when they laughed. There were also new friends, including the usual sprinkling of ladies besotted with Ben, such as a Miss Frere, of whom Arthur's somewhat irritated recollection was of 'an ear and the rim of a cheek, her face being set towards Jerusalem—i.e. M.B.'. All ended up in long conversations with Ben, on the lawn or at the fireside. A young American friend of Arthur's, expecting a dowdy and austere hostess, was agreeably surprised. 'But it's astonishing!' he said to Arthur in the smoking room. 'Here is your mother, living in a remote country place, getting on in years, who has all the freshness of youth, has everybody and everything at her fingers' ends, and holds her own in argument from American politics to Greek metaphysics—and what is more keeps a poetical touch on life all the time. How is it done?' The young man may, though, have been the same American who persisted in cornering Ben and whose ceaseless stream of talk made her feel 'as if I had been listening to bagpipes for a week'.

Without its visitors (even, much of the time, with them) Tremans remained a house of women—Ben and Lucy in their big mahogany bed, Maggie in her room with quaint recesses; often Nettie, too, on one of her long visits, and Beth in her room in the attic, from which, as time went on, now often fretful and tearful, she seldom stirred. Into this well of oestrogen—for weekends, on holiday, to write books—came Ben's sons, hardly renowned for their excess of testosterone, and they frequently brought guests of their own. These friends were, as Fred put it, a most heterogeneous collection. Hugh produced some rather strange visitors, clerics, mostly, with the oddest habits of behaviour. Arthur brought denizens of his literary world—Percy Lubbock and the writer and critic Edmund Gosse, both of whom became his lifelong friends. There was an Eton colleague, the 'picturesque' H. E. Luxmoore, 'in a low collar and Liberty-fabric tie, knickerbockers, and stockings that showed his small feet and, in the evening, a brown velvet dinner-jacket', and later a Cambridge undergraduate George Mallory, eventually famous for tackling Mount Everest, but then a sublimely decorative young man, much captivated by Arthur. Ben developed a discreet passion for the delicately featured youth. 'Mr Mallory is here,' she wrote once to Hugh, 'such a dear boy looking so absolutely young—and Oh isn't he "pretty"! I like him immensely but I want to call him by his Christian name, and don't know it—and Arthur is so exquisitely polite to him, that if I did, I mightn't dare to use it.'

Fred brought a series of comparably decorative young men, often someone no one had seen or heard of before, generally very much younger than he and flattered by a famous novelist's attentions; one such was Wilfred Coleridge, a descendent of the poet, just eighteen and fresh out of Eton. 'He is a cheerful creature,' said Arthur, 'not very attractive, with an odd rather assured manner; he admires Fred devotedly, and Fred seems to have an affection for him, half paternal half sentimental. He is always with him and yet seems to snub him a good deal in a jovial way.' Fred's young men and Arthur's young men, if they were at Tremans simultaneously, appear to have had little to do with each other, and between the brothers, what Arthur once termed 'the homo sexual question' was simply not discussed—not, at least, until some decades later.

In addition to his alluring friends, Fred embarked upon a series of handsome young valets, much to Ben's disapproval, as she thought he was getting above his station. 'A footman! My! That's his Lady Charles,' she quipped, referring to one of

287

Fred's London 'Earls and Countesses', Lady Charles Beresford. More seriously, she commented: 'His manservant really sticks in my throat . . . A strong young man, with all his income to make should scarcely go about with a man do you think.' Fred had to ask Mrs Moss the cook to teach the first of his valets, Sidney, some simple breakfast dishes, though breakfast-making skills might have been expected to be a prerequisite of the young man's profession.

*Fred Recollects the Conversational Flow
of Lady Charles Beresford,
once the focus of a great Society scandal and in
later life renowned for her auburn wig, pink-
blancmange dress sense and startlingly haphazard
make-up, with clouds of face powder and
eyebrows in unexpected places*

I've read the manuscript you sent me. Where are my dogs? Blackie, come here at once, and don't make nuptials with Orange among the petunias. I read it in bed last night, and Blackie was lying on my chest, so that when I giggled he fell off . . . The turquoise brooch? No, don't bother: they'll find it. Let's have lunch . . . Did you go to the opera last night? Tristan: such a bore! And the love-duet! it was time for their golden wedding before they got to the end . . . Yes: Tristan! How marvellous! Why does nobody love like that now? and for heaven's sake let's go in out of this awful sun. It ought to be electric light. Where is Orange? . . . Have you seen Maisie? I am told she has gone into deep mourning over Tim's death like a widow. Of course everybody knew, but she needn't remind them: so silly to dot the i's when the man's dead, and the i's have all been dotted again and again already. But crape, swathed in crape, like a crow, and almost tumbling out of her box last night at the Liebestod . . .

When Arthur, Fred or Hugh were down at Tremans, afternoon walks and cycle tours stretched farther afield. After Arthur took to motoring, he would bowl them all across the countryside in his car, then send Ben and Maggie (who despite her recovery could still not walk very far) on ahead with the driver; meanwhile he, Lucy and whoever else had been persuaded to come took a brisk hike through the countryside, to be met some miles later in time to drive home in the magnificent green motor for the sacred hour of tea, at five o'clock. With the family at home, evenings were taken up with whist, parlour games and '*fine* arguments'. The old word and literary games resurfaced. One evening Maggie read out a gentle satire on Lucy, Fred a parody of Keats, Ben a funny essay on growing old, and Hugh a series of nightmarish adventures that recalled the gory stories he had told as a child. Even Lucy contributed a poem of her own. Ben, who had once shared an evil-smelling pipe with Fred, and sometimes had a cigarette with Hugh or Fred after dinner, out of sight of Lucy who disapproved of smoking quite as fiercely as Edward had, also composed a little verse poking fun at Fred's habit.

To Whom Did Fred Write After Dinner?
A poem by Mary Benson

Mysterious, secret, dark as night—
The names of all his friends.
He only says 'I go to write',
And there my knowledge ends.
I pry not, I—I only feel
Whenever he comes back O!
That through his letters loudly peal
The pleasures of Tobacco.

Family talk of an evening was, Arthur noted, 'remarkably good—very brisk, humorous, fanciful; and even serious. Arguments are sustained with force and ingenuity ... It might appear forced and smart, like the crackling of thorns. But perhaps it is saved from that by a vein of poetry. Lucy talks less than we do: but argues with greater tenacity; and her laugh is delightful.' Lucy had, Arthur noted elsewhere, 'great and gentle decisiveness ... a pleasant touch of amicable combativeness, and a firm grasp of practical issues'. Maggie may have found a new 'sphere' outdoors, and Ben might be the animating spirit of Tremans, but Lucy ran life there, and held sway over Ben.

The old Queen died in 1901, and the dissipated Prince of Wales—dubbed 'Edward the Caresser' by some in his private circle —succeeded her as King Edward VII, ending a long and noisy wait in the wings. 'Most people pray to the Eternal Father,' he had quipped, 'but I am the only one afflicted with an Eternal Mother.' Arthur thought the new monarch 'bourgeois, ungraceful, small-minded, gross' and said caustically of the Coronation that it 'was to the King, I fear, the Apotheosis of Buttons not the consecration of life to service'. The tone at Court changed quickly. Attending a special command performance at Windsor Castle of J. M. Barrie's comedy *Quality Street*, in 1902, Arthur observed that the old Victorian atmosphere had gone completely. 'It is much more genial, considerate, *equal*—it lacks the grim and ugly stateliness of the old time; but it also lacks dignity. When it was said that the Queen is coming—that she wd receive, courtiers ran about like frightened hens— and were horribly afraid of her, knowing she would notice everything. Now, no one could be exactly *afraid* of the King!' Not just the Court, but the country as a whole was undergoing a massive shift of gear. A long and (to the British) surprisingly difficult war against the Boers in South Africa had unsettled

A Visit to Tremans

Lucy	Archbishop	Mrs Mary	Arthur	Beth
Tait	Davidson	Davidson	Benson	Benson

firm convictions of imperial might. Women were becoming increasingly vociferous in demanding the vote. Money was beginning to barge ahead of breeding in the corridors of power. It was an age of millionaires, Arthur conceded to the Duchess of Bedford in a conversation at Tremans, with the old despots being replaced by a 'tyranny of wealth', and to many the new King epitomized the brash new times.

These swirling currents of change swept past Tremans. Ben regretted this, but was not sufficiently fired by any fervour of her own to involve herself in politics. 'How the Political Situation thickens,' she wrote to Hugh during a period of worker unrest and a government crisis. 'I wish I was in the middle of it all—or at any rate were Watching on a Hill with a Staff and having messages coming and going.' Ben had loved talking with politicians, but she remained disengaged from politics. She was in touch, but old-fashioned—and conservatively disapproving of Ethel Smyth's increasing involvement with the movement for women's suffrage. Ethel, who was to compose 'The March of the Women', the anthem of the Suffragette Movement, argued fiercely with Ben on the subject—on one occasion, in the little revolving summerhouse, growing so vehement on the Church's attitude to the struggle that she felt moved later to write to Ben and apologize. This drew a characteristic response: 'Now you speak of it I *do* remember a few stormy moments in the Shelter that day, but my dear, you never *were* given to understatement, were you?'

Arthur was moving in increasingly grand social circles. Gruff and more reticent than his sparkling socialite younger brother, Arthur was nevertheless charming company, and had inherited Ben's genius at conversation, 'keeping the stickiest ball nimbly rolling, with the effect that the rest of the talkers got the encouraging impression that they were in peculiarly good form themselves'. After one especially stimulating Windsor lunch party, Arthur had been taken up by Lady Ponsonby, wife of Sir Henry Ponsonby, Queen Victoria's private secretary, who had effected all manner of influential introductions. The young Duke of Albany, the Queen's grandson, was entered for Arthur's house at Eton in 1894, and Arthur had been drawn into his mother the Duchess's inner circle. Throughout the 1890s, Arthur published small volumes of verse, and within time he was accepted as an unofficial Poet Laureate to the Court at Windsor, the work of the official incumbent Alfred Austin being so awful that even the Queen and the then Prince of Wales could tell. When Edward Elgar adapted part of his *Pomp and Circumstance March No. 1* into the finale of a Coronation Ode for Edward VII, the King himself suggested that Arthur should come up with some words. Arthur rather disarmed the composer during one requested rewrite by complaining that the metre was a difficult one, and suggesting that if Elgar 'could string a few nonsense words just to show me how you would like them to run I would construct it, following the air closely'. Nevertheless, words and tune proved immediately popular, becoming—and remaining—a second national anthem. 'Land of Hope and Glory' received its premiere at a concert performance at Covent Garden in 1902, sung by the redoubtable Clara Butt, whose voice at times rolled down the slopes of rich contralto into a deeply impressive baritone.

In the summer of 1903, Arthur was invited to assist Viscount Esher in the editing of Queen Victoria's letters. The following year he left Eton for Cambridge, where he had been offered a fellowship at Magdalene College, to concentrate on the Queen's letters, on his poetry, and on writing biographies and novels. Leaving Eton brought him a freedom he had yearned for. 'I should like to make some younger friends,' he had written in his diary in January, 'in a way which is impossible when one is in authority over them. But one schemes and schemes.' For Arthur, fulfilled desire lay behind glass. His emotions were tightly held back, kept in 'a carefully locked and guarded strong room' to which he barely had entry himself. He had been brought up, he thought, 'to regard all sexual relations as being rather detestable in their very nature, a thing *per se* to be ashamed of', regretted that he had 'never been in vital touch with anyone—never either fought anyone, or kissed anyone'. He lived 'on the edge of life; on the green margin', the eternal observer, ever 'on the edge of Paradise and never quite finding the way in'.

Arthur Benson Views Paradise

. . . while on an evening walk at Eton
Such a little picture coming back: the lane was still as death, fragrant and cool. Impey's house loomed up, mostly dark. There was a window lighted up, full of flowers: the room inside still: but just as I came past there came a boy in a nightgown to the window with a candle, put it down; and began to move the flowers, smiling. It seemed so strange to see this, hung like a

The 'Boys' at Tremans

| *Arthur,* | *Hugh,* | *Fred* |
| *Aged Fifty-One* | *Aged Forty-Two* | *Aged Forty-Six* |

picture, high in the air: like a window opened to heaven; and yet he was so unconscious that anyone saw him, down in the dark. And then came a further surprise, of which I will not speak, but which I shall not easily forget.

... *on a summer's day in Cambridge*

The flash of the naked body of a bather, up by Byron's Pool, across the meadow grass and among the trees gave me an indescribable thrill of romance and desire. Winterbottom looked in, very gracious and smiling; and I nearly gave way to a somewhat sentimental impulse; but did not, and left the words unuttered. I have a strong feeling that one must not be silly in friendship—and yet one loses many beautiful things so; if only one could just be natural!

... *yet cannot reach it*

Watching two poor lady-birds, who are perambulating the window, one inside one outside, stopping to make signals, and bewildered that they can't touch the little body that is so close, just beneath their feet. That is a parable.

From A. C. Benson's Novel Beside Still Waters

He could clasp hands with another soul, he could step pleasantly and congenially through the anterooms and corridors of friendship; but as soon as the great door that led to the inner rooms of the house came in sight, a certain coldness and shamefacedness held him back; the hand was dropped, the expected word unspoken.

[He] found himself with a great number of close friends, and without a single intimate one. He had never bared his heart to another, he had never seen another heart bare before his eyes. He had never let himself go.

Fred, meanwhile, was glittering in London, turning out books at a rate. In 1900 he had used Arthur's standing with Henry James to elicit an invitation to visit James at home, at Lamb House, in Rye. Afterwards, James wrote to Arthur: 'Your brother Fred *is* personal, and I found him a very interesting, charming, acute and observant youth—modern highly, as you say; with only (it's my own criticism) a tendency to place Golf too high in his intellectual interests.' Fred had, the venerable author noted drily, a great 'affinity with town', but he was glad to see that the young man had 'work to his hand there'—and indeed Fred did. In the first years of the new century he produced book after commercially successful book, including such novels as *The Challoners*—about an imperious, overmastering clergyman who checks the 'innocent and sunny impulses of joy' in his child-bride and terrorizes his children. He wrote it in three weeks, and it sold over 10,000 copies within a year.

Ben adored Fred's wit, shrugged off his flippancy, enjoyed his stories from town. He remained her favourite, now that his flat on Oxford Street (and later a little house in Chelsea) had eased the tensions of living at Tremans—in addition to siphoning off some of the excess furniture. Maggie

297

was happy, Arthur well-placed and Fred a tremendous success. It was Hugh's turn to cause his mother concern.

Hugh had long been drifting towards Rome, and his approach accelerated considerably once his father was dead. While Ben was still in Winchester, Hugh had left his curacy in Kent to join the monastic Community of the Resurrection, founded by the theologically controversial Canon Gore, at Mirfield, in Yorkshire. The fraternity was celibate, lived under common rule and with a common purse. Hugh clashed furiously with his father's successor, Archbishop Temple, over the decision. Even Beth was perturbed that the 'greedy things' would run off with Master Hugh's socks and vests in their fervour for communal property. Ben knew that any attempt to restrain her impulsive, headstrong youngest son would simply lead to further foot-stomping, and remarked, 'he has acted so hastily that to do anything [to prevent him] is almost impossible now ... I feel that we mustn't give him the idea of a wilful boy thwarted.' Soon after the move to Tremans, Hugh left Mirfield, spending long periods with them in Sussex and in 1903 publishing his own first book, *The Light Invisible*, a series of short stories centred on an old Roman Catholic priest. By July of that year, after three months at Tremans and many a long conversation with Ben, Hugh went to a Dominican convent in Gloucestershire to put himself under instruction for the Roman Catholic Church. In September he travelled to the College of San Silvestro in Rome. After nine months there— during which he managed to pick up not one word of Italian—Hugh was ordained as a Roman Catholic priest.

The voluntary submission of the son of an Archbishop of Canterbury to (in the phrase of one early Anglican litany) 'the Bishop of Rome and all his detestable enormities' caused something of a scandal among readers of the *Church Times*, but Ben, who had known religious crises of her own, and whose overriding impulse was love for those around her, in preference to any broader theoretical, theological or social concern, stood behind Hugh, despite her own feelings of 'special sadness'. Besides, experience had taught her that opposition to the unbending Hugh served only to exaggerate his wayward behaviour. She had long talks with him while he made his decision, but once he was ordained wrote: 'We know you are ours still, and nothing will ever shake that fundamental blessed reality of love . . . you know now where your heart feels you can be truly loyal, where it finds its home, where you deeply feel God has led you. . . only *let us in*, always, whenever you rightly can—my heart cries out for that.' Arthur was not as tolerant, snorting that Hugh had acted on a whim, in a light-hearted and self-absorbed way, 'like a child flying a kite', and that the one thing he wanted was 'authority and the luxury of not having to make up a confused and not very profound mind'. He noted that Hugh still loved dressing up and wore his biretta all day long. Ethel Smyth, who had never liked the boy and had been irritated by the way he swept around Lambeth in a long coat as his father's chaplain, observed that 'it was a relief to think of him safe in a cassock', while Arthur's friend H. E. Luxmoore (he of the knickerbockers and brown velvet dinner-jacket) was unimpressed—even by Hugh's official purple trim when he was eventually made a Monsignor—

declaring that he was just the same 'sharp insignificant little scug as he had been at Eton'.

Talk at Tremans when Hugh was present was apt to flare into vehement rows. The family, Fred noted, 'required little provocation to be argumentative', but even so it was impossible to be silent in response to Hugh's dogmatic, often ill-thought-out pronouncements, or the arrogantly dismissive 'But I belong to a Church that happens to know'. Even the preternaturally silent Nettie was sometimes moved to say 'Rubbish!' under her breath. Lucy brought her own line of smug superiority to the fray, which exacerbated the situation. Ben listened quietly and threw water on white-hot fury with a 'Dear me, how pleasant it is to hear young people talk!' (slightly misquoting Mrs Vincy in *Middlemarch*)—at which point her progeny would reconcile temporarily to fall upon her for flippancy.

Hugh appropriated another attic room at Tremans for a Roman Catholic chapel, painting the windows with images of saints (visible to tradesmen, and known in the village as 'Mrs Benson's Dolls'). Here he said Mass every morning, and conducted other offices during the day. He sought out a little server, a village boy, and went on long walks with him once religious duties had been seen to. Hugh tore about Tremans, a tornado in cassock and tippet, rushed into breakfast, ripped open his mail, rattled through stories (often profane) with his staccato stammer, shrieked with laughter at his own jokes, and once offered an alarmed Anglican cleric some newly arrived communion wafers to taste, smacking his lips and saying they were delicious. (The wafers were not as yet consecrated, but the visitor was horrified nonetheless.) In his quieter moments he set about

300

writing polemical Catholic novels, with such titles as *Come Rack! Come Rope!*, *The Winnowing*, and *Confessions of a Convert*. In 1905, Hugh moved to Cambridge, to work for the university's Roman Catholic chaplaincy—with such startling success that complaints about his proselytizing were soon being made to Arthur at Magdalene. Later, he took to public preaching, achieving popularity across Britain and in tours through the USA. When he preached, Hugh's histrionic daily energy was channelled into high melodrama and his stammer entirely disappeared. He became the Mrs Patrick Campbell of the pulpit.

Father Hugh Benson is Encountered
Preaching at the Church of San Silvestro
in Rome
By Robert Hichens, who once as a young man in
Egypt was so enamoured of Fred Benson's tan
and wit

In the pulpit ... he was, I thought, startlingly sensational. His changes of voice were so abrupt as to be alarming. But even more surprising were his movements of body. Sometimes he would suddenly lower his voice and simultaneously shrink down in the pulpit until only his head and face were visible to the congregation. Then he would raise his voice almost to a shriek and, like a figure in a Punch and Judy show, dart up diagonally and lean over the pulpit edge until one almost feared that he would tumble out of it and land sprawling among his fascinated, yet apprehensive hearers below.

I have in my time heard a good many preachers, both English and foreign. . . But Father Benson surpassed them all in exaggerated emotionalism of manner and voice . . . he almost stupefied me on that occasion . . . I have heard him called dramatic. I thought him melodramatic.

Hugh wrote his books, Fred said, 'in furious haste' with a 'terrifying fecundity', surely a case of the pot calling the kettle black. Arthur, too, was able to spin phrases with astonishing celerity—an Ode for the *Eton Chronicle* in ten minutes, two hymns for the confirmation of Prince Leopold of Battenberg while on the train from London to Horsted Keynes, entire books at a rate of tens of thousands of words a month, as well as some three thousand letters a year and a diary that eventually ran to over four million words.

At Tremans, Arthur sat every day, for the hours between tea and dinner, in an armchair in his room, writing on a board placed on his knees and dropping completed sheets—neither reread nor corrected—into a basket at his side, ready for the typist. Much of this activity went into producing what Fred described as 'those reflective volumes by which he was now getting so widely known', books that brought 'guidance and uplift' to their readers, but which were 'deplored by those friends who saw his humour, his critical incisiveness, his keen intellectual interests unused or unexercised' in a stream of works which they judged to be 'wholly unworthy of his gifts'. Literary friends pronounced the writing as vapid, silly and fatuous. Henry James had praised the 'charm' and 'loveability' of Arthur's early verse, but wrote to him that he felt 'a certain desire to screw you up just a peg higher. . . to make you squeeze your subject just a little tighter—press on it with a harder thumb', criticism that held even more true of these later works. Even Arthur felt that his mind was 'wanting in grip', and noted that his books went 'straight to the heart of a few hundred of the unctuous and sentimental middle-class'. Yet these sweet, anodyne works of comforting commonplaces, with such titles as *Through a College Window, The Thread of Gold* and *Thy Rod and Thy Staff* attracted a devoted following—including large numbers of importunate widows and spinsters, to each of whose letters Arthur diligently replied. It was almost, Fred said, as if his brother had two personalities with no single connecting point between them—the incisive, genial, intellectual side, and this tender, tranquillizing personality that wrote books as if by dictation without pause for thought. Arthur himself admitted: 'In my books I am solemn, sweet, refined; in real life I am rather vehement, sharp, contemptuous and a busy mocker.' Yet the books brought in a healthy income, and Arthur continued to publish prolifically. In 1906, *Punch* ran a cartoon in its 'Signs of the Times' series, with the caption 'Self-denial week: Mr A. C. Benson refrains from publishing a book.'

Punch's satire could quite easily have been directed at any one of Arthur's productive siblings. Maggie once joked in a letter to Hugh, 'I think it's hard that with 3 brothers there should be nary a new book ready for me this week', but commented more seriously to Ben, 'the real difficulty is that none of the Benson Bros. *can* stop writing. They are like the wild huntsman.'

Ben once observed that writing was 'the one solace of a Benson under all difficulties'. Since their childhood days, when fearsome Papa might be subject to the odd sting in the family magazine, Benson tensions, contradictions and perplexities—both awkwardnesses between themselves, and those personal vexations that tugged inwardly—had been deflected into the written word. The Benson mind, Arthur wrote once, 'naturally thinks that anything which concerns itself is of the nature of a national crisis and a local convulsion. It is all lit up in a kind of golden glory, and the actors have tongues of fire on their heads.' As the boys grew older, this eloquent and dedicated self-absorption was becoming mightily profitable. The 'odd outburst of books', Maggie wrote to Arthur, 'in an unmarrying family is better than marriage'. Unlike marriage, which loosened bonds between siblings, her brothers' writing drew them closer, because it gave her an insight into their personalities she would otherwise not have had. 'One gets to know you in a double way, by a sort of second channel,' she wrote to Arthur, adding that through Hugh's and Arthur's books, she came to understand a part of them that 'could not and should not be too much expressed in daily life, but which enlightens us all'.

In the bookcase in her sitting room at Tremans, Ben had an Arthur shelf, a Fred shelf and a Hugh shelf, guarding the contents fiercely, never lending them out. That is not to say, Fred noted, that the books gave her any joy at all. She was a severe and candid critic of her sons' work. Fred was convinced that she never read any of it twice, nor would have read much of it once had they not written it: 'She liked "bits" in most volumes of this library, but not one spark of inspiration, not one crumb of the bread of life, did she find in any of them.' Arthur, too, acknowledged Ben as his 'most trusted and eager critic', one who had 'a remarkable perception for what was otiose, inappropriate or disproportioned', who might praise certain passages, but who 'laid her fingers infallibly on weaker episodes'. She told him more than once that she did not feel him to be altogether behind his books. Ben dismissed Arthur's sentimentality, and berated Fred's superficiality, claiming that the latter did not apply himself to his writing with his full capabilities. There she had a point. Fred became the most frequently cited author in early editions of H. W. Fowler's *The King's English*, in the 'Antics' chapter of the Style section, under such headings as 'Intrusive smartness', 'The determined picturesque' and 'Patronizing superiority expressed by describing simple things in long words'. About Fred's novel *The Money Market* (which he himself had admitted was 'twaddle'), Ben was scathing, saying that it was amusing, but light, and though she had been swimming along reading it, suddenly 'a thumping impossible incident (of the usual worst order) cuts clean across all the weavings of character and is followed by equally impossible mawkish sentimental Christian forgiveness'. It all rang false, she went on, was not true to real human nature, only to the superficial world he had sketched: 'I am rather tired of smart people and should have liked him to have struck a deeper vein.' Ben's critique bore weight with her sons. The prolific Arthur paid her the ultimate compliment and 'suppressed half a dozen books out of deference to her views', an impressive tally given the rarity of such restraint on his part.

Ben was not the only family critic. One evening, when all three brothers were at Tremans, working on books, someone suggested they suspend their literary labours and that each attempt a parody of one of the others. 'This was a congenial job,' noted Fred, for though these three men took their work very seriously, 'there was not a vestige of mutual admiration between them, and they thought it would be pleasant to give frank expression to the lack of it.' So like three Cains, each prepared to murder an Abel. Ben 'much looked forward to this feast of fraternal candour'.

Arthur had to read Hugh's mystical religious novel *The Light Invisible* before he could begin his task. He composed a piece about a saintly Roman Catholic priest, who took surreptitious sips of port while sitting in his parlour communing with the Unseen; or doddered about the garden recounting such clairvoyant spiritual experiences as his vision of a woman dressed in blue with stars in her hair, standing by a rosemary bush. 'She smiled and vanished, so it was not difficult to guess who *she* was.' Arthur was so overcome by mirth as he read that his eyes streamed and he had to wipe his spectacles, and Ben laughed 'helplessly and hopelessly, with her face all screwed up', though Hugh sat puzzled and enquiring, smiling politely.

Next, Fred tackled Arthur, with a story of 'a wise patient wistful middle-aged gentleman called Geoffrey', who 'sate' (an irritating anachronism, favoured by both Arthur and his father) by his mullioned window, looked out at meadows and wild flowers, and mused—at length—about his gardener being rude to him. Geoffrey wondered how people could be so discourteous in a world where a Divine

Hand had scattered such loveliness, mused again, tranquilly, on his own boyhood, and (inspired by a hymn the gardener was whistling) on how he and the gardener would both one day face the great mystery of death. Then, instead of dismissing the gardener, Geoffrey called him to the window where he sate, and thanked him for the lesson his whistling had imparted, and the two sang the final verse together. Once again, Ben was reduced to helpless giggles—while Arthur sat (or sate) frosty, looking pained.

Next came Hugh, on Fred, with a composition full of babbling puppets whose inane, inconsequent talk had no individuality at all—one which, Fred thought, missed the mark entirely, while Ben and the others were convulsed. 'Oh you clever people!' said Ben when it was all over. 'Why don't you all for the future write each other's books instead of your own? You do them much better. Give me all those stories. I shall read them when I feel depressed.'

In 1904, Chatto & Windus published a book entitled *Hadrian the Seventh* by one Frederick Rolfe, the self-styled Baron Corvo, in which the protagonist rises from a life of obscurity and literary poverty to become Pope. It was a work of fantasized autobiography, of outrageous wish fulfilment liberally laced with venom, as a man pitted against the world trounces his enemies. Rolfe furiously—and eloquently—poured vitriol on the hierarchy of the Holy Roman Church, who had thwarted his own attempts to become a priest, while maintaining a fervent, if somewhat recondite, Catholicism. (He circumvented the Church's snub by abbreviating his first name to Fr.) Shatteringly arrogant, Rolfe sustained a supreme self-belief in the face of public indifference to his work, scathing criticism in the press, and the betrayal he eventually perceived in almost anyone who dared befriend him. Generally in a state of abject poverty, he did battle by letter with publishers he thought had cheated him, and in turn implored money of friends, or hailed abuse upon them, with accusations of perfidy and deception. In 1908, he moved to Venice, where he alternated between being lauded in palazzos and sleeping rough. In certain circles he developed some renown for the introductions he could make to sexually obliging adolescent boys there, and for the extraordinarily vivid letters he wrote describing his own encounters.

Hugh read *Hadrian the Seventh* in February 1905, and was entranced. He wrote to Rolfe, declaring his admiration, saying it was impossible to express how much pleasure the book had given him, and that he had read it three times. He said it was brilliant, and put it among the three books from which he wished never to be separated. A correspondence ensued which grew more intimate and frequent, with each writing to the other almost daily. In August, Hugh suggested a walking tour—starting out from Cambridge with one or two shirts, a toothbrush and a breviary, eating where they could and staying in out-of-the-way inns in any village where a 'mass house' was available. The tour was such a success that it was immediately followed by an invitation to Tremans.

The whole family was at Tremans that summer. Fred (with hindsight) wrote of Rolfe as 'picturesque and depraved and devil-ridden'. Arthur took against the man instantly. He thought him sinister, felt he brooded over the house 'like the spirit over chaos'. Rolfe was badly dressed, as well as wearing enormous rings, and managed to make Arthur feel constantly ill-tempered, despite (or perhaps because of) all they might have found they had in common. This bespectacled, long-nosed, priest-like visitor was, Arthur harrumphed to his diary, 'very silent and deaf at dinner; but not in the least shy or humble or conciliatory. I discovered, by his talk in the chain-room, while we smoked, that he was a great egotist and fancied himself a great writer.' He was relieved when Rolfe left.

Hugh had departed in a fit of pique at what he saw as his family's rejection of his new friend. Once again, it was up to Ben to restore the peace, with her customary tactful turn of phrase. 'You haven't got it at all right abt Mr Rolfe,' she wrote to Hugh. 'I should like to see more of him very much—it wasn't a fair seeing of him with the unsympathetic element of Arthur's mind. Not that Arthur wasn't quite nice, but a mind which works in such a very different manner introduces an element not favourable to unfettered talk.'

For a while it looked as if another visit was in the offing. Hugh and Rolfe decided to collaborate on 'a really startling novel' about St Thomas à Becket. The project went horribly awry when Hugh's agent and publisher advised against an association with Rolfe's name on the title page. Relations between the two men spiralled downwards, finally to shatter into fragments of Rolfeian abuse that continued (often publicly) for years.

Frederick Rolfe Paints a Picture of his
Former Friend and Collaborator,
Father Hugh Benson, in his Novel The Desire
and Pursuit of the Whole

The Reverend Bobugo Bonsen was a stuttering little Chrysostom of a priest, with the Cambridge manners of a Vaughan's dove, the face of the Mad Hatter out of *Alice in Wonderland*, and the figure of an Etonian who painfully neglects to take any pains at all with his temple of the Holy Ghost but wears paper collars and a black straw alpine hat. . . By sensational novel-writing [his formula was Begin-so-that-you-must-go-on-till-there-is-nothing-left-for-you-to-do-but-to-end-with-a-Bang-(for choice)-of-the slammed-door-of-a-Carthusian-convent-behind-your hero], and by perfervid preaching, he made enough money to buy a country-place. . . He did not exactly aspire to actual creation: but he certainly nourished the notion that several serious mistakes had resulted from his absence during the events described in the first chapter of Genesis.

Apart from the momentary shudder caused by Rolfe's visit, the summer of 1905 was a happy one. These were halcyon days at Tremans, with all the family often there. Arthur seemed to speak for them all when he wrote that the old house offered a 'perpetual feast of little, simple, ancient homely beauties: always waiting at every turn; never flaunted. The quiet, the twitter of the birds, the rustle of trees, the green hills and woods in all directions: make it the very sweetest home imaginable.' The world shrank around Tremans; the life of its inhabitants was painted in watercolours, with small strokes. At the end of December 1905, Maggie wrote to a friend of a busy—even chaotic—morning:

8.30. Mother came in, before going to London with Lucy for the day.

9. Beth, conversation about shortcomings of the cook, especially what was done with some sausages.

10.15. While I had my hair done, my mother's maid came in much gloom about the Stool-ball [an old Sussex game] Club's entertainment.

10.30. Coachman. Acute crisis about new horse. Then to cook with tactful and leading questions and suggestions.

11. To Arthur and my aunt, when there came a stream of telegrams so that the boy who brought one carried away four, and another arrived directly after.

11.45. Began my book; fire, sofa and bedroom.

11.50. Nurse for an interview, in the middle of which came Arthur about a book. Back to my room and book.

12.15. Midday letters. Horse crisis more acute; up to Arthur about the other book, and back to my room.

12.30. My aunt to say one telegram hadn't gone, consequent rush downstairs. Back to book and room.

12.45. Stool-ball entertainment crisis more acute. Back to book. Then a message from the cook.

1. Beth to say she wouldn't interrupt me. Back

311

to book till 1.20—and then there's the gong for lunch.

And since then another telegram; and the blacksmith's daughter on the Stool-ball Club crisis. I fear I do rather waste time in small ways!

Maggie had been happy during her first years at Tremans, much occupied with her new outdoor 'sphere', even largely at peace with Lucy in their mutual love for the place. But tending poultry, coping with crises about horses and organizing village amusements were pitiful occupations for a mind like hers. Their petty distractions could only temporarily deflect the forces that had begun to create cracks at Winchester. The forces regathered. By 1906 they threatened an implosion.

Chapter Fifteen

In 1906 Ben turned sixty-five and Lucy fifty; Maggie and Nettie were in their early forties, while Beth had reached the grand old age of eighty-eight. Anyone staying at Tremans, Fred wrote, even an intimate friend, would see only an ideal seemliness and tranquillity, 'a widowed mother and her daughter living each with the friend of her heart in a beautiful house in great comfort'. But beneath this placid surface welled a 'profound disturbance'. The first signs were subtle. Maggie was restless, her jealousy of Lucy rekindled; once again she grew certain her mother had turned against her. She was sullen with Ben; little frays with Lucy became more frequent. Maggie wanted a Penzance hedge, perhaps, in front of the tiled sitting-out place in the garden. Lucy thought that that would cut off the view of the South Downs. Maggie bridled, but at a glance from Ben, Lucy said no more, instead rather agreed about starting some ducks, as the weedy pond near the stable-yard seemed destined for them.

Slowly the Winchester strains resurfaced. Maggie was still, painstakingly, working on *The Venture of Rational Faith*, but day-to-day life at Tremans induced a depressed listlessness in her. 'I have given up chasing turkeys, and am gradually

313

giving up fussing about anything,' Maggie wrote to her friend Gladys Bevan in August 1906. Some weeks earlier she had said that there was really 'nothing the matter except tiredness. I *am* a little tired still. In fact I feel I shall have to relinquish a good deal a certain tattered remnant of pride that I retain.' To Nettie she had once blamed her moods on fatigue: 'It's odd, when one gets tired, the way in which vague fears and depressions and feelings of powerlessness. . . come dimly back, just the way clouds grow and fade on a hot day.' In the summer of 1906 the clouds of fears, depressions and feelings of powerlessness did not fade but gathered, darkly. Maggie and Ben had deep, difficult conversations.

Maggie became convinced that Ben and Lucy were trying to exclude her. These feelings had never entirely disappeared after Winchester. To Ben, they seemed to have caused Maggie to inhabit a world of unreality. Even in 1902, Ben had felt the need to write to her: 'My dear and Precious Person. . . I feel as if you were wandering further and further in some strange region and my voice can't reach you. But it SHALL. It seems as if you were following a mirage and I love you far too well not to try and tear you back. . . *You know in your soul that you have been mistaken in your idea of me.*' Maggie insisted that she did not judge, but she could be every bit as censorious as Edward had been—perhaps even more so. 'I never knew anyone judge more rapidly, promptly and without appeal,' Ben wrote to her. Maggie herself acknowledged that she lacked 'elasticity', yet sensed that the daily round at Tremans was doing little to help her: 'I think one gets less elastic when

314

one can't escape by activities from the circle of oneself.' She laid her accusations before Ben— that Ben cared nothing for her, that she was subservient to Lucy, that Lucy was trying to oust them all. Like Edward, Maggie demanded Ben's love, yet was coldly domineering, at times attempting to exercise the power of an authoritarian patriarch, then making a more subtle bid for control with the demands for attention of an invalid child.

Once again, Ben was in bondage, and not only to Maggie. Lucy, too, was controlling, and something of a bully. 'Last night,' Ben wrote in her diary, in the midst of Maggie's illness, 'something prompted me to ask Lucy whether she considered me a grumbler. She said very promptly, "Yes." I asked, "Let 20 be the maximum grumbler, what mark do you give me?" and she answered "15". . . There is all told. She tried to water it down, but it was a facer.' There follow pages of the same analysis of her own faults and self-blame that Edward once induced. Although Maggie's claim that Tremans was 'a *republic*, but that Lucy was dictator!' might be seen as part of her jealous imaginings, yet there was truth in it. Lucy could be combative, smugly convinced that she was right, holier-than-thou in all her good works, certainly holier-than-the-Benson-brood. She would frequently interrupt people as they began to talk, riding them down—and Ben would retreat mildly, as had been her habit of more than forty years. After one 'militant conversation' with Ben and Lucy, Arthur noted in his diary:

The fact really is that Lucy, who is very strong and unimaginative and good-

315

humoured, has a subtle effect. She has been *everything* to Mama, and I am everlastingly grateful to her—but I think she has really rather broken us up as a family. She *disapproves* of us all, for various reasons, and is quite unable to see another point of view. It is she, I think, who is really the provocative element.

Later, he was even more forthright:

She is the evil genius of the family. I think it is she who has done most to disintegrate us. She doesn't assert herself, she just goes her own way.

Maggie's condition worsened during the summer. She began to get into 'fusses about detail, paroxysms of anxiety', felt like 'a piece of old and frayed elastic', as if a shadow were creeping over her mind. She tried to strangle herself with a piece of string. She set her bedroom curtains alight. One morning, the day after a long talk in which Maggie had revealed to Ben how she longed for her motherly love and kisses as of old, Ben went in to see her (Maggie had taken to breakfasting in bed) and found her almost paralysed by depression, in a state Ben recognized only too well from her years with Edward. She asked Maggie what the matter was. 'Oh, I am killing it!' came the perplexing reply. At the end of August it was decided that Maggie and Nettie should go to Cornwall for a month, for Maggie to rest and recuperate.

*An Intelligent Woman, Frustrated by the
Inactivity Forced upon her by her Gender, is
Taken to a Country House for a Rest-Cure
Following a Nervous Collapse,
but has disturbing experiences there*

If a physician of high standing, and one's husband, assures friends and relatives that there is really nothing the matter with one but temporary nervous depression—a slight hysterical tendency—what is one to do?. . . So I take phosphates or phosphites—whichever it is, and tonics, and journeys, and air, and exercise, and am absolutely forbidden to 'work' until I am well again.

Personally I disagree with their ideas.

Personally, I believe that congenial work, with excitement and change, would do me good. [. . .]

The paint and paper [in the bedroom] look as if a boys' school had used it. . . I never saw a worse paper in my life.

One of those sprawling flamboyant patterns committing every artistic sin.

It is dull enough to confuse the eye in following, pronounced enough to constantly irritate and provoke study, and when you follow the lame uncertain curves for a little distance they suddenly commit suicide— plunge off at outrageous angles, destroy themselves in unheard of contradictions.

The colour is repellent, almost revolting; a smouldering unclean yellow, strangely faded by the slow-turning sunlight [. . .]

But in places where it isn't faded and where the sun is just so—I can see a strange, provoking, formless sort of figure, that seems to skulk about behind that silly and conspicuous front design. [...]

I peeled off all the paper I could reach standing on the floor. It sticks horribly and the pattern just enjoys it! All those strangled heads and bulbous eyes and waddling fungus growths just shriek with derision!

From 'The Yellow Wallpaper',
a short story by Charlotte Perkins Gilman,
1892.

From Cornwall, Maggie wrote to Arthur about her depression. He responded with typically egocentric musings on his own sorrows. On the way home she stopped off to visit Fred in London, saying as she left, 'I wanted to see you again first,' leaving him wondering what that 'first' meant. Back at Tremans, through the winter and into the spring of 1907, Maggie's despair deepened, and her behaviour grew ever odder. Beth was worried by the way she wandered through the corridors, 'with a fixed and deadly gaze'. Maggie told Arthur that she saw 'underlying darknesses and vilenesses, old animal inheritances and evil taints of blood' in the faces of people passing in the street; that the world was phantasmal, as though everything except the actual objects on which her eyes rested were falling into dust and nothingness. To Fred she mentioned the spirits of dreadful beasts and demons lurking behind mask-faces of men and women.

Ben and Lucy had plans to go to Venice on holiday. Doctors diagnosed Maggie's problem as a mild liver upset, and assured Ben that she could go ahead with her arrangements. A sense of desertion and betrayal outraged Maggie. To her mind, she was right about Ben and Lucy. Lucy had stolen her mother. They cared nothing for her and were happy to go off to Venice together, leaving her in this state. She would show them. In a frenzy, she flagellated herself with a carriage whip, to see—she said—what pain would do. She tied her own hands together, saying she was frightened she would lose control. The night before Ben and Lucy were due to leave, Maggie could not sleep and in the morning summoned Lucy to her room, placing guilt and responsibility firmly in Lucy's hands by telling her she was afraid she might kill herself or do harm to somebody. Ben and Lucy put off their trip, and called Dr Todd.

At dinner Maggie did not utter a word. She rocked, put her head on her hands, rested her forehead on the table, and slipped from her chair on to the floor. The others would not believe how bad she was, she told Dr Todd, she needed to be tied up. Only by agreeing to do so did he manage to persuade her, sobbing loudly, to leave the room. At eleven o'clock that night she cried out loudly in her bedroom. Lucy and Dr Todd went to her. Here accounts differ. Fred records that Maggie was gripped by a 'homicidal mania' and implies that (even earlier, perhaps, over dinner) she tried to kill Ben; others that Maggie tried to kill herself. It took Todd, the parish nurse and three servants four hours to restrain her, and indeed, eventually, to tie her up.

Dr Todd summoned two colleagues, one of whom was an expert in such matters, Dr George Savage (who two years earlier had treated Virginia Stephen, later Woolf, after her breakdown following the death of her father). Arthur was called, and Ben sent a telegram to Fred telling him, 'We are in very deep waters.' Arthur arrived, regretful that in his earlier letters to Maggie he had focused so wholly upon himself, but soon doing so once again. He determined to stay at Tremans for at least a week, he said, 'or at all events for as long as I can stand it. A few bad nights and such pleasant reveries as mine of this morning would soon embark me on the same course ... what a beautiful, desirable, sad, treacherous, unjust world it is, little things punished so heavily, big things left alone.'

When Dr Savage saw Maggie, he advised that she be transferred to an institution for the insane. Arthur signed the committal order. On 8 May, in the morning, Ben and Lucy went out for a walk, the servants were told to stay in their rooms, and Arthur occupied Beth in helping him to pack. A carriage drew up to take Maggie to a private asylum, St George's Convent, run by the Sisters of Mercy, a few miles away at Wivelsfield. Fred noted that Ben bore this 'without any shrinking of the spirit', and Arthur thought Lucy's stalwartness 'simply beyond words'. All three brothers went to see Maggie within a few days. She was serene with Hugh, distant towards Fred, and confided in Arthur her fears that the demons would return. On visits over the next few weeks, Ben found her daughter disturbed and erratic, though on her better days she was calm enough to sit knitting. Maggie made no recovery. At the end of August Arthur went to see her, and found her wildly unsettled and convinced that the Sisters were trying to poison her. As he left the convent, he heard another inmate screaming, a tormented cry that moved him to 'as dark and dreadful a depth of despairing bewilderment' as he had ever felt. Next morning Arthur awoke in deep depression: 'Something seemed to crumble in my brain and clutch at my heart. I thought I was going to die.' He began to dread that he was joining his sister on a downward spiral.

In October, Dr Todd suggested that Maggie be transferred to The Priory, at Roehampton, in South London, where she could receive closer clinical care. The Priory cost a steep £550 a year, and Maggie's own money had run out. Ben and Lucy agreed to add what they could, and Arthur and Fred to contribute according to their respective incomes. Hugh refused to help (it was not merely from malice that Rolfe, in his ranting letters, accused Hugh of grotesque meanness). Hugh was in the process of buying himself a country property, Hare Street House, in the village of Buntingford in Hertfordshire. Towards the end of October, Dr Todd made the necessary arrangements. Arthur's depression deepened. He, too, consulted Dr Todd. On 1 November Todd placed him in the care of a nerve specialist at a residential nursing home in Mayfair. A few days later, Maggie was moved to The Priory.

From Maggie Benson's 1901 Short Story,
'The Soul of Cat', about Persis, 'a dainty lady,
pure Persian', who hated her kittens 'with a
hatred founded on jealousy and love'

She was a cat of extreme sensibility, of passionate temper, of a character attractive and lovable from its very intensity. . . should we let her go about with a sullen face to the world, green eyes glooming wretchedly upon it, an intensity of wretchedness, jealousy and hate consuming her little cat's heart[?]. . . as the kittens grew older maternal tenderness and delights faded, maternal cares ceased, and a dull, jealous misery settled down over Persis. . . she, not responding to my caresses, sat staring out before her with such black, immovable despair on her face that I shall not easily forget it. . . the cat's life was a series of violent changes of mood. . . she became sullen, suspicious, and filled with jealous gloom. . .

[Persis disappears one day]
So vanished secretly from life that strange little soul of a cat—a troubled soul for it was not the animal loves and hates that were too much for her—these she had ample spirit and courage to endure, but she knew a jealous love for beings beyond her dim power of comprehension, a passionate desire for praise and admiration from creatures whom she did not understand, and these waked a strange conflict and turmoil in the vivid and limited nature, troubling her relations with her kind, filling her now with black despairs, and painful passions, and now with serene, half understood content.

'A letter from Dr Chambers last night shows to our great comfort that the darling feels among friends,' Ben wrote to Nettie, a few days after the move. 'She sent for him several times and begged for him not to "send her away".' Ben (and sometimes Lucy) wrote regularly to Nettie, keeping her up to date with doctors' reports on Maggie's progress. Ben signed her letters 'Your lovingest Mother'; and when mentioning Ben to Nettie, Lucy often referred to her as 'Ma'. Nettie had become part of the family. Ben also shared news of Beth (whose health was beginning to fail), life at Tremans, and how Arthur was progressing.

'She has asked for none of us, so we must just wait,' Ben wrote to Nettie in mid-November about Maggie. 'One must just co-operate with all one's might.' Ben needed all her might. She was not to see Maggie again for nearly two years. Maggie's clinician at The Priory, Dr Chambers, considered that the possible emotional disruption might be harmful unless Maggie consented to visits—and Maggie refused. That Christmas, the family were given leave to send cards to Maggie, but not to include any letters. Ben had to content herself with written reports from Dr Chambers or a nurse, charting Maggie's 'great confusion', her restlessness, distress, brooding silences, refusal of food, her at times incoherent ranting and violent delusions—and her continued denunciations of Ben and Lucy, which at times extended to other family members as well, and sometimes were turned in upon herself. When letters were allowed, Ben received pages of poisonous hatred, and accusations that she and Lucy wanted to exclude Maggie from Tremans so that they could be alone together. Arthur thought Maggie's ingenuity at inflicting pain on Ben was 'satanical'— if not consciously malicious, then a result of demonic possession. Ben responded with characteristic self-effacement. 'I just lie low,' she wrote. She sought solace in religious meditation, and confided in Hugh, whom she thought understood that side of her life better than the others. 'She surpassed

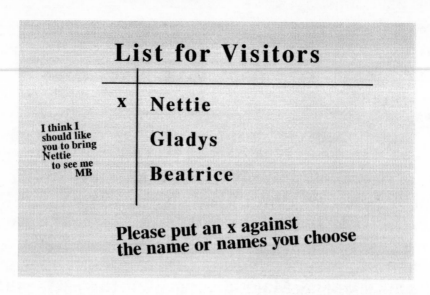

List for Visitors

X	Nettie
	Gladys
	Beatrice

I think I should like you to bring Nettie to see me MB

Please put an x against the name or names you choose

Maggie Benson Indicates Whom She Wishes to See

anything she has ever said before in bitterness and dislike and reproach and fulminations,' Ben wrote to Hugh after one vitriolic attack, 'so I have passed into silence again. Oh how I wish one could find the source of this poisonous hatred! Bless her.' Ben turned the situation over and over in her mind, 'and in my ears one deep throb is always going on, Maggie, Maggie Maggie—and what it all means'. 'No storms are more terrible than those that rage at high altitudes,' wrote Ethyl Smyth, pondering what inner conflicts had brought about 'the clouding of that wonderful brain'.

A Letter to Maggie Benson, from her Mother

Dearest Child. Why do you write me such unkind letters? You know they can do nothing but give pain, and all is so untrue. When you feel it would be a pleasure to see me, you must

324

Beth, Aged Seventy-Eight

write and say so—I believe you love me deep down, but you have allowed these poisonous thoughts with all their falseness to take possession of you. I love you, as I always have, with my whole heart—and you can imagine therefore what a letter like this is to me.

Always your Mother.

Had Dr Chambers been *au fait* with the thought of Sigmund Freud, whose book *Die Traumdeutung* had recently been published in Vienna (though not yet in James Strachey's translation as *The Interpretation of Dreams*), he may well have seen Maggie's jealousy of Lucy as one of a sexual rival, as an antagonism to someone who had usurped her father's male role in a way Maggie herself subconsciously desired to do. As it was, Chambers took the more orthodox view that the causes were gynaecological. 'An operation' was considered, and his reports linked Maggie's loss of control to the 'special reason' for which she was confined to bed each month. Ben thought Maggie's accusations were more than just 'a cry for help'. To Nettie she wrote: 'I have come to the conclusion that it is more an *utterance of her feeling* than an *asking*. I mean I don't think *answers have any effect*. The Cry is always repeated in exactly the same words. . . It seems often like the moaning of a person in delirium. . . God Bless the darling—the one comfort is he loves better than we do.'

As Ben neared her seventieth birthday, her life was once again consumed with the welfare of her children. 'Arthur is the great problem,' she wrote to Nettie, soon after Maggie had been removed to The Priory. For the two years following his first spell in the Mayfair nursing home (where he had stayed for three weeks), Arthur never entirely shook off his depression, and was at times gripped by a crippling despair. He tried hypnosis, foreign travel, further cures in nursing homes, was looked after by friends and spent a month in the care of a

326

Hampstead doctor, as well as long periods at Tremans. At times he was suicidal, and he became convinced his condition was hereditary. There had been mad and depressive forebears on both sides of the family, and Arthur thought that he and Maggie both carried their father's malady. It was a relief, he thought, that none of them had married, and that the Benson line was coming to an end. His illness drew him closer to Fred, whom he had always thought flighty and superficial, but who offered caring and stalwart support. At Tremans Ben gave him what comfort she could, though confided to Nettie a feeling of powerlessness, of not quite understanding the source of Arthur's wretchedness or really knowing what to do about it.

From A. C. Benson's Novel Beside Still Waters

One night he went to bed late, and found it difficult to sleep; thoughts raced through his brain, scenes and images forming and reforming with inconceivable rapidity; at last he fell asleep, to awake an hour or two later in an intolerable agony of mind. His heart beat thick and fast, and a shapeless horror seemed to envelop him. He struck a light and tried to read, but a ghastly and poisonous fear of he knew not what seemed to clutch at his mind. At last he fell into a broken sleep; but when he rose in the morning, he knew that some mysterious evil had befallen him. . . For that day and for many days he wrestled with a fierce blackness of depression. . .

Gradually, through the first months of 1909, Maggie began to show some signs of improvement. She was able to dress herself, she stopped refusing food, and for the first time joined other patients in the communal drawing room. The nurse's notes to Ben, which had once lamented that 'Miss Benson takes so little interest in anything that it is very difficult to fix on anything that would give her pleasure', began to report walks in the garden, short carriage drives and even the occasional game of croquet. Ben sent her a canary, as Maggie had always loved animals, and though Maggie at first said 'nothing thrives here well', she started taking an interest in it, as well as caring for some plants Nettie had sent. In March, Ben wrote exultantly to Nettie: 'O NETTIE, YOU are the First Person to whom she has sent a message'—a verbal one, via Dr Todd, thanking Nettie for the plants, sending her love and regrets for the harm she had done. A letter to Nettie followed a few weeks later. Maggie requested visits from Hugh and Fred (who went weekly when he was in London), but still not from her mother. In August, Ben was at last permitted to visit. Maggie was polite, gave Ben her own chair because it was higher, picked up Ben's walking stick when it fell, offered to pour the tea when she saw that Ben's arm was rheumatic—but she still seemed confused, concentrated on little of what Ben said to her, and at times reverted to her old accusations. There was an unfortunate incident when Ben rose to go, and Maggie wanted to come away too—a scene re-enacted on subsequent visits, on one occasion Maggie wrenching at Ben's heart as she came right up to the final communication door, crying 'Mother!'

Once, Maggie had to be assured that Ben was 'the Real one'; she also (after imagined sightings) asked to see 'the Real Miss Gourlay'. On 15 January 1910 Maggie wrote Nettie a touching letter beginning, 'My dearest, I don't forget that to-morrow was the day on which I first saw you. We had some happy times after that, at least I thought them happy,' but it was not until March—and then only after many pleas by Ben to Dr Chambers—that Nettie was allowed to visit. Ben might have considered Nettie to be one of the family, but to the doctors she was merely a friend.

In 1911, Beth died, in her ninety-fourth year, after being bedridden for some months following a stroke. Beth had been with the family for seventy-seven years. She had nursed little Minnie, been her girlhood confidante, a comfort to the frightened young Mary Benson in the first years of her marriage, and nurse in turn to each of her six children. In her final months, as Beth lay in her room, Ben would make her own stiff-jointed ascent to the top of the house to comfort her, read to her and reminisce. Beth had given her the unstinting love of a mother. Yet, as ever, Arthur noted, there was 'neither bitterness nor dumb endurance' about Ben's grief. 'The silence, the gap brought my mother neither horror nor dismay. She did not love anyone less nor think of them as less alive, because they had quitted the earthly scene. Life might be shifted, but love could not be broken.' Fred cherished Beth's 'utterly beautiful life of love and service'; Arthur, who had generally strangled love at birth, said that 'the love I had and have for her is almost the deepest emotion

329

of my life'. To the end, Beth adored Hugh. When he returned from the disastrous Egyptian trip following his father's death, Beth (who had been sent to Yorkshire) made the long journey to London to meet him at the railway station. She brought a little gift of a packet of cakes, an orange and a book—as she used to do when he took the train to school. Hugh was with a friend. He laughed gaily, pecked her on the cheek and was gone within minutes, dropping the gift into a rubbish bin.

All except Maggie came to Beth's funeral, at the village church in Horsted Keynes. Maggie was suffering frequent relapses, with recurrences of delusions and bouts of violence. Her treatment of Ben on some visits was so vile that Ben stayed away for long stretches at a time. At one point Maggie thought Fred was dead, that he had been accused of killing her; she told Arthur (who, still concerned for his own health, had stayed away, and was only persuaded to visit her again well into 1910) that she was afraid to use some stationery he had brought as a gift, as doing so courted disaster—a chimney at The Priory might fall down; somehow she was convinced that taking out the envelopes might have the impact of pulling out bricks. Eventually, the family decided that Maggie would benefit more from being in private care, and in October 1913 she was moved as a paying guest to the home of a Dr and Mrs Barton, in Wimbledon. At £800 a year, this arrangement was considerably more expensive than The Priory. Once again, Arthur and Fred contributed sums commensurate with their literary earnings (£225 and £175 respectively), Ben and Lucy said that together they could find £300 (though Arthur suspected they could afford more), and

Hugh was unco-operative, saying that Maggie should stay where she was.

Hugh had established a small community at Hare Street House in Buntingford, an odd ménage comprising a dangerous and gossiping Mrs Lindsey, who was clearly in love with him, her little son Ken, with whom Hugh was besotted, a strange Dr Sessions, who had given up his practice to concentrate on an interest in demonic possession, and an old, silent priest who suffered from melancholia. Arthur felt profoundly uncomfortable there, and avoided visiting. The house was filled with cast-off furnishings from Tremans, and together with one Gabriel Pippet and other nimble-fingered brethren, Hugh had snipped and stitched wall-hangings of coloured figures sewn on to brown canvas, including a disquieting Dance of Death (which hung in the room where visiting Anglicans stayed, as a gruesome reminder of their fate). The latest vituperative postcard from Frederick Rolfe might be propped on the chimney-piece. In the midst of all this flitted Hugh, 'in flannels of inconceivable shabbiness and such shoes as a tramp discards by the wayside', his only luxury being 'a prodigious consumption of the cheapest cigarettes he could find'—infuriating, but insuppressible, with his air of: 'Oh, isn't it fun?'

'Life pumps along,' Ben wrote to Hugh. She continued to confide her religious meditations to him, but delighted most in Fred's company—although he was spending long periods in Capri, where he had taken a villa, and in 1913 visited India, to stay with the latest (and most enduring) of his attractive young friends, Francis Yeats-Brown. After months of ill-health there, Fred returned to England, where he consulted a faith healer (with Ben's approval, though to the horror of the rest of the family), but eventually had to be operated on to have a kidney removed. Fred recovered well. Arthur—after a momentary relapse into depression that lasted the course of Fred's operation and kept him from visiting—was in good spirits once more, and was standing in for the Master of Magdalene, who was away under doctor's orders. In Wimbledon, Maggie's condition had slightly improved—though on one of Arthur's visits she lay on her back in the grass after a walk, and refused to return to the house, and he feared she might be carrying a knife. She was allowed on short excursions to London with a nurse, and once came to an awkward tea with Ben and Lucy, who were staying at Lambeth Palace. Arthur came down for the day from Cambridge. Maggie spoke bitterly about motherly love, removed a necklace Ben had given her and tried to hand it back, leaving it lying on a table when Ben refused to take it and lapsing into sullen silence. Hoping to avoid an unpleasant scene in front of the Davidsons, Ben asked Arthur to take Maggie away. Passively, Maggie allowed the necklace to be put back on, but as she parted company with Arthur, said: 'Well, when Mama has manoeuvred us all into our graves, perhaps she will be content.'

One day in the spring of 1914, instead of taking her afternoon rest, Maggie calmly left the Bartons' house in Wimbledon, boarded a train to Victoria Station and took another to Horsted Keynes. She walked the mile or so to Tremans, greeting a servant she encountered with 'I have come home, Mary'. The sight of Maggie's drawn, wizened face suddenly appearing at the drawing-room window shocked a shy young friend of Arthur's, Geoffrey

Madan, who had just arrived on his first visit. Maggie insisted on going around the house. On the old ottoman in Ben's sitting room she found a whip.

'What's this?' Maggie demanded.

Ben told her it was the whip Joey the parrot liked to bite.

'It's the whip I used on myself,' said Maggie. 'Did you put it out on purpose?'

She flung accusations at Ben, who tried to talk her down quietly. When Dr Barton arrived with a nurse to take her away, Maggie screamed abuse, flew into a rage, and begged to stay, but was manhandled into a cab, and returned to Wimbledon. Arthur was much shaken by the incident. What made matters worse, it seemed to Arthur, was that Maggie's intellect was as sharp as ever, 'but the emotions. . . all atrophied or perverted'.

A few weeks later, Fred left for Capri, for a long stay at the Villa Cercola, the house he had leased jointly with Somerset Maugham (though the two never stayed there at the same time), and which was occupied year-round by their flamboyant—Arthur thought distasteful—friend, John Ellingham Brooks. One resplendent day at the end of June, after an early breakfast in the shade of the pergola, Fred walked out of the gate, past the garden wall draped with passion-flower and morning glory, and down the stone path to Bagno Timberino, where he spent the morning alternately swimming and basking in the sun. On the way home, he stopped at the post office to pick up mail and the Italian papers, which came over on the noon steamer from Naples. Back at the villa, Brooks skimmed the papers over lunch.

'Hullo,' he said, 'an Archduke was assassinated yesterday. Franz Ferdinand?'

'What an awful thing,' responded Fred. 'Who is he? And where did it happen?'

'He's the Emperor of Austria's heir,' said Brooks. 'He was attending manoeuvres at Sarajevo.'

'Never heard of it . . . I want to go up Monte Solaro after tea. Do come. Those tawny lilies should be in flower.'

'Too hot,' said Brooks. 'Besides, I must water the garden.'

After siesta, Brooks took down *The Times Atlas*, out of curiosity, to ascertain where Sarajevo was. He told Fred it was the capital of Bosnia, which left Fred little the wiser. The two did not allude to the incident again. Fred travelled back to England, as he had intended, a fortnight later and was mildly surprised by talk of the Serbian Government's complicity in the Archduke's assassination, of Austro-Hungarian anger and German aggression, of the tugs of treaties with Britain's allies. He was at a country-house party on 4 August, when a telegram arrived from a well-connected friend of the host with the news that the Prime Minister was addressing the House of Commons that morning, that an ultimatum sent to Germany had been ignored, and that the country was at war.

The Duchess is Disturbed after Dinner

Adeline, Duchess of Bedford was taking coffee alone after the evening meal, at her house on Berkeley Square, when Woburn, the butler who ran her household with paralysing dignity entered, shutting the door noiselessly. Soundlessly, he approached to exactly the correct distance and said: 'The Zeppelins have arrived, your Grace,' as if they were guests for her *soirée*, come rather early. As a Zeppelin raid had not long before caused some considerable damage to the flat of her sister, Lady Henry Somerset, the Duchess in great agitation told Woburn to telephone to see if Lady Henry was safe. 'Very good, your Grace,' said the imperturbable butler, gliding out and closing the door noiselessly behind him. He came back, again shut the door, and advanced to exactly the spot where he had stood before. 'Her ladyship's flat has been blown to bits, your Grace,' said he, 'but her ladyship wasn't at home.'

At fifty-two, Arthur was beyond consideration for enlistment. Before the outbreak of hostilities, he had commented: 'I personally am against war in any guise, I think it an anachronism in civilised nations, like duelling.' After war was declared, his view changed, but he felt too old, too ill to be of use; imprisoned by his personality, and superfluous. 'I was made to be of use in peace,' he wrote. 'I am useless in war. . . I feel today an embarrassed loiterer on the fringe of life.' He criticized Archbishop Davidson for his gloom at the war, indeed felt 'really rather *ashamed* of him' for his reticence in firing up spirits, though he was also scathing of the braying jingoism of the newspapers, and scornful of a Church that prayed for victory. God either could not or would not avert war: 'If he cannot, it must be only aggravating to be prayed to—if he will not, why ask him?. . . If I were almighty and meant to send war, the prayers of individuals would be no more than the chirping of sparrows.' He took a personal dislike to the First Lord of the Admiralty, Winston Churchill, when he met him one afternoon at the Athenaeum, thinking him 'a horrid little fellow. . . like some sort of *maggot*. His head is big, he stoops. He has thin nervous limp sort of hands. He looks like a drug-taker, or at least as if there were something wrong to be ashamed of.' For the rest, Arthur's life went on much the same after 1914 as it had done before, a gentle round of writing and lectures—although he did compose a further two rousing verses for 'Land of Hope and Glory'.

Hugh became convinced that Armageddon was at hand, after reports at the end of August 1914 of angels appearing before the battle at Mons, and when the death of Pope Pius X occurred almost simultaneously with an eclipse of the sun. 'It is extremely like Armageddon,' he said to Fred, 'and why shouldn't the Kaiser be Antichrist?' He maintained firmly that the 'great and terrible day of the Lord' was at hand. Nevertheless, he offered to serve as chaplain to Catholics on the Western Front, but was turned down. Hugh died, unexpectedly, in October 1914, shortly before his forty-third birthday. He had been overtaxing himself with preaching engagements, and felt constantly exhausted, confiding to Arthur that he had rather taken to whisky, 'not for drinky but for drunky'. Earlier in the month he had developed severe chest pains, which doctors diagnosed as 'false angina'. Hugh's comment was that although false, it was extremely plausible, and he continued with his usual workload. Ben had known such a situation before, during Edward's last weeks. She tried to persuade Hugh to slow down, but knew of

Mary Benson, Aged Seventy-Three

old the hopelessness of ever influencing her wayward youngest son. 'I tell Hugh exactly what I think,' she said to Arthur. 'I warn him that he will have a crash, and will be obliged to give up the greater part of his work—but he won't or can't listen; and I am not going to bore him by becoming a mere anxious mother. People must live their lives in their own way, and this is what he chooses—he says he will take the risks.' During a Mission at Salford, in Manchester, Hugh's chest pains worsened, and he developed pneumonia. He was taken to Bishop's House, but even with pneumonia insisted on going to see a performance of the cinematograph, which amused and exhausted him. His condition grew worse and Arthur was called. 'I don't feel like dying at all,' Hugh said to his brother when he arrived. Hugh was buried at Hare Street House—not, as he had requested, in a vault with a light-wood coffin that could be broken open from the inside, and with a duplicate key to the vault beside it, just in case he had been buried alive in error—but (once requisite Home Office permission had been obtained) near a rose-plot in the garden.

Monsignor Robert Hugh Benson's Plan
for a Novel on the European War

I *Priest coming out of Mass: Post Office: sees*
   it is war
II *Barracks: he comes out, in uniform:*
   reminiscences: meets a student: then a
   Jesuit priest
III *The march: sees churches: knows very little.*
   Smoke of shells: aeroplane
IV *Under fire: his failure with a dying man:*

338

   Jesuit dies
V   *Belgian village: horrors: priest shot*
VI   *English cheer him up: he sees them fight*
VII   *His wound and capture: tells them he is a*
   priest: trial: condemnation
VIII   *Simply sent off under guard in train:*
   escapes: help of Bavarians
IX   *Gets back to his regiment: sent to a line of*
   communications: peace and quiet: his
   mother's house
X   *Garrison: pious Colonel. He says Mass:*
   and he is shot: a priest-soldier hears his
   confession
   Uhlans' patrol

Maggie survived her younger brother by just over a year, dying of heart failure in May 1916, a few weeks before turning fifty-one. 'There is nothing to mourn for,' Arthur admitted. 'It was a heavenly deliverance.' Yet for the few days before Maggie died, the cloud seemed to lift from her mind. Fred had been visiting her almost weekly for some months. They had always been close and his liveliness and lightness of touch seemed to revive her. In the fortnight before she died, Maggie smiled, quoted Browning, was full of old stories and humorous talk. She asked to see Ben, and even Lucy, and on the last evening of her life chatted with them, repeated family jokes and reminisced affectionately, saying as they left: 'Well, I *have* had a happy day.' This miraculous last-minute clarity helped relieve Ben of an enormous sense of defeat and guilt. She was sure Fred had a hand in the transformation, and wrote him ecstatic letters expressing her gratitude and sense of release. Ben thought of Maggie's 'Freedom, and Life, and Joy' in those final days, and that meant 'all those nine years wiped away, or perhaps more truly and better still, *understood*. How one's heart revels and is satisfied . . . O BLESS YOU. A mother may bless her son, I suppose, just for the pure joy of *what he is*. I'll take the risk, anyhow.' Maggie was buried beside her sister Nellie, at Addington.

Fred, at forty-seven, was, like Arthur, too old for enlistment. At Tremans, he irritated Arthur with his inside gossip about the war 'from mysterious unnamed people, in high official positions, who only confide in Fred'. Ben was amused by his name-dropping, hints of privileged information, and then hasty retraction, as if he had made a gaffe. Yet Fred did make a direct contribution to the war effort. He was assigned by the Ministry of Information to write a report on German activity in Turkey, and the Foreign Office asked him to investigate the morale of the Italians, and to ascertain whether or not the Pope really was neutral, or secretly favoured Germany and Austria. With a pass to travel without hindrance in neutral Italy, Fred headed to the Villa Cercola, and wrote his report from Capri. Back in London, he noted that the civilian population 'were beginning to find the unaccustomed routine quite intolerably dull, and they discovered that (wholly apart from the great issues, from the horrors and sorrows and splendours) the war was, above all things, the most frightful bore'.

In April 1915, Arthur received an extraordinary offer from one of his woman correspondents. He had for years been answering letters from a

Madame de Nottbeck—née Astor—who had both inherited a fortune and married a rich man. Madame de Nottbeck wished to give Arthur the sum of £40,000, without any conditions, to do with absolutely what he liked. She did not even desire to meet him. It was a considerable amount of money—Arthur calculated that in all his twenty years at Eton, he had earned, writing included, just £20,000; in the cash-for-honours scandal that embroiled Lloyd George in the 1920s, the recognized tariff for a knighthood was £10,000, with £30,000 for a baronetcy, and £50,000 for a peerage. After much hesitation, and further correspondence with Madame de Nottbeck, Arthur accepted the money. It was to be the first of a number of gifts, making him an exceptionally rich man. Arthur immediately made generous offers to friends. He had already made many gifts to Magdalene College—for fellowships and building work—and these he increased immensely. When the Master of Magdalene died at the end of October, Arthur was invited to fill the role he had often held in proxy in earlier years. In the two days after the announcement was made, Arthur received over four hundred letters and telegrams of congratulation. He swept down to Tremans, via the Athenaeum where Archbishop Davidson, among others, greeted him as 'Master'. Ben was delighted at the news, and solemnly kissed his hand. The household treated him with great dignity—though Fred feigned ignorance of university affairs. Yet, by the end of the year, Arthur was again feeling twinges of depression. Over the following months their severity increased, coming at him 'like a breath from Hell'. In the summer of 1917, he

341

suffered a total collapse. Dr Todd arrived to take him to a nursing home near Ascot, where Arthur remained until long after the war was over.

Lucy responded to the national crisis with her usual pragmatism, throwing herself into work for children orphaned by the war. Ben, when war was declared, saw it more transcendentally, as an indication that 'Greed and Selfish Desire and Desire for Possession and Position are the things that are Wrong with us,' and opining that no amount of talking about peace could 'prevent this hideous outcome, which is from Within'. She remained mostly cocooned at Tremans, where—Arthur noted—a 'touch of the tranquillity of age' descended on her, and she lived more in and for the day, hardly looking ahead, and thus spared much of the misery of what was happening in the wider world. But then, Arthur went on, 'all her life long the march of external events and political forces had meant less to her than the little circle so brightly illuminated by her own bright mind.' That circle was becoming more proscribed. Few except family came to Tremans now, and Ben seldom went to London.

Ben had grown old. For years, gout and rheumatism had gnawed at her. She had long quipped that a walk with her was 'a totter with a tortoise'. The gout 'with its Hydra nature' crept through her and seemed 'to spare no organ but the TONGUE— That is in quite good working order'. When her eyes began to fail—a 'mistiness which slides across'—she echoed Dickens's formidable Mrs Squeers with a flippant 'IS THIS THE HEND?' More seriously, she wrote: 'I am endeavouring to see how to turn disabilities into powers. That must be the task of advancing years, and ought to be true right up to the Gates of Death—and that it is difficult is part of the going, something to set one's teeth in.' What really bothered Ben was 'a certain shortage of hearing'. As she grew more deeply deaf, she fell silent. Low tones, especially of male conversation, escaped her. She did not join in for fear of appearing stupid. At moments like these, denied the conversation that had ever been her sustenance, she felt 'the Rest of Life stretches before me a Desert Track from which Death will be a thankful emergence'. Yet the old spark was still there. In the spring of 1917 the seventy-six-year-old Ben, on a visit to Lambeth Palace, was given the task of diverting the Liberal statesman Viscount Morley, three years her senior. She wrote to tell Arthur:

Lord Morley dined here—older and crocker— and having close behind him 2 or 3 months of Flue—and being deafer than I—We had a time! and it not being thought good for him to go to Chapel I was invited to lure him to sit out with me instead and you should have seen my shameful feminine appeal to him—though one foot in the grave for both of us we hopped together on the other, and I got him to talk about Ireland, and to indulge in reminiscences personal and other.

But such visits to Lambeth were rare. Back at Tremans—deaf, deprived of the nourishment of conversation, and as Lucy busied herself with her good works and her surviving children got on with their lives—Ben slipped into silence.

Death of Mrs Benson
Widow of the Archbishop

We regret to announce the death of Mrs Benson, widow of the late Archbishop Benson. Mrs Benson died peacefully in her sleep during the night of 15th June 1918. It is 22 years since the Archbishop died at Hawarden. Mrs Benson's surviving sons, Mr A. C. Benson, Master of Magdalene, and Mr E. F. Benson, are well known by their writings. Mrs Benson was buried yesterday beside the graves of her deceased daughters at Addington Palace. Among mourners at her funeral were Adeline, Duchess of Bedford, the composer Miss Ethel Smyth, and Miss Lucy Tait, a family friend.

Fred kept Tremans on for a year after Ben's death. Lucy could not bear to remain there, and bought a smaller house in the neighbourhood, living there and at Lambeth with her sister and Archbishop Davidson. Arthur was still in the nursing home, and Fred had no desire to live alone in the country. Around the time that he was thinking of giving up the remainder of the lease on Tremans, Henry James's old home—Lamb House in Rye—became available (James had died in 1916). Fred secured a tenancy, which he shared with Arthur when Arthur eventually recovered, and before he died in 1925, coming down there from Magdalene for his holidays. Lamb House and Rye came to be at the heart of Fred's 'Mapp and Lucia' novels, which met with greater success than anything he had ever written, ensuring a place for E. F. Benson on bookshelves for decades to come.

It fell to Fred alone to pack up Tremans. Room by room he presided over the fate of objects that had been gathered into the stream of Benson family life for over half a century—Ben's old bed, the now-collapsed ottoman, the altarpiece sideboard from Wellington and the organ from the chapel at Addington, the bronzed dessert service from Lincoln, engravings that had hung at Lambeth Palace, Maggie's statue of Rameses the Great. Somewhere, over the years, the blancmange-like beaded velvet pincushion made for Queen Victoria had disappeared. There were packets of letters from old Mrs Sidgwick to Minnie, in browned envelopes with early Victorian stamps, childhood scribblings from Truro, one of little Martin's first copybooks. There were Ben's diaries, Edward's sermons, files on the Lincoln Judgement and unused invitations to Speech Day at Wellington College. There were poems and scrapbooks, quickly jotted postcards and long expressions of love—as well as Maggie's vile letters to Ben, which Fred burnt along with other 'dangerous stuff that had better perish'.

For days Fred sifted, reminisced, made hard decisions. He selected treasured items to keep, dispatched much to the auctioneers, made gifts to servants, chose pieces to go to Cambridge, to await Arthur's recovery.

Piece by piece the Bensons were drained out of Tremans, till the old house stood empty and silent, its contents crated and removed, dispersed to anonymous new owners, sent on to Rye, or consigned to the bonfire.

Acknowledgements

I am most grateful to the Authors' Foundation for an Elizabeth Longford Grant, which was of considerable help in meeting travel costs incurred while researching this book.
The Bodleian Library, University of Oxford, kindly granted me access to the Benson Family Papers, and permission to quote from Mary Benson's diaries and letters. I am especially grateful to Colin Harris and the staff in the Special Collections department for their help and support. I should also like to acknowledge, with thanks, access granted by the Wren Library, Trinity College, Cambridge, to E. W. Benson's diaries, and the Master and Fellows of Magdalene College, Cambridge, for allowing me to consult and quote from A. C. Benson's diaries.

The discerning eye and sound judgement of my editor, Ravi Mirchandani, enhanced this book considerably, and I am thankful, too, for the encouragement and good faith of my agent, David Miller. Thanks, also, to Sarah Norman and all at Atlantic, who so enthusiastically took the book on board. Katie Derham and John Vincent were generous in their hospitality, and a special thanks goes to Hans Nicolaï, Jo Beall and Linetta de Castle, all of whom offered warmth and conviviality to a distracted guest. As ever, heartfelt thanks goes to Britta Boehler, Chris Chambers, Andrew May, Gerard van Vuuren and all those friends who have offered succour, advice, and help with research.

Select Bibliography

Primary Material

Mary Benson's diary, together with substantial Benson family correspondence, manuscripts, photographs and other Bensonia are held with the Benson Family Papers, Bodleian Library, University of Oxford.

A. C. Benson's diaries are at the Pepys Library, Magdalene College, University of Cambridge.

E. W. Benson's diaries, and other papers, are at the Wren Library, Trinity College, University of Cambridge.

Published Works

Abbott, Evelyn, *The Life and Letters of Benjamin Jowett*, 2 vols, John Murray, London, 1897

Ackroyd, Peter, *London: The Biography*, Chatto & Windus, London, 2000

Anon., *The Duties of Servants: A Practical Guide to the Routine of Domestic Service*, Copper Beech reprint of 1894 original, London, 1993

Asquith, Betty, *The Bensons, A Victorian Family*, E. F. Benson Society reprint, London, 1994

Bailin, Miriam, *The Sickroom in Victorian Fiction*, Cambridge University Press, Cambridge, 1994

Baring, Maurice, *The Puppet Show of Memory*, Little Brown & Co., New York, 1922

Benkowitz, Miriam, *Frederick Rolfe: Baron Corvo*,

Hamish Hamilton, London, 1977

Benson, A. C. *Memoirs of Arthur Hamilton*, Henry Holt, New York, 1886

——*The Life of Edward White Benson, Sometime Archbishop of Canterbury*, 2 vols, Macmillan, London, 1899

——*Beside Still Waters*, G. p.Putnam's Sons, London, 1907

——*Hugh, Memoirs of a Brother*, Smith, Elder & Co., London, 1915

——*Life and Letters of Maggie Benson*, John Murray, London, 1917

——*The House of Quiet*, John Murray, London, 1919

——*The Trefoil*, John Murray, London, 1923

Benson, E. F., *Dodo, An Omnibus*, Hogarth Press, London 1986 [1893]

——*The Challoners*, William Heinemann, London, 1904

——*Across The Stream*, John Murray, London, 1919

——*Our Family Affairs 1867–1896*, George H. Doran, New York, 1921 [1920]

——*Rex*, Hodder & Stoughton, London, 1925

——*Mother*, George H. Doran, New York, 1925

——*As We Were, A Victorian Peep-Show*, Hogarth Press, London, 1985 [1930]

——*The Tale of an Empty House and Other Ghost Stories*, Black Swan, London, 1986

——*Final Edition*, Hogarth Press, London, 1988 [1940]

Benson, E. F. (ed.), *Henry James, Letters to A. C. Benson and Auguste Monod*, Elkin Mathews & Marrot, London, 1930

Benson, Margaret, *The Soul of a Cat, and Other Stories*, Heinemann, London, 1901

Benson, R. H., *The Sentimentalists*, Pitman & Sons, London, 1906

——*The Necromancers*, Bernhard Tauchnitz, Leipzig, 1910

Davidson, Randall, *Life of Archibald Campbell Tait, Archbishop of Canterbury*, Macmillan, London, 1891

Delmont, Sara, and Duffin, Lorna, *The Nineteenth-Century Woman, Her Cultural and Physical World*, Croom Helm, London, 1978

Flanders, Judith, *The Victorian House: Domestic Life from Childbirth to Deathbed*, HarperCollins, London, 2003

Gilman, Charlotte Perkins, *The Yellow Wallpaper and Other Stories*, Dover, New York, 1997

Hichens, Robert, *Yesterday*, Cassell, London, 1947

James, Henry, *The Turn of the Screw*, Penguin Books, Harmondsworth, 1984

Lubbock, Percy (ed.), *The Letters of Henry James*, Macmillan, London, 1920

——*The Diary of Arthur Christopher Benson*, Hutchinson & Co, London, 1926

Marcus, Sharon, *Between Women: Friendship, Desire, and Marriage in Victorian England*, Princeton University Press, Princeton, 2007

Martindale, C. C., *The Life of Monsignor Robert Hugh Benson*, 2 vols, Longmans, London, 1916

Masterman, Lucy (ed.), *Mary Gladstone (Mrs Drew), Her Diaries and Letters*, E. p.Dutton, New York, 1930

Masters, Brian, *The Life of E. F. Benson*, Chatto & Windus, London, 1991

Money, James, *Capri, Island of Pleasure*, Hamish Hamilton, London, 1986

Nethercot, Arthur Hobart, *The First Five Lives of*

Annie Besant, University of Chicago Press, Chicago, 1960

Newsome, David H., *Godliness & Good Learning: Four Studies on a Victorian Ideal*, Cassell, London, 1961

——*On the Edge of Paradise: A. C. Benson, the Diarist*, University of Chicago Press, Chicago, 1980

——*The Victorian World Picture*, John Murray, London, 1997

Oppenheim, Janet, *The Other World: Spiritualism and Psychical Research in England, 1850–1914*, Cambridge University Press, Cambridge, 1985

——*'Shattered Nerves': Doctors, Patients, and Depression in Victorian England*, Oxford University Press, Oxford, 1991

Page, Frederick (ed.), *The Poems of Coventry Patmore*, Oxford University Press, London, 1949

Palmer, Geoffrey and Lloyd, Noel, *Father of the Bensons*, Lennard Publishing, Harpenden, 1998

Partridge, Michael, *Gladstone*, Routledge, London, 2002

Paterson, Michael, *Life in Victorian Britain: A Social History of Queen Victoria's Reign*, Robinson, London, 2008

Paxman, Jeremy, *The Victorians: Britain through the Paintings of the Age*, BBC Books, London, 2009

Raverat, Gwen, *Period Piece: A Cambridge Childhood*, Faber & Faber, London, 1987

Rolfe, Frederick, *The Desire & Pursuit of the Whole*, Quartet Books, London, 1993

Roper, Michael and Tosh, John (eds), *Manful Assertions: Masculinities in Britain since 1800*, Routledge, London, 1991

Showalter, Elaine, *The Female Malady: Women,*

Madness, and Culture in England 1830–1980, Pantheon, New York, 1985

Smyth, Ethel, *Impressions that Remained*, 2 vols, Longmans, London, 1919

——*As Time Went On. . .* , Longmans, London, 1936

——*The Memoirs of Ethyl Smyth*, Faber & Faber, London, 2008

Stanley, Arthur Penrhyn, *Life and Correspondence of Thomas Arnold*, John Murray, London, 1881

Stephenson, Glennis (ed.), *Nineteenth-Century Stories by Women, An Anthology*, Broadview Literary Texts, Peterborough, Ontario, 1993

Tangye, Michael, *Tehidy and the Bassets: the Rise and Fall of a Great Cornish Family*, Truran, Redruth, 2002

Taylor, Anne, *Annie Besant: The Biography*, Oxford University Press, Oxford, 1992

Tosh, John, *Manliness and Masculinities in Nineteenth-Century Britain*, Pearson Longman, Harlow, 2005

Vicinus, Martha, (ed.), *Suffer and Be Still: Women in the Victorian Age*, Indiana University Press, Bloomington, 1972

——(ed.), *A Widening Sphere: Changing Roles of Victorian Women*, Indiana University Press, Bloomington, 1977

——*Intimate Friends, Women who Loved Women, 1778–1928*, University of Chicago Press, Chicago, 2004

Watkins, Gwen, *E. F. Benson & His Family and Friends*, E. F. Benson Society, Rye, 2003

Whitehouse, J. Howard, *Vindication of Ruskin*, Allen & Unwin, London, 1950

Williams, David, *Genesis and Exodus: A Portrait of*

the Benson Family, Hamish Hamilton, London, 1979

Wilson, A. N., *After the Victorians*, Hutchinson, London, 2005

Wohl, Anthony (ed.), *The Victorian Family, Structures and Stresses*, St Martin's Press, New York, 1978